LITERACY IN AMERICAN LIVES

Literacy in American Lives traces the changing conditions of literacy learning as they were felt in the lives of ordinary Americans born between 1895 and 1985. The book demonstrates what sharply rising standards for literacy have meant to successive generations of Americans and how – as students, workers, parents, and citizens – they have responded to rapid changes in the meaning and methods of literacy learning in their society. Drawing on more than 80 life histories of Americans from all walks of life, the book addresses critical questions facing public education at the twenty-first century: How does rapid economic restructuring affect the ways that individuals acquire reading and writing? How do families pass the skills of reading and writing on to children under conditions of relentless social and technological change? What is the role of economic change in maintaining inequality in access and reward for literacy? What is the human impact of the nation's growing reliance on the literacy skills of workers? Using extended case studies, this book gets beyond the usual laments about the crisis in literacy to offer an often surprising look into the ways that literacy is lived in America.

Deborah Brandt is Professor of English at the University of Wisconsin–Madison. She is author of *Literacy as Involvement,* which won the 1993 David H. Russell Award for Distinguished Research from the National Council of Teachers of English. In 1998–1999, she was a Visiting Fellow at the U.S. Department of Education in Washington, D.C.

D0030041

LITERACY IN AMERICAN LIVES

Deborah Brandt

University of Wisconsin–Madison

CAMBRIDGE
UNIVERSITY PRESS

PUBLISHED BY THE PRESS SYNDICATED OF THE UNIVERSITY OF CAMBRIDGE
The Pitt Building, Trumpington Street, Cambridge, United Kingdom

CAMBRIDGE UNIVERSITY PRESS
The Edinburgh Building, Cambridge CB2 2RU, UK
40 West 20th Street, New York, NY 10011-4211, USA
10 Stamford Road, Oakleigh, VIC 3166, Australia
Ruiz de Alarcón 13, 28014, Madrid, Spain
Dock House, The Waterfront, Cape Town 8001, South Africa

http://www.cambridge.org

© Deborah Brandt 2001

First published 2001

Printed in the United States of America

Typeface Plantin Light 10/13 pt.   *System* Quark XPress™   [HT]

A catalog record for this book is available from the British Library

Library of Congress Cataloging-in-Publication Data

Brandt, Deborah, 1951–
    Literacy in American lives / Deborah Brandt.
        p. cm.
    Includes bibliographical references and index.
    ISBN 0-521-78315-1 — ISBN 0-521-00306-7 (pb)
        1. Literacy – United States – History – 20th century.   I. Title.
    LC151 .B72 2001
    302.2′244 – dc21   00-045425

ISBN 0 521 78315 1 hardback
ISBN 0 521 00306 7 paperback

For Hannah Brandt,
who showed me how to write.

And Del Brandt,
who showed me why to write.

CONTENTS

ACKNOWLEDGMENTS

This book has been long in the making and my debts are many. My first thanks are to those who provided the invaluable resources of time and space. Much of this work was done at the Madison wing of the National Research Center on English Learning and Achievement (CELA), housed at the Wisconsin Center for Educational Research. I am grateful to the funder, the U.S. Department of Education Office of Educational Research and Improvement (OERI); CELA directors Arthur Applebee, Judith Langer, and Martin Nystrand; and all the Madison-based researchers who provided unforgettable afternoons of rousing discussion. At the Wisconsin Center for Education Research, I thank Andy Porter, Debbie Stewart, and Lois Turner. Thanks especially to my long-time colleague Marty Nystrand for his confidence, patience, and support at strategic times. The OERI also provided a stimulating year of research leave in Washington, D.C. where I was a Visiting Scholar at the National Institute on Post-Secondary Education, Libraries, and Lifelong Learning. Thanks to Kent McGuire and to all the institute members, especially Irene Harwarth, for making my time there productive. Joan Trumble of the National Library of Education provided excellent research help and introduced me to intricacies of electronic searching, and I am also grateful to the staff of the Library of Congress for help during my many inspiring days there. Also while at OERI, I had the good fortune of working with other Visiting Scholars: Anne Bouie, Pam Keating, and Diane Horm-Wingerd. A fifth fellow, Clifford Hill of Teacher's College, provided especially wise counsel and helped to keep me moving forward. Through the many stages of this project, I benefitted from grants from the Research Foundation of the National Council of Teachers of English and the University of Wisconsin Graduate School and Vilas Foundation.

At Wisconsin, two research assistants, Anna King Syvertsen and Julie Nelson Christoph, provided indispensable archival assistance, tracking down sometimes obscure facts without raising an eyebrow or missing a beat.

Too many individuals to mention provided leads and introductions that connected me to the nearly 100 people I interviewed for this project. Thanks to all of the people who were instrumental in that way, but especially Larry Hamlin, Margaret Wajda, Larry Kohn, Francie Saposnik, Pam Parsons, Dora Silva, Consuelo Lopez Springfield, George Thomas, and John Romano. Friends and colleagues who provided research leads also are too many to mention, but special thanks to Mike Rose, Michael Smith, Beverly Moss, Tom Fox, Bobby Austin, Catherine Hobbs, Peter Mortensen, and Kurt Spellmeyer. I had the chance to try out the ideas of this book at various campuses where I was invited to share work in progress, so I am grateful to colleagues and students at the University of Oklahoma, University of Minnesota, Drake University, University of Illinois, Kent State University, University of Louisville, Pennsylvania State University, University of New Hampshire, Gallaudet University, Western Maryland College, and the State of Wisconsin Department of Public Instruction. This project has brought me happily into the orbit of other researchers doing very fine work on literacy in the field of writing studies, and I especially have benefitted from stimulating discussions with Beth Daniell, Kim Donehower, Peter Mortensen, Beverly Moss, Min-Zhan Lu, and Bruce Horner. Several people have read various parts of this manuscript with care and sensitivity; I am thankful to Bob Gundlach, John Odom, Anne Gere, and Jackie Royster for their insights. I owe particular debts to Steve Witte, who provided important methodological guidance, and Harvey J. Graff, whose unflagging generosity has been almost as important to my work as his unsurpassable research. Again, I thank all who have read and commented on versions of the manuscript and apologize for not always realizing sound suggestions.

I also wish to acknowledge the current and former graduate students at Wisconsin who have worked with me in classes and projects over the nearly 10 years that I was at work on this research, with special appreciation to my CELA partners, John Duffy and Karen Redfield. Studying with intelligent and committed individuals is a treasure to me. And to the young people in the Madison Urban League Project Jamaa, in whose after-school company I spent many a good hour reading, writing, and reflecting, and to one of my teachers there, Keith Burkes, I extend my hearty thanks. At home, Steve Wajda and Mike Wajda were there when necessary to set me right with their unsparing wit and down-to-earth love. Thanks to Mike, too, for straightening out my files and fixing computer glitches.

An inadequate thanks to Julia Hough at Cambridge University Press, an ace of an editor.

My deepest debt is to those neighbors who opened their lives to my scrutiny. Through this project, I came to know where I live. Now, when I pass through a corner of town or ride a rural highway, my head may flood with the voices and experiences of people who have lived and died there. Their enlargement of my life will be a lasting source of gratitude.

Madison, Wisconsin
December 2000

INTRODUCTION

The Pursuit of Literacy

Literacy is so much an expectation in this country that it has become more usual to ask why and how people fail to learn to read and write than to ask why and how they succeed. In a society in which virtually every child attends school and where some kind of print penetrates every corner of existence, only the strongest sorts of countervailing forces – oppression, deprivation, dislocation – seem able to exclude a person from literacy. Asked to imagine how their lives would be different if they didn't know how to read and write, people I have spoken with are often baffled and pained. "I would be totally in the dark," they say. Or, "It would be like not having shoes."

To think of literacy as a staple of life – on the order of indoor lights or clothing – is to understand how thoroughly most Americans in these times are able to take their literacy for granted. It also is to appreciate how central reading and writing can be to people's sense of security and well-being, even to their sense of dignity. At the same time, these analogies ask us to take a deeper look. They remind us that, as with electricity or manufactured goods, individual literacy exists only as part of larger material systems, systems that on the one hand enable acts of reading or writing and on the other hand confer their value. Changes in these systems change the meaning and status of individual literacy much as the newest style of shoes – or method of producing shoes – might enhance or depreciate the worth of the old. Further, these analogies remind us that, despite a tendency to take the resource of literacy for granted, acquiring literacy – like acquiring other basic staples of life – remains an active, sometimes daunting process for individuals and families. This process is exacerbated by turbulent economic changes that do not merely raise standards for literacy achievement from one generation to the next but often ruthlessly reconfigure the social and economic systems through which literacy can be pursued and through which it can find its worth.

This book is about how ordinary people have learned to read and write during the century just concluded. It is also about how they have made use of that learning at various stages of their lives. Learning to read and write has taken place amid convulsive changes in economic and social life, educational expectations, and communication technologies. This has been a time when the meaning of what it is to be literate has seemed to shift with nearly every new generation. Inevitably, pursuing literacy in the twentieth century entailed learning to respond to an unprecedented pace of change in the uses, forms, and standards of literacy. One of the major aims of this book is to look closely at the sources of the changing conditions of literacy learning and especially at the ways that Americans have faced the escalating pressure to provide for themselves and their children the kinds of literate skill demanded by life in these times.

Literacy has proven to be a difficult and contentious topic of investigation largely because its place in American culture has become so complex and even conflicted. Expanding literacy undeniably has been an instrument for more democratic access to learning, political participation, and upward mobility. At the same time, it has become one of the sharpest tools for stratification and denial of opportunity. Print in the twentieth century was the sea on which ideas and other cultural goods flowed easily among regions, occupations, and social classes. But it also was a mechanism by which the great bureaucracies of modern life tightened around us, along with their systems of testing, sorting, controlling, and coercing. The ability to read and, more recently, to write often helps to catapult individuals into higher economic brackets and social privilege. Yet the very broadening of these abilities among greater numbers of people has enabled economic and technological changes that now destabilize and devalue once serviceable levels of literate skills. Unending cycles of competition and change keep raising the stakes for literacy achievement. In fact, as literacy has gotten implicated in almost all of the ways that money is now made in America, the reading and writing skills of the population have become grounds for unprecedented encroachment and concern by those who profit from what those skills produce. In short, literacy is valuable – and volatile – property. And like other commodities with private and public value, it is a grounds for potential exploitation, injustice, and struggle as well as potential hope, satisfaction, and reward. Wherever literacy is learned and practiced, these competing interests will always be present.

This study explores these complexities and contradictions through the perspectives of 80 Americans born between 1895 and 1985. In interviews conducted in the early 1990s, they explored with me their memories of how they learned to write and read, from their earliest childhood memories to the present day. Through their testimonies, I especially hoped to understand better what sharply rising standards for literacy have meant to successive generations of Americans and how – as students, workers, parents, and private and public citizens – they have responded to rapid changes in the meanings and methods of literacy learning.

For at least 20 years, there have been serious research efforts to treat literacy "in context." From different disciplinary perspectives, studies in psychology, anthropology, linguistics, child development, and critical education have provided persuasive evidence that literacy abilities are nested in and sustained by larger social and cultural activity. Reading and writing occur instrumentally as part of broader activities (for instance, working, worshiping, governing, teaching and learning, relaxing). It is these activities that give reading and writing their purpose and point. Contexts constitute the meanings for which we reach during reading and writing and in that way help to constitute (and can hinder) our ability to read or write. Contextual perspectives tend to emphasize the relational nature of reading and writing: People build up and exercise skills through participation with others in particular contexts. This perspective also tends to recognize the multiplicity of literacy abilities and their legitimacy: As social groups differ in their cultural expressions or class locations, for instance, so will preferred ways of reading and writing differ. In fact, this perspective tends to eschew references to skills or abilities at all, focusing instead on the concept of literate practices, emphasizing the grounded, routinized, multiple, and socially sanctioned ways in which reading and writing occur. Attention to the situated nature of literacy also has provided avenues for treating the ideological dimensions of literacy, the politics by which reading and writing preferences of elite groups get installed as the measure against which other versions are deemed inadequate or undesirable.[1]

Contextual perspectives have developed in challenge to views that equate literacy only with the technical matters of decoding or encoding of written language, a literacy lodged merely in discrete linguistic and scribal skills such as sounding out, spelling, or semantic fluency. This narrower approach has been faulted for treating literacy as if it were a decontextualized skill, neutral, self-contained, portable, a skill that can be acquired once and for all and used and measured transparently without regard to contextual conditions. Although this narrow, technical approach continues to influence literacy instruction and assessment in schools, there are growing calls for approaches to literacy that more rigorously incorporate the realities of its situated dimensions. From a contextual perspective, literate abilities originate in social postures and social knowledge that begin well before and extend well beyond words on a page. Serious programs of literacy instruction, many argue, must teach toward these contextual and contextualizing dimensions of literacy if they are to be successful and just.

Literacy in American Lives shares generally in this contextual perspective on literacy, if for no other reason than it was only through attention to specific material facts of people's experiences with literacy that I could address the questions that mattered to me most: How has literacy learning changed over the last century and how have rising expectations for literacy been experienced as part of felt life? Answers to those questions demanded that I pay close attention to what people could remember about the specific scenes of their learning: where they were, who else was present, what materials they used, and so on. I also knew when I started that I would be foregrounding some aspects of context, namely, the biographical context of learning over a lifetime and the comparative context of generational cohorts, that are not usually treated in research and theory on literacy.[2] As the analysis proceeded, additional elements of context – especially economics and history – surged into view and became vital for explaining what I found. Economic transformations, as they appeared in family work, regional restructuring, communication systems, and political organization, were the engine of change in literacy learning, setting an especially brisk pace over the last several decades. And history, by which I mostly refer to the society's collective accumulation of experience, materials, know-how, and education, as well as the forward and backward projections of its institutions, laws, and social movements, provided the principal means to which people appealed as they made, or tried to make, these changes. In fact, as we will see, as the forms and products of literacy proliferated across time and across generations, the accumulating history of literacy itself came to press on the scenes of new literacy learning in increasingly complicated ways, serving to enable and sometimes to impede acts of learning.

The analysis that follows focuses, then, on relationships between individual literacy development and large-scale economic development, as the two played out in specific ways and in specific places in the 80 lives that I studied. It was in this relationship that both the major pressures for change and the major opportunities for learning came into relationship. It was also this intersection that illuminated the competing interests that came to surround literacy as it rose in exploitable economic value, especially in the second half of the last century. Certainly the role of economic change in raising standards and expectations for literacy is widely recognized and much discussed. No government report or labor forecast or educational mission statement these days goes without mentioning that postindustrial conditions now require all Americans to attain higher levels of skill, especially in reading and writing.[3] This study, however, considers these changes in work and economic relations as they have affected the contexts in which literacy learning itself takes place: how the persistent demand for higher and higher levels of skill became the overriding condition in which literacy learning would be conducted. The investigation is meant to capture a dual dynamic in the experiences of the people I talked with: the ways that they have pursued literacy and the ways that it has pursued them.

For purposes of this study, literacy skill is treated primarily as a resource – economic, political, intellectual, spiritual – which, like wealth or education, or trade skill or social connections, is pursued for the opportunities and protections that it potentially grants its seekers. To treat literacy in this way is to understand not only why individuals labor to attain literacy but also to appreciate why, as with any resource of value, organized economic and political interests work so persistently to conscript and ration the powers of literacy for their own competitive advantage. The status of literacy as a valued resource in this society accounts, then, for both the value of literacy for individual learners and the value that literate individuals have in wider arenas of economic competition into which their skills are recruited. As a resource, literacy has potential payoff in gaining power or pleasure, in accruing information, civil rights, education, spirituality, status, money.[4] To treat literacy as a resource is to appreciate the lengths that families and individuals will go to secure (or resecure) literacy for themselves or their children. But it also takes into account how the resources of literacy skill are exploited in competitions for profit or advantage that go on within the larger communities in which people live and work and in which their literacy learning takes place.

Of course, acquiring the resources of reading or writing, even in ample amounts, cannot guarantee desired ends. Nor does gaining literacy inoculate against discriminations of various kinds.[5] Further, calling literacy a valued resource is not meant to imply that reading and writing are morally or functionally superior to other forms of human activity. Rather, this way of treating literacy simply acknowledges the practical meaning that literacy has for most citizens at the start of the twenty-first century. Literacy counts in life as people find it, although how much it counts, what it counts for, and how it pays off vary considerably.

The concept of resource may remind some readers of Pierre Bourdieu's notion of cultural capital: the conglomeration of skills, credentials, and relationships of obligation that families and individuals use to jockey for and maintain class status. It may remind others of Gary Becker's sense of human capital: the ways that individuals and companies invest in and profit by the development of intellectual capacities.[6] But the term also invites, I hope, broader connotations that will take on resonance as this study unfolds. Literacy is a resource in the way that electricity is a resource: Its circulation keeps lights on. Literacy is also a productive resource, a means of production and reproduction, including a means by which legacies of human experience move from past to future and by which, for many, identities are made and sustained. At the same time, seeing literacy as a productive resource in economic terms makes it analogous in some ways to natural resources or raw materials. What land was to the agricultural economy or iron to the manufacturing economy, people's skills are to the information economy.[7] Workers these days produce wealth not only by processing raw materials but by supplying those raw materials themselves in the form of knowledge and skills, including communication skills. The struggles that have always raged over ownership of the means of production can only confound the struggles that have always accompanied literacy learning and teaching in this society.

In terms of the analytical methods of this study, treating literacy in such broad, connotative ways tries to do justice to the simultaneous forces at play in the complex episodes of literacy learning as people described them. In addressing the question of how they learned to write and read, people sometimes turned their attention to the resources on hand for developing as writers or readers – that is, where it was that they found opportunity, assistance, inspiration, or information. Quite frequently, people's learning registered as an effort to improve their skills – to enlarge their resourcefulness, in a sense, to meet new conditions. Learning also appeared as surplus, as a by-product of performing tasks, an inevitable outcome of putting literacy resources into service. And on a more abstract level, the resource of literacy appeared as an available collective good, a cultural equivalent of water or air that connected individuals to the human systems of their time and place. It was in trying unsuccessfully to separate and categorize these expressions of learning that I profoundly appreciated why definitions of literacy prove so difficult and contentious. In any case, in treating literacy as a resource, the discussion will move frequently among three closely related themes: *Literacy learning* principally will refer to specific occasions when people take on new understandings or capacities; as we will see, literacy learning is not confined to school settings or formal study. *Literacy development* refers to the accumulating project of literacy learning across a lifetime, the interrelated effects and potentials of learning over time. It is closely connected to the life span and to historical events that affect literacy as a collective good. *Literacy opportunity* refers to people's relationships to social and economic structures that condition chances for learning and development. Realistically, these three dimensions are not easy to separate and, as literacy is lived, seem to be three sides of one coin.

To treat literacy as a resource is to emphasize that it takes its shape from what can be traded on it. This perspective attends to the competitions that surround literacy, the struggles to harness it for profit or ideological advantage, the struggles for the prerogative to manage or measure it, and the ways that these incessant struggles set the terms for individual encounters with literacy. Above all, this perspective emphasizes the instability of literacy, its links to political and economic changes and to the shifting standards of value and conditions of access that accompany those changes. Literacy was at the heart of recent transformations in work and life. Tracing the dynamics of literacy learning over the twentieth century inescapably puts these changes at the center of consideration.

This study, by design, focuses on economic and other material influences in literacy. I do not wish to imply strict economic determinism nor to underestimate many other cultural aspects that figure into literacy (for instance, the ways that reading and writing can express a sense of self or group identity or other cultural dimensions). However, because economic and material conditions have been, in my view, underestimated and at times ignored in descriptive studies of literacy, I wanted to offer some useful directions for bringing economic issues more fully into view. Many recent ethnographic studies of literacy in the United States and elsewhere have worked to chronicle the diversity of literacy practices among ordinary people. These studies underscore the fact that reading and writing serve many functions, appear in many places, take many forms. They demonstrate how people achieve literacy by various avenues, how reading and writing and learning about them go on in many contexts beyond formal schooling, and often hand in hand with other cultural activities like storytelling, child rearing, and collective problem solving. Together, these studies strongly imply that literacy among the U.S. citizenry has been underestimated by standardized tests and other narrow, usually school-based measurements that miss the meanings and forms of literacy in everyday life. Uncovering as they do the often surprising vigor and ingenuity of what David Barton and Mary Hamilton have called "hidden" or "vernacular" literacy, many of these studies challenge stereotypes of low literacy that are often pinned on people who already carry other kinds of stigmas. In addition, these often fine-grained explorations of out-of-school literacy practices provide educators with conceptual tools for bridging between the resources students bring to school and the different literacy practices they must learn to control – a model that is equally appropriate in adult and workplace literacy instruction. By expanding the perspective on literacy, by treating it fundamentally as cultural and con-textualized, these studies try to democratize the worth and importance of all literacy practices. Above all, in their sheer accumulation they compli-cate treatments of literacy as merely a set of technical, drillable, portable skills. They display instead the complex social and cultural orchestrations that even the simplest acts of reading or writing entail. They also invite interrogation into the implications of literacy in the maintenance of racism, sexism, and other undemocratic interests.[8]

Literacy in American Lives shares many of the perspectives and motiva-tions of this line of recent research. Indeed, this study is in deep concep-tual debt to these predecessors. At the same time, however, this study tries to offer new critical frameworks for approaching everyday literacy. The diversity and multiplicity of literacy practices may rightly bear witness to cultural variety and human resourcefulness. But that is not all they tell. Multiple literacy practices are also a sign of stratification and struggle. Their variety speaks of different and often unequal subsidy systems for literacy, which often lead to differential outcomes and levels of literacy achievement. Literacy practices trail along within themselves histories of opportunities granted and opportunities denied, as well as ascending power or waning worth, legitimacy or marginality of particular literate experience. Just as illiteracy is rarely self-chosen and rarely self-created, the literacy that people practice is not the literacy they necessarily wish to practice. Focusing merely on the uses of literacy as they seem to arise from local goals and interests can obscure these complications. Ethno-graphic descriptions do not often speak directly enough and in a sus-tained way to the histories by which literacy practices arrive or do not arrive in local contexts, flourish or not in certain times and locales. Nor do they often invite a search for the interests beyond those of the local users that hold literacy practices in place, give them their meaning, or take them away. Nor do they often fully address the mixed motives, antipathies, and ambivalence with which so much literacy is learned and practiced. This study focuses heavily on the arrival of new literacy learning through a life span and across generations, brought in mostly on the coattails of eco-nomic change. It was those aspects of literacy that became salient to me as this research unfolded and came to demand my focused attention.

Parameters of the Study

This is a study, then, about how people across the past century learned to read and write, actively, passively, willingly, resistantly, and, always, persistently, over a lifetime. It focuses on the experiences of ordinary people, some who read or write constantly and some who do so rarely, some who are able to take reading or writing with them into virtually any sphere of life where it can do some good and others who usually must trade on other means to make out. In any case, in this study, an understanding of literacy is built up from people's accounts of their lived experiences, embracing those instances in which anyone said they learned anything about reading or writing. Although encounters with literacy often blended with other activities (some people learned about writing, for instance, while drawing, calculating, reading, listening to the radio, watching television, talking), the study maintains a primary focus on the acquisition and use of alphabetic script. The interest is in reading and writing as people would mundanely and practically distinguish them from other sorts of recognizable activity (or at least as they were being recognized in the 1990s!). The study makes no attempt to measure people's literacy skills against any kind of standard (although it notices, at times, how such measurements are made). Rather, the driving concerns have to do with how people say they came to acquire or develop the resources of reading or writing – at all.

It has been commonplace, as I mentioned, to consider literacy in the plural, as sets of social practices, diverse routines that must be understood in relationship to the particular social aims and habits associated with their contexts of use. In this study, perhaps because the focus is less on how people practice literacy and more on how they have pursued it, literacy appears less settled than the term *practice* might imply. It appears more elusive, as a want, as an incursion, as an unstable currency. When literacy does appear in this study as a social practice, it is as a practice that is often jumping its tracks, propelled into new directions by new or intensifying pressures for its use.

This study is based on 80 in-depth interviews I conducted in the mid-1990s with a diverse group of Americans ranging in birth date from the late 1890s to the early 1980s. In the interviews, we traced together their memories of learning to write and, to a lesser extent, their memories of learning to read. The inquiry focused especially on the people, institutions, materials, and motivations that contributed to literacy learning, both in school and out, from birth to the present. I also explored with the people I interviewed the uses and values that literacy has had for them at various stages of life. This study follows in the tradition of life-story research, which is a loose confederation of historical, sociological, psychological, and phenomenological inquiry. This form of research serves multiple purposes and employs various methodologies, including the collection of open-ended autobiographical monologues, structured and less structured interviews, and biographical surveys. What these diverse traditions have in common is an interest in people's descriptions of their own life experiences. A significant focus for analysis is the life span. Social psychology uses life stories to explore people's subjective worlds, seeking relationships among social structure, personality, and behavior. Other sorts of inquiries examine the linguistic forms and functions of narrative accounts themselves to uncover the meaning structures that people call on to bring order to their experiences. Perhaps the best known line of life-story research is oral history, which uses interviews to gather information about the social conditions of ordinary lives, information that is otherwise unrecorded and often overlooked in conventional histories of important people and events. In other cases, oral history is used to document multiple perspectives on public events. My study is aligned in many ways with oral history perspectives as articulated by Paul Thompson (1975, 1988, 1990) and Trevor Lummis (1987) and with the biographical sociology of Daniel Bertaux (1981, 1984).[9] I treat autobiographical accounts for their historical value, for their illumination of people's relationships to the social structures of their times and places, especially those in which literacy learning is implicated. Rather than searching for uniqueness or subjective differences, this study concerns itself with similarities of experience among people who experience similarly structured positions and relations. As Trevor Lummis explained,

> ...people live their lives within the material and cultural boundaries of their time span, and so life histories are exceptionally effective historical sources because through the totality of lived experience they reveal relations between individuals and social forces which are rarely apparent in other sources. Above all, the information is historical and dynamic in that it reveals changes of experience through time.[10]

Direct accounts about how ordinary people have acquired reading and writing and their motivations for doing so are largely missing from the record of mass literacy development. Most studies of the past have had to rely on indirect evidence, such as signature rates, book circulation, or the growth of schooling, with only an occasional excerpt from diaries or letters or autobiographies to provide a more contextualized sense of the means and meaning of literacy in various eras. Only recently have we begun to accumulate more systematic and direct accounts of contemporary literacy as it has been experienced. Nevertheless, many current debates about literacy education and policy continue to be based largely on indirect evidence, such as standardized test scores or education levels or surveys of reading habits. It is the persistent interest of this study to characterize literacy not as it registers on various scales but as it has been lived.

The point of view of this investigation is roughly through birth cohorts, a method of analysis meant to capture literacy learning within what Lummis called "material and cultural boundaries" of a time span. Norman Ryder discussed the merits of birth cohort analysis in studying social change:

> Each new cohort makes fresh contact with the contemporary social heritage and carries the impress of the encounter through life. This confrontation has been called the intersection of the innovative and the conservative forces in history. The members of any cohort are entitled to participate in only one slice of life – their unique location in the stream of history.[11]

This approach has proven especially amenable to a treatment of the changing conditions of literacy learning, especially given the ways that literacy-based technologies have been introduced across the century, entering people's lives at different ages and so with different impacts and possibilities. At the same time, though, tracing literacy through successive generations illuminates the "conservative forces" that Ryder mentioned, as we can see how older, fading forms of literacy roll along with new and emerging ones, creating new material and ideological configurations for literacy learners at any stage of life. Literacy preserves, and one of the things that it is best at preserving is itself, so an encounter with literacy will always in some sense be an encounter with its history. Consequently, what is new in literacy learning comes not merely from new technologies and their implications but from the creation of new relationships to older technologies and ways of writing and reading. Cohort analysis is especially useful for apprehending this process. Finally, the comparative perspective recognizes the close connections between social structures and communication systems and how changes in both are interrelated; literacy is not merely an expression of social structure but a dynamic element in it. What people are able to do with their writing or reading in any time and place – as well as what others do to them with writing and reading – contribute to their sense of identity, normality, possibility.

Of course, as with any investigative approach, life stories have their limitations and dangers. Especially complicating is the fact that accounts of past events inevitably are rendered through the perspective of the present. People reflect on – indeed, refashion – a memory in terms of its significance for how things have turned out, whether in terms of personal circumstances or shared culture. This is a thorny matter for the interviewer as well as those interviewed. It is especially tricky in an investigation of changing meanings of literacy, as past senses of writing or reading are apprehended through more recent realities and perspectives and the blend is hard to separate. One way to mitigate this problem, as Daniel Bertaux has suggested, is to focus people's attention on the past by remembering concrete activities and material surroundings.[12] Such a tactic cannot claim to yield something more objective or true but does potentially grant a return to the material scenes of past learning, a move that especially interested me. I devised an interview script by which I tried to lead participants through a chronological account of both ordinary and extraordinary encounters with writing and reading, lingering to explore their detailed recollections of the literal settings, people, and materials that animated their memories. (See Appendix.) Of course, such an approach only leads to the additional complication of the role of the questions and questioner in structuring life-story accounts. In an effort to be cooperative, those being interviewed will try to render their responses according to the perceived desires of the questioner.[13] Undoubtedly, the heavy hand of my interview script, shaped by the theoretical interests motivating my study, imposed itself on the participants, becoming at times at odds with the communication norms they preferred and knew best. Other times, of course, the script receded as conversations meandered into stories, jokes, jibes, and other tangents during which I tried to listen closely for the lessons about literacy that they offered. In any case, one of the great advantages of conducting autobiographical interviews at the end of the twentieth century was the ubiquitous models of the interview format available through television, radio, and print, making the roles of interviewer and interviewee not quite so strange for either party. Nevertheless, the methodological limitations I mention as well as the ones I fail to notice myself are indelibly present in (and absent from!) this presentation, there (and not there) for the discriminating reader to weigh against my claims.[14]

A few more deliberate limitations must be noted. First, although reading development is not ignored in this study, the central focus is on writing and learning to write. One reason is simply to help to redress the neglect of the social history of writing in comparison to reading. As

Michael Halloran has observed, "Writing has been a virtually invisible topic in the material history of modern culture."[15] I have been amazed throughout the process of researching for this book at how invisible writing remains as a researched phenomenon in economics, history of education, and communication studies.[16] Although the situation is improving, much more is left to be known about the practices, meanings, and values of writing for ordinary citizens. A focus on writing is especially pertinent now because the pressure to write is perhaps the main new feature of literacy to have emerged in the second half of the twentieth century. It is a second wave, one might say, of the mass (reading) literacy achieved for many groups by the second half of the nineteenth century.

Second, I decided early on not to ask participants to show me their writing. Partly this was a practical matter, for most of the writing done by ordinary people is by nature transitory, consumed, discarded. Most of the texts people recalled no longer existed anyway. Partly this was a philosophical matter, for too much of our understanding about literacy and writing development is based on the analysis of texts, and this study is meant to emphasize other dimensions. Partly, too, this was a personal matter, a reluctance to force into my relationship with the participants the long shadow of the teacher ready to uncover shameful inadequacies of expression. As the interviews demonstrated, the disapproving teacher looms large enough still in many people's memories and was best, I thought, left alone. In several cases, people spontaneously offered me examples of their writing, sometimes journals, letters, poems and fiction, autobiographies, old school reports, or professional projects and publications. But they were never solicited.

Finally, I steered away in the interviews and certainly in the write-ups from probes and disclosures of most personal matters. These excisions from the presentation, even when bits of the shape of literacy learning might have been cut along with them, were motivated by a desire not to hurt or embarrass the people who helped me so much in this project. I hope I have succeeded.

A note about transcriptions: All quotations from the interviews have been edited into standard written English with hesitations, misstarts, and pauses eliminated. Such editing indeed washes out the dialectical diversity of the people I spoke with. However, not trained as a linguist, I lacked the skill to transcribe accurately the range of regional accents and dialects that I heard. Although the racism of our society often invites researchers to hear and inscribe aspects of the most stigmatized dialects (for instance, Ebonics or the "broken" English of second-language speakers), the speech of the nonstigmatized is not so closely scrutinized for its deviations from the accepted standard. It is out of a sense of evenhandedness, then, that I have converted all the speech that I quote into standard edited English. Dropping the hesitations and misstarts risks loss of nuance, but in each case I listened carefully to the contextual meaning of passages I have chosen to quote to be sure that such editing would not flagrantly distort meaning as I understood it. What is gained by these decisions, I hope, is greater clarity and efficiency for the reader.

The Setting of the Study

This study involved 80 people ranging in age at the time of the interviews from 98 years old to 10. All the participants were living in south central Wisconsin, virtually all of them in the county surrounding the university that employs me. This area, whose population numbered more than 367,000 at the time of the 1990 census, is diverse geographically and economically. Nearly three fourths of the county is still farmland (although in the late 1990s it was being lost quickly to commercial and residential development), and the county has often been referred to as the dairy capital of the United States. Small towns provide commercial hubs for rural areas, yet the county also embraces a dense urban area around the state capital, which is also home to a large public university. Sprawling suburban communities ring the capital. State government and the university are leading employers, followed by the medical industry, insurance, food processing, and light manufacturing. By the mid-1990s, retail shops, restaurants, and other services were burgeoning. Settled originally by the Fox, Sauk, and Ho-Chunk, the area was populated by the midnineteenth century by German and Norwegian immigrants attracted to the rich farmland. It remains today an area with high concentrations of European Americans in both rural and urban areas. Small but growing populations of African, Mexican, and Asian Americans join a few Native Americans (about 1% of the population) and newly arrived immigrants from Europe, Asia, Mexico, and Central America to round out the ethnic profile. Seventy percent of the county's residents were born in Wisconsin. At the time of the study, unemployment in the county was below the national average and level of schooling above it, yet ethnic disparities in income and education achievement were significant. Although 10% of the population overall was living below the poverty line, the proportion grew to close to 33% among residents of color, most of them working poor.[17]

Originally, this study was to draw participants who would represent the 1990 U.S. census profile of the county in terms of ethnicity, education level, occupation, and region of birth. But as interviewing progressed and the vicissitudes of conducting the study set in, it became harder – and of less interest, frankly – to maintain this goal. I sought and found a group of people who, overall, were diverse in terms of ethnicity, income, education, occupation, religion, and experience. Fifty-four of the people were European American, 16 African American, 4 Mexican American, 2 Native American, 2 of Asian descent, and 2 of Middle Eastern descent. Eleven grew up in households where languages other than English were spoken and, in some cases, written and read. Twenty-two of the participants had been born and raised in the county where the study was conducted. Another 15 had been born and raised in other parts of Wisconsin. The rest grew up out of state, in the east, west, southwest, west, and other parts of the Midwest. Four were foreign born, although schooled as children in the United States (a requirement I imposed in my selection). Fifty of the participants grew up in rural areas or small towns; 20 were raised in metropolitan areas; the rest, in big cities. Ten of the participants had fewer than 12 years of schooling. Twenty-five had earned high school diplomas or their equivalent. Twenty-three had some years of post-secondary education, with 22 attaining a bachelor's degree or more.

It is through the life circumstances of the people interviewed for this study, about which much more will be said later, that a better sense of this society will emerge. Many of the elderly European Americans I interviewed had been raised on small, family-owned farms in the Midwest and had attended one or two-room country schools. Now retired from jobs in sales, clerical work, transportation, or dairy production, they were living in area retirement centers or public housing projects or nursing homes, attracted to the county by its good health care and transportation systems. Many of the older African Americans I interviewed belonged to families who had migrated to the upper Midwest from Southern sharecropping communities during and after World War II, to work for the railroad or the auto industry and later for the post office, government services, public utilities, and business. Other African Americans, typically younger and poorer, arrived in the 1980s or 1990s to escape violence and political neglect in nearby big cities, bringing their school-aged children and finding work in low-paid service positions. Many Mexican Americans in the area arrived originally as farm workers or children of farm workers, up in the summer from Texas border towns, eventually to settle in year-round with jobs in canneries or in small family businesses. Other Mexican Americans arrived to attend the university and decided to stay. The diaspora following the Vietnam War brought southeast Asians into diverse occupations in the area. A large bulk of the participants arrived from various parts of the country to study or work at the university or to take positions in the thriving professional and technical economy. All in all, participants in this study made their living as postal workers, farm laborers, factory workers, bus drivers, social workers, secretaries, dairy farmers, journalists, educators, classroom aides, domestics, executives, lawyers, hairdressers, homemakers, technicians, small-business owners, nurses and nurses' aides, salespeople, government workers, and more. Thirteen interviewees were students, attending area public or parochial schools, small local colleges, or the university. Twelve participants lived in households that fell into the government category of low income.

Thus, this study offers a profile that cannot be said to be statistically representative of any population. But I recognized early on that I could not include all of America's voices nor did I wish to force participants in this study to stand for the entire ethnic group, region, or occupation from which they came. By matters of feasibility, this study bears a regional bias toward the conditions in the county where I live and work, toward the experiences of its natives and the people who have been drawn there since early in the twentieth century. Yet I take heart from Bertaux's observation that any life is representative "not as the result of statistical practices but because ... its social determinations simply are shared by many others as a matter of reality."[18] So, as a matter of reality – if not proper proportion – the 80 lives represented here articulate a vast range of literacy learning over the twentieth century in America.

This is also to say that this study accounts for the details reported in the life stories of 80 particular individuals. Consequently, many aspects of the history of literacy in the twentieth century are missing from this book – because they either did not touch the lives of the individuals studied here or failed to arise as topics during the interviews. A different interviewer, a different setting, and different questions all might have yielded dimensions of literacy learning other than those with which I work here. This research began with individuals and not with the institutions around which literacy instruction is typically organized. For instance, I did not approach for systematic study any adult basic education programs, workplace literacy programs, Headstart, or family literacy programs. Though all of these are active initiatives in the region that I studied, the stories of these agencies are not told here. Neither does this study treat the official histories of school curriculums or teaching methods, except insofar as they were recalled and remarked on in interviews. In part because curricular and institutional histories already exist in the scholarship and because most contemporary literacy research is based in organized, mostly instructional settings, this study takes a different tack. As a result, it omits sites within its broad geographical setting where literacy learning goes on and where a great deal of human resources are concentrated in that effort. It is useful to remember, however, that literacy programs, chronically underfunded in the United States, still engage only small numbers of the population. Further, virtually all of the people I interviewed made multiple points of contact over the course of their lives with a wide array of institutional agents – some traditionally associated with literacy and many that are not – and these contacts are explored through the context of the individual history. The claim, however, is never to comprehensiveness. Indeed, I have not even been able to be comprehensive with the individual histories I have collected. Many angles, major and minor, have been let go – at least for now. What is here, though, is as true as I can get it to what I think is of widest public importance.

Volunteers for the study were recruited through nursing homes, retirement, and senior citizen centers, unions, schools, social service, community and housing agencies, professional organizations, churches and synagogues, and through networks of associates and friends. In some cases, intermediaries approached potential participants and then I followed up with phone requests. Almost all of the interviews were conducted in private homes; a few were conducted in workplaces and hospital rooms. Interviews lasted between one and three hours; occasionally, I followed up interviews with additional phone queries. In some cases, I made personal monetary donations to nonprofit organizations that assisted me and in several cases provided some favors and reciprocal services for participants. All interviews were tape recorded and subsequently transcribed. Throughout the study, pseudonyms replace personal names, locations, and other potential cues to the identity of the participants.

The following section continues to explain the conceptual and analytical approach of the study.

The Analytical Framework: Sponsors of Literacy

In his sweeping history of adult learning in the United States, Joseph Kett described the intellectual atmosphere available to young apprentices who worked in the small, decentralized print shops of antebellum America. Because printers also were the solicitors and editors of what they published, their workshops served as lively incubators for literacy and political discourse. By the midnineteenth century, however, this opportunity faded when the invention of the steam press reorganized the economy of the print industry. Steam presses were so expensive that they required capital outlays beyond the means of many printers. As a result, print jobs were outsourced, the processes of editing and printing were split, and, in tight competition, print apprentices became low-paid mechanics with no more access to the multiskilled environment of the craft shop.[19] Although this shift in working conditions may be evidence of the deskilling of workers induced by the Industrial Revolution,[20] it also offers a site for reflecting on the dynamic sources of literacy and literacy learning. The reading and writing skills of print apprentices in this period were an achievement not simply of teachers and learners or of the discourse practices of the printer community. Rather, these skills existed vulnerably, contingently within an economic moment. The pre–steam press economy enabled some of the most basic aspects of the apprentices' literacy, especially their access to material production and the public meaning or worth of their skills. Paradoxically, even as the steam-powered penny press made print more accessible (by making publishing more profitable), it brought an end to a particular form of literacy sponsorship and a drop in literacy potential.

Kett's study, which focused on the competition among providers of education in the United States, helped me to formulate an analytical approach to literacy learning that I came to call sponsors of literacy. As I suggested earlier, literacy looms as one of the great engines of profit and competitive advantage in the twentieth century: a lubricant for consumer desire, a means for integrating corporate markets, a foundation for the deployment of weapons and other technology, a raw material in the mass production of information. As ordinary citizens have been compelled into these economies, their reading and writing skills have grown sharply more central to the everyday trade of information and goods as well as to the pursuit of education, employment, civil rights, and status. At the same time, people's literate skills have grown vulnerable to unprecedented turbulence in their economic value, as conditions, forms, and standards of literacy achievement seem to shift with almost every new generation of learners. In my analysis of the life histories, I sought ways to understand the vicissitudes of individual literacy development in relationship to the large-scale economic forces that set the routes and determine the worldly worth of that literacy.

My own field of writing studies has had much to say about individual literacy development. Especially in the last quarter of the twentieth century, we have theorized, researched, critiqued, debated, and sometimes even managed to enhance the literacy potentials of ordinary citizens as they have tried to cope with life as they find it. Less easily and certainly less steadily have we been able to relate what we see, study, and do to these larger contexts of profit making and competition. This even as we recognize that the most pressing issues we deal with – tightening associations between literacy skill and social viability, the breakneck pace of change in communications technology, persistent inequities in access and reward – all relate to structural conditions in literacy's bigger picture. When economic forces are addressed in our work, they appear primarily as generalities: contexts, determinants, motivators, barriers, touchstones. But rarely are they systematically related to the local conditions and embodied moments of literacy learning that occupy so many of us on a daily basis.[21]

This study does not presume to overcome the analytical failure completely. But it does offer a conceptual approach that begins to connect literacy as an individual development to literacy as an economic development, at least as the two have played out over the last century. The approach is through what I call sponsors of literacy. Sponsors, as I have come to think of them, are any agents, local or distant, concrete or abstract, who enable, support, teach, and model, as well as recruit, regulate, suppress, or withhold, literacy – and gain advantage by it in some way. Just as the ages of radio and television accustomed us to having programs brought to us by various commercial sponsors, it is useful to think about who or what underwrites occasions of literacy learning and use. Although the interests of the sponsor and the sponsored do not have to converge (and, in fact, may conflict), sponsors nevertheless set the terms for access to literacy and wield powerful incentives for compliance and loyalty. Sponsors are delivery systems for the economies of literacy, the means by which these forces present themselves to – and through – individual learners. They also represent the causes into which people's literacy usually gets recruited.[22] Sponsors are a tangible reminder that literacy learning throughout history has always required permission, sanction, assistance, coercion, or, at minimum, contact with existing trade routes.

Intuitively, *sponsors* seemed a fitting term for the figures who turned up most typically in people's memories of literacy learning: older relatives, teachers, religious leaders, supervisors, military officers, librarians, friends, editors, influential authors. Sponsors, as we ordinarily think of them, are powerful figures who bankroll events or smooth the way for initiates. Usually richer, more knowledgeable, and more entrenched than the sponsored, sponsors nevertheless enter a reciprocal relationship with those they underwrite. They lend their resources or credibility to the sponsored but also stand to gain benefits from their success, whether by direct repayment or, indirectly, by credit of association. *Sponsors* also proved an appealing term in my analysis because of all the commercial references that appeared in these twentieth-century accounts – the magazines, peddled encyclopedias, essay contests, radio and television programs, toys, fan clubs, writing tools, and so on, from which so much experience with literacy was derived. As the twentieth century turned the abilities to read and write into widely exploitable resources, commercial sponsorship abounded.

In whatever form, sponsors deliver the ideological freight that must be borne for access to what they have. Of course, the sponsored can be oblivious to or innovative with this ideological burden. Like Little Leaguers who wear the logo of a local insurance agency on their uniforms, not out of a concern for enhancing the agency's image but as a means for getting to play ball, people throughout history have acquired literacy pragmatically under the banner of others' causes. In the days before free public schooling in England, Protestant Sunday schools warily offered basic reading instruction to working-class families as part of evangelical duty. To the horror of many in the church sponsorship, these families insistently, sometimes riotously demanded of their Sunday schools more instruction, including in writing and math, because it provided means for upward mobility.[23] Through the sponsorship of Baptist and Methodist ministries, African Americans in slavery taught each other to understand the Bible in subversively liberatory ways. Under a conservative regime, they developed forms of critical literacy that sustained religious, educational, and political movements both before and after emancipation.[24] Most of the time, however, literacy takes its shape from the interests of its sponsors. And, as we will see throughout this book, obligations toward one's sponsors run deep, affecting what, when, why, and how people write and read.

The concept of sponsors helps to explain, then, a range of human relationships and ideological pressures that turn up at the scenes of literacy learning – from benign sharing between adults and youths to euphemistic coercions in schools and workplaces to the most notorious impositions and deprivations by church or state. It also is a concept useful for tracking literacy's materiel: the things that accompany writing and reading and the ways they are manufactured and distributed. *Sponsorship* as a sociological term is even more broadly suggestive for thinking about economies of literacy development. Studies of patronage in Europe and *compadrazgo* in the Americas show how patron–client relationships in the past grew up around the need to manage scarce resources and promote political stability.[25] Pragmatic, instrumental, ambivalent, patron–client relationships integrated otherwise antagonistic social classes into relationships of mutual, albeit unequal, dependencies. Loaning land, money, protection, and other favors allowed the politically powerful to extend their influence and justify their exploitation of clients. Clients traded their labor and deference for access to opportunities for themselves or their children and for leverage needed to improve their social standing. Especially under conquest in Latin America, *compadrazgo* reintegrated native societies badly fragmented by the diseases and other disruptions that followed foreign invasions. At the same time, this system was susceptible to its own stresses, especially when patrons became clients themselves of still more centralized or distant overlords, with all the shifts in loyalty and perspective that entailed.[26]

In raising this association with formal systems of patronage, I do not wish to overlook the very different economic, political, and education systems within which U.S. literacy has developed. But where we find the sponsoring of literacy, it will be useful to look for its function within larger political and economic arenas. Literacy is a valued commodity in the U.S. economy, a key resource in gaining profit and edge. This value helps to explain, of course, the length people will go to secure literacy for themselves or their children. But it also explains why the powerful work so persistently to conscript and ration the resource of literacy. The competition to harness literacy, to manage, measure, teach, and exploit it, intensified throughout the twentieth century. It is vital to pay attention to this development because it largely sets the terms for individuals' encounters with literacy. This competition shapes the incentives and barriers (including uneven distributions of opportunity) that greet literacy learners in any particular time and place. It is this competition that has made access to the right kinds of literacy sponsors so crucial for political and economic well-being. And it also has spurred the rapid, complex changes that now make the pursuit of literacy feel so turbulent and precarious for so many.

Each of the following chapters applies the analytical concept of the sponsor to life-history accounts to address fundamental questions about literacy learning in the twentieth century: How do regional economic transformations change the conditions for literacy learning for people in that place? What do sharply rising standards for literacy feel like in the lives of ordinary Americans? How is literacy passed across generations under conditions of rapid social change? What barriers and opportunities in social structures matter to literacy learning at the current time? In several chapters, I have chosen to concentrate on extended exemplar cases to provide detailed examination of the material and ideological conditions that carry potential answers to these questions. Where exemplar cases are used, they have been chosen for the clarity and robustness with which they illustrate findings from the larger body of life accounts. In other chapters, the data have been sliced more thickly, across groups and at times across the entire set of interviews. Although in the end it has been necessary to focus in depth on only a few of the many interviews that I collected, it was only by collecting and analyzing many interviews (indeed, I wish there could have been more) that I could find the recurrent patterns and themes that I here illustrate with fewer, in-depth cases.

Chapter 1, Literacy, Opportunity, and Economic Change, treats literacy learning in relationship to regional economic restructuring over a 60-year period. The chapter follows the lifelong literacy experiences of two women born and raised on small, family-owned dairy farms, one at the beginning of the twentieth century and one near the end. Their literacy learning is set within the growing intrusions of corporate agribusiness into dairy communities, rising poverty in rural communities, and the takeover of former farmland by urban and suburban interests. The chapter considers how affiliations with dominant and minority economies, including gender expectations within those economies, affect paths for literacy learning. As economies rise and fall in salience, size, or value, the literacy opportunities of people linked to those economies also rise and fall, along with their overall potential to trade on that literacy.

Chapter 2, Literacy and Illiteracy in Documentary America, inquires into the meanings of sharply rising standards for literacy: how these standards arrive in people's lives and how people respond to them. In the twentieth century, as print became more and more useful for selling products, integrating systems, managing bureaucracies, waging war, and so on, sponsors of literacy proliferated as did the ferocity of their competitions. Caught up in these competitions, more and more Americans felt the demand to do more and more things with their literacy. The chapter investigates patterns of sponsorship in the literacy learning of two adult men during 20 critical years of their lives. One, an auto worker turned union representative, struggled to adjust to an increasingly legalistic context in which union bargaining and grievance proceedings occurred. In this transition, his skills as a debater and negotiator were eclipsed by the growing importance of written documents within union–management competitions. The second man, a former sharecropper growing up in the jaws of racism, entered prison in the 1970s unable to read or write. He began a gradual project of self-rescue within the context of a modernizing prison. In synchronization with a series of legal rulings that expanded prisoner rights and access to legal knowledge, he left prison a literate man. In both cases, analysis focuses on competitions within what Edward Stevens has called "advanced contractarian society" as it served to sponsor literacy learning in the latter half of the twentieth century.[27]

Chapter 3, Accumulating Literacy: How Four Generations of One American Family Learned to Write, revisits the same regional landscape as is studied in Chapter 1. However, here, the story is told through the perspective of four consecutive generations of the May family, all of whom lived within a 20-mile radius of one another in a dynamically developing county in Wisconsin. The chapter follows the family as it moves, with the nation overall, from the village to the city to suburbia, from farming to manufacturing to a high-tech, service economy. The chapter looks at how reading and writing are passed from one generation to the next, and how the larger economic and cultural transformations in which the family is engaged affect that process. The Depression, World War II, the expansion of educational opportunities, the arrival of mass media, and the tightening association between social viability and literate skill are all considered through the life experiences of the May family. The chapter demonstrates how histories of economic competition in which families have been engaged supply many of the resources through which later generations encounter literacy. However, as economic change accelerates, the time span shrinks in which these resources remain durable and relevant. The challenges to literacy learning and life chances are explored.

Chapter 4, "The Power of It": Sponsors of Literacy in African American Lives, looks at the experiences of people whose literacy expanded dramatically during a period in which they were experiencing systematic exclusion from educational and economic opportunity. Throughout the twentieth century, the literacy development of African American citizens was rarely figured into the needs of the nation's changing economy, and even when African Americans attained high-level literacy, the worth of that literacy was usually honored only within the African American community itself. How does literacy develop in the absence of broad economic sponsorship and subsidy? This chapter looks at how self-help systems developed by African Americans to survive slavery and legal segregation worked during the twentieth century to sponsor literacy learning. The chapter considers specifically the role of the African American church, African American educators, and the African American–oriented media as they appeared as sponsors of literacy in the lives of 16 individuals born between the 1910s and the 1970s. These traditional cultural agents formed the deep wells that fed a steady rise in literacy and education rates among African Americans. The chapter ends by tracing these major sponsorship networks as they converged in the writing development of one man during nearly 50 years of experience.

Chapter 5, The Sacred and the Profane: Reading versus Writing in Popular Memory, treats all 80 life histories to consider some surprising differences in the cultural contexts in which people remembered learning to read versus learning to write. Although reading appears as a deeply sanctioned activity in most families and communities, writing is a more ambivalently encouraged enterprise and is fraught, more than reading, with secrecy, punishment, and surveillance. Reasons for these discrepancies are sought both in the reconstructed memories of the people interviewed and in the different cultural and economic traditions by which reading and writing have developed in America. The implications of these legacies are explored in light of the central role that writing is coming to occupy in work and social relations at the start of the twenty-first century.

Chapter 6, The Means of Production: Literacy and Stratification at the Twenty-First Century, addresses issues of literacy and social equity. It follows the literacy learning in the lives of two young people who were born in the same year, 1969. The chapter asks how, despite ostensible democracy in educational chances, stratification of opportunity continues to organize access and reward in literacy learning. The chapter looks behind the static socioeconomic factors that typically explain differential outcomes in literacy achievement (i.e., family income, race, and education). It goes more deeply into the patterns of literacy sponsorship that lie behind those profiles. The two young people are linked to very different economic histories, which, in the same place at the same time, supply different access routes, different degrees of sponsoring power, and different scales of monetary worth to the reading and writing practices they learn. This chapter also explores the emerging prominence of mass media and computer technology in the lives of young learners as well the multicultural and ideologically complex forms of literacy that many Americans practice. This chapter considers how schools and other interested parties could mount more inventive methods for intervening, as sponsors, to equalize chances and rewards for literacy learning.

The Conclusion, Literacy in American Lives, wraps up the inquiry, revisiting the main findings across focus topics. The chapter argues that contemporary literacy learning is caught up in unprecedented transformations in the role of literacy in modern technological societies. Through most of its history, literacy was associated with the conservative interests of central authorities, principally church and state. Over the last century, however, literacy and its spinoffs have become most associated with revolutions in communication technologies, diversification of forms and formats, destabilization of knowledge, and decentralization of authority. It is in and through these conditions that writing and reading are now learned. The chapter ends with an exploration of the implications of this shift for schools and other instructional sponsors of literacy.

1

LITERACY, OPPORTUNITY, AND ECONOMIC CHANGE

The foundation of national wealth is really people – the human capital represented by their knowledge, skills, organizations, and motivations. Just as the primary assets of a modern corporation leave the workplace each night to go home for dinner, so the income-generating assets of a nation are the knowledge and skills of its workers – not its industrial plants or natural resources. As the economies of developed nations move further into the post-industrial era, human capital plays an ever more important role in their progress. As the society becomes more complex, the amount of education and knowledge needed to make a productive contribution to the economy becomes greater [Johnson & Packer, 1987, p. 16].

With this policy blueprint, called *Workforce 2000,* the U.S. Department of Labor bluntly exposed the way that literacy ability, corporate profitability, and national productivity have all become entangled. At one time, American workers had value for their capacity to transform raw materials into consumable goods. But by the start of the twenty-first century, they had become the raw material itself. The nature of work in the United States puts a premium on the ability to traffic in symbols generally and in verbal symbols particularly, as print and print-based technologies have penetrated into virtually all aspects of money making. In an information economy, reading and writing serve as input, output, and conduit for producing profit and winning economic advantage. Systematic information has replaced direct experience as the basis for knowledge making and decision making, turning texts into the principle tools and literacy into the principle craft of the information economy.[1] If the ability to read and write was once regarded as a duty to God or democracy, it is now, according to the government, a duty to productivity, and one with increasingly sharp consequences for those not in compliance. Unrelenting economic change has become the key motivator for schools, students, parents, states, and communities to raise expectations for literacy achievement. It is also considered the key reason for widening gaps in income between skilled and unskilled workers.

But for all of the attention paid to this modern-day literacy crisis, in which the demand for literacy seems chronically to outstrip supply, not enough concern has been paid to how economic change itself affects people's ability to become and stay literate. The economic shifts that move us "further into the post-industrial era" do not merely apply pressure for a more highly literate workforce; they also, more profoundly, constitute the turbulent conditions in which individuals, families, and entire regions must collect resources for literacy learning. Fierce economic competitions, including the changes in communication they stimulate, can destabilize the public meanings and social worth of people's literate skills. They also can reconfigure the social and economic systems through which people must pursue literacy and pass it along to others.[2]

This chapter looks at the effects of rapid economic change and regional restructuring on opportunities for literacy learning as they manifest themselves in local ways of life. The perspective will be through the lifelong literacy learning of two twentieth-century women, each born into the family farm economy of the upper Midwest. The focus especially will be on how regional restructuring can alter access and reward for literacy and how the interplay of receding and emerging economies affects the social contexts that sustain possibilities for learning.

As explained in the Introduction, the cases are built on an analysis of what I call the sponsors of literacy, those agents who support or discourage literacy learning and development as ulterior motives in their own struggles for economic or political gain. Sponsors became a particularly illuminating lens for tracking the presence of economic forces at the scenes of literacy learning, for tracing connections between the ways that money gets made and the way that literacy gets made. Sponsors appeared all over people's memories of how they learned to write and read, in their memories of people, commercial products, public facilities, religious organizations, and other institutional and work settings. As we will see below, sponsors are an especially tangible way to track connections between literacy as an individual development and literacy as an economic development because of how closely literacy in the twentieth century grew integral to the interests of corporate capitalism. Sponsors, as I came to understand them, embody the resource management systems of literacy, particularly avenues to access and reward. Sponsors also introduce the instability in the worth of people's literacy. As various sponsors of literacy emerge and recede, and as their prospects rise and fall as part of economic and political competition, so go the prospects of those they sponsor, both in terms of opportunity for literacy learning and the worth of particular literacy skills. Analysis of sponsorship exposes the ways that individual acts of literacy learning partake of social and economic conditions around them and pinpoints the changing conditions of literacy learning across time.

Previous social histories of literacy have paid particular attention to material and cultural conditions that spread mass literacy in its initial stages in the United States and elsewhere, especially in the periods before mandatory public schooling. Where once investigations into the spread of mass literacy relied on crude measurements such as signature rates or book ownership,[3] revisionist historians try to recover the broader contexts that favored or disfavored literacy in particular times and places. They seek an understanding of both the "pull" of literacy (i.e., the various economic, political, and social factors that induced literacy use or denied it) and the "push" for literacy (i.e., the motivations, aspirations, and struggles by which common people gained access to reading and writing). These investigations have considered, among other factors, religion, imperialism, occupations, population density, slavery, urbanization, commercialization, democratization, schools, political stability, transportation, trade, family relations, and various pressures of supply and demand as they contributed or not to the spread of literacy. Disagreements abound as to which factors accounted most for the entrenchment and continued growth of literacy. Historians variously emphasize one factor over another, although more recent thinking suggests that regions arrived at literacy (or didn't) by differing constellations of conditions. Blanket claims about the causes of literacy are extremely difficult to apply.[4]

Histories of the spread of mass literacy are filled with information about the major sponsoring agents responsible for the pull toward learning to read and write. This history demonstrates how, until relatively recently, the major agents of literacy have been church and state. Missionaries, conquerors, conscriptors, and nation builders throughout time imposed literacy and literacy teaching as part of the mass conversion of hearts and minds required for their causes, just as resistors, critics, heretics, and revolutionaries could use literacy to withstand or transform indoctrination. In the United States, the aim of universal literacy began as an imperative of the Christian mission and, by the middle of the nineteenth century, had shifted to secular interests of nation building, social conformity, and civic responsibility. Commercial interests, of course, produced and distributed Bibles, books, newspapers, writing utensils, and other such material goods and stimulated growth in the occupations that supported these products.[5] But until only quite recently literacy was principally a form of consumption, not of production; serviceable forms of reading and writing were practiced in society long before literacy was required by or relevant to most occupations.[6]

This history is enlightening as a general reminder of how the meaning of literacy and the means by which it arrives to people is always under historical change. Specifically, historical accounts demonstrate how newly emerging sponsors of literacy can take over the ideological apparatus associated with earlier forms of literacy. Work by Soltow and Stevens (1981) and Graff (1979, 1986) illustrates how the moral basis of religious literacy could be appropriated, nearly wholesale, by the "civic religion" of literacy for citizenship. Reading could retain an association with virtue and industry even while moving into a secular context. In a related vein, this history illustrates how one wave of literacy development enables the next. Without the efforts of churches to establish schools and inculcate a moral imperative for literacy teaching within families, the state would not have been able to use literacy so effectively for social control and nation building. Likewise, the relative democratization of reading and writing skill that accompanied state sponsorship of schooling became an irresistibly exploitable resource for corporate capitalism as it developed in this century. As we will see below, these dynamics of literacy sponsorship and ideology enter quite specifically into individual experiences with learning to read and write. This cumulative history of religious, political, and economic interests remains embedded in the systems and practices through which people encounter the meanings and means of literacy today.

Many histories of the initial spread of mass literacy focus on regions as the basis of their analysis.[7] Because they have had to account for uneven growth in literacy, historians have looked at geographical and demographic factors that distinguished areas of widespread literacy from areas of moderate or low literacy. From a regional perspective, historians are able to demonstrate how unequal distributions of literacy related to unequal distributions of other things – wealth, roads, schools, trade, political privilege. How closely people lived together, the kinds of work they did, their relationships to centers of political power, the relative cost of educating children or purchasing books – all of these material conditions affected rates of literacy growth in the past. These histories, of course, turn up inequities within regions as well as among them; women's literacy grew more slowly than men's, blacks' more slowly than whites'. However, these studies show that members of disenfranchised groups had better chances of gaining literacy when they lived in regions where literacy was otherwise abundant.[8]

Regional histories also illuminate the value of literacy as a resource. In the early days of mass literacy, the worth of individual literacy would rise with the rates of literacy in a region. The greater number of people who could read or write, the more those skills could be traded on to conduct social and economic relations and the more likely that reading and writing skills learned in youth would not be lost. (Falling out of literacy was a frequent occurrence in contexts where the uses of reading and writing were few).[9] It is a question whether these same conditions pertain now in quite the same way. Although literacy today obviously still takes its value from its widespread currency, economic changes have brought complications to this formula. Rising values of advanced skills, propelled by new literacy-based technologies, deflate the value of basic literacy in the marketplace today and threaten to make many forms of reading or writing obsolete.[10] Where in the past, social and economic stratification determined one's chances of sharing or not in a common literacy, today literacy itself is more complexly stratified and contributes to widening gaps in social and economic status. Even further complicating are the impacts of information technologies and global consolidations of capital, which, as Castells (1989) observed, is changing the relationship between geography and wealth production. Be that as it may, these historical accounts are a useful reminder that the spread of literacy in the past was fitful, fragile, and vulnerable to disruptions and uneven terrain (geographical, economic, and political). Although much changed during the twentieth century, these histories provide useful conceptual clues for approaching contemporary literacy learning. Based primarily in the eighteenth and nineteenth centuries, these histories treat the arrival of literacy as an agent of change in regional societies, as a new ingredient in social and economic relations. What is left to consider is how a changing literacy, linked to a changing economy, affects regional societies and opportunities for learning within them.

The following discussion, then, looks at two people who learned to read and write within the context of the family farm economy of the upper Midwest. Their accounts can provide a stark and immediately accessible illustration of relationships between literacy learning and economic competition because changes to rural life in American are both dramatic and familiar to the society. Yet the patterns to which this essay draws attention also can be traced – in various degrees and configurations – in the lives of scores of other Americans who participated in an array of rural, urban, and suburban economies over the course of the twentieth century. The analysis will pursue the following general lines of inquiry: What bearing does membership in an economic system have on the sponsorship of literacy learning? How do regional economic competitions enter into experiences with literacy? What opportunities and barriers for literacy learning arise during economic transition and transformation?

Let us, then, consider the parallel lives of two European American Midwestern women I will call Martha Day and Barbara Hunt. Both were raised on 80-acre, low-income dairy farms that their fathers had inherited, Day in northern Indiana and Hunt in southern Wisconsin. Both grew up in sparse, rural settlements of 500 families or fewer, some distance from stores and schools. Both were the middle of three children. Both found much of their academic writing less memorable and satisfying than their extracurricular writing: Day with the high school yearbook and Hunt with her state forensics association. Both read often for pleasure, and both kept journals. Neither had much money or family encouragement for schooling beyond the twelfth grade, and both left home and went to work shortly after high school graduation. For all of these striking similarities in background, however, the differences in their life circumstances are more pronounced. For one thing, they were born 68 years apart, Day in 1903 and Hunt in 1971. Further, although Day found her way after high school into a journalism career, becoming a columnist and women's editor for a regional magazine, the *Mid-Plains Farmer,* Hunt, at 22 years old, was cashiering at the Mid-Plains Mobil Station,[11] doing child care on the side, and taking an occasional course in the human services program at a two-year technical college 25 miles from her home.

This contrast speaks directly of course to the rising standard for literacy and school achievement across a 60-year span. Martha Day's high school graduation in 1920 made her among the best-educated members of her community, whereas in the 1980s the only thing guaranteed to a high-school graduate like Barbara Hunt was that she would earn several hundred thousand dollars less over her lifetime than college graduates. But these accounts also point up subtler cultural changes that affect literacy development. Day came of age when the small family farm economy in the Midwest was worth more, literally in terms of dollars and jobs but also culturally and socially. At the turn of the twentieth century, Day belonged to the 40% of the U.S. population engaged in the agricultural sector. By the time of Hunt's birth in 1971, farm kids belonged to the 2% of the population left in agriculture. Day's residence on an 80-acre farm and her attendance at a two-room country school made her background typical of European Americans in her predominantly rural state. Sixty years later, rural schools joined urban schools in being chronically under-financed in comparison with suburban districts, and family-owned dairy farms were disappearing from the Wisconsin landscape at a rate of 1,000 farms a year.[12] Although Martha Day and Barbara Hunt both were pro-foundly affected by wrenching transformations in rural life, Day was able to trade more seamlessly on the status of her farm-girl background to make the transition from physical to mental labor. For Hunt similar fea-tures of the farm-girl background found little resonance within the econ-omy in which she was competing.

"The Typical Little Village of That Day": The Case of Martha Day

At the risk of oversimplifying, we could say that Martha Day's earliest literacy learning took place within a local society that was growing together while Barbara Hunt's took place within a local society that was coming apart. Many elements of Day's earliest literacy memories are set within an emerging infrastructure of electric lights, paved roads, rural mail delivery, rising farm prices, farm journalism, and expanding schooling that developed as part of a turn-of-the-century boom time in Midwestern rural areas.[13] Like many people I have talked to from this time and place, Day shared proudly in a progressive identity that seemed to be delivered into many rural households along with the local newspaper. Reading of periodicals was linked to forward-looking think-ing, intelligent farming, and political participation, including people like Day's parents, who, like most of their neighbors, had but grade-school educations. Here is Day's recollection of the presence of newspapers in her home:

> Dad always subscribed to [the nearest daily] and took it by the year. My dad was smart and a good scholar and a most interested man in politics and everything that was going on. I don't remember reading it much, but I remember when my father came in from working in the fields, the first thing he'd do [was], if the paper, if the mail had come, he would sit down and read the newspaper. He was very sharp on that kind of thing. For that day.

Martha Day attended grade school about one mile from her farm in one of the many two-story brick schoolhouses that had been scattered around her county in the late nineteenth century.[14] Because her community did not provide public education beyond tenth grade, she and her brother finished high school in a larger town, carpooling with neighbors to make the 10-mile drive. It was in high school that Day discovered her love of writing, primarily through work on the yearbook and through the school library. Current books also arrived at her home by mail, sent at birthdays and holidays by a favorite aunt who was a librarian in Washington, D.C. "I got the feeling of emotions coming through words on paper," Day recalled. "I think reading makes people want to write."

At the time of our interview in 1992, Day was still stinging from the gender discrimination that sent her brother away to college while she stayed in the area to care for her invalid mother. "[My brother's] teachers encouraged him," she explained. "They got a rector scholarship. Told him about it. Nobody told me. I made grades just as good as his. But they didn't push girls, and my parents couldn't have sent us on." Instead, when her mother was well enough, Day moved to the nearest city, worked in the book department of a large department store, and took secretarial courses at night.

Day was part of a major migration of the 1920s – an outflow from the countryside that would help to radically alter the community into which she was born.[15] Nevertheless, many social aspects of a lingering nineteenth-century agrarian tradition seemed to follow her to town, significantly conditioning her literacy opportunities. Chief among these was the broad overlap of homogeneous social institutions that had organized her childhood and would subsidize her "love of writing" well into adult life.

Early in the interview, Day recalled attending grade school in what she described as "the typical little village of that day." "There was," she said, "a school, a church, and a general store." Education, religion, and commerce were located, literally, at the same intersection of her village, so it is not surprising that Day remembered her early literacy learning taking place within a small and local social network. In such a system, you were defined by the family you belonged to, its reputation, and its social standing. Nelson (1995) has written about the economic function of the ethnic homogeneity on which many Midwestern rural communities were founded, calling their close-knittedness "an essential feature of the labor system." Residential segregation was perceived "as a prerequisite for material as well as social success," which in turn depended on "informal bargains and implicit understandings" (pp. 6–7). Despite the fact that so many people were on the move at that time – or perhaps because of it – this network was still in place for Day when she relocated to the city, 50 miles away. "I never did have to hunt for jobs," she said. "Somebody from my area always said, 'Call me' or 'We've got a job. Would you be interested in it?'" Both the informality and the redundancy of these social networks were evident in Day's account of her break into journalism, which occurred shortly after her marriage to a bookkeeper in 1925. She and her husband began attending a Methodist Sunday school class for young married couples that was taught by the then managing editor of a local newspaper. Aware of Day's interest in writing, he asked her to put together a monthly newsletter for the Sunday school group. A few years later, this man bought a small, regional farm magazine and invited Day to become a part-time "rewrite man," as she called herself. Her job was to recast into short news items the press releases and bulletins that were pouring out of the state agricultural university and experimental stations at that time.

Day worked at home, with a typewriter, desk, and filing cabinet that the editor provided. Each Sunday, she brought her rewrites to church and received a new batch of assignments. Occasionally, the editor asked her to write a feature story, usually about a farm woman. Occasionally, Day's husband would go along on her feature assignments to take photographs that illustrated her published articles. The editor was instrumental in teaching Day classic elements of journalistic style. She recalled:

> He kept building me up, you know, giving me a little more instruction. How the first paragraph had to do this and so forth. He would try to coach me along. He'd say, "Now that might have been better if you'd included a little less in that paragraph and things like that."

At the same time, the editor encouraged Day to appeal to her farm background as she imagined topics and audiences. "He'd say, 'Imagine you are a farm woman,'" she recalled. "That I grew up on a farm helped me in some respects. It wouldn't today."

When commercial farm publishing entered a bonanza period in the 1940s, the newspaperman's local farm journal was bought out by a much larger conglomerate, which I call here the *Mid-Plains Farmer*.[16] Day was invited to move to corporate offices and, between several more buyouts and mergers, gradually assumed more editorial responsibility. She contributed a bimonthly column on domestic topics, compiled cookbooks that were distributed as complimentary promotions, and traveled regularly to Chicago and other big cities for editorial meetings or conventions of the National Association of Women Farm Editors (whose membership numbered 16 nationwide). She retired in 1968. At the time of our interview in 1992, she was widowed and residing in a residential care facility near her daughter, some 400 miles from her birthplace. She wrote letters to church friends, some from the original adult Sunday school class, and showed me extensive memoirs she had written in several bound journals that her daughter had bought for her. Although her eyesight was deteriorating, she had recently composed a humorous poem about osteoporosis that a nurse helped her to get published in a health magazine for senior citizens.

This account urges us to consider two significant dimensions of literacy development: first, how the cultural and social organization of a particular economy creates reservoirs of opportunity and constraint from which individuals take their literacy, and second, how these backgrounds can later become exploitable by agents of change. Day's memories of early literacy learning carry the paradoxes and tensions alive in rural, white societies at the turn of the twentieth century, as young people were shaped by conservative values of farm and village even while they were heading for lives elsewhere. For Day, these paradoxes registered most painfully in the gender inequality in which her expanding educational and geographical horizons were encased. Although both she and her brother left the farm, he went to college and to an eventual science career in the nation's capital. She took her interest in reading and writing 50 miles to her state capital for jobs selling books and taking dictation. Yet staying back left her tethered to the conservative social institutions out of which her later literacy opportunities (and their exploitable value) would come. Although village life was already under radical change, the legacies of the village economy, in which religious, educational, and commercial interests blended so routinely, were still intact in her social sphere. This tradition provided the point of contact for Day's entrance into paid, professional writing and sanctioned the informal apprenticeship by which she learned her trade. Local ownership of newspapers and farm journals was part of this social milieu, helping to make Day's local identity part of her qualifications for her first job. Interestingly, in the small, nonspecialized operation of the local farm journal (in which news stories and columns were often contributed by farmers themselves), gender specialization was less pronounced, and Day took on the assignments of a "rewrite man," dealing with technical and agricultural information coming from the landgrant college. Only with her later transfer to the larger corporation would her duties become exclusively that of a "women's" editor.

One more aspect of cultural and social organization is worth noting here. This was a period when print, although becoming more widespread, nevertheless was most readily identified with and experienced through particular institutions in society: the church, the school, the popular press. These were the basic institutions that had promulgated an initial mass literacy in the latter half of the nineteenth century in America. These institutions and their practices came forward into the twentieth century as dense sites of literate resources. This concentration of literate heritages into a few institutions made it common to find people like the Sunday school teacher/newspaper editor, in whose very figure coalesced the religious and secular print traditions that lie deep within the history of the United States. Several members of Day's generation recalled influential teachers who seemed literally to embody these print traditions and make them available in informal, apprenticeship relationships. These strong figures were principal forms by which literacy opportunity appeared in the social arrangements of this time and place.[17]

What remains most interesting about Day's background is how attractive and exploitable it became when the farm magazine industry took off in the 1940s. This was a period of favorable growth in agricultural journalism. Farm outputs were up; fertilizers, irrigation, and other commercial products were being sold, principally through print advertising. A rapid rise in education levels was under way. Agricultural colleges continued to pump out information, which had to be translated into popular treatments. Magazines in this period attempted to appeal to the entire farm family and to uphold feel-good elements of the agrarian tradition even as they subtly changed habits and practices of farm families toward a new, much more business-oriented mode of farming.[18] Women's news was crucial to the commercial success of these magazines, in part because, as Day explained, wives typically were the family members who placed the subscriptions. Although eventually overcome by the growing popularity of full-scale, national women's magazines like *Ladies' Home Journal* or *Good Housekeeping*, women's sections in regional farm journals carried features on topics ranging from gardening and canning to dress, diet, faith, and marital advice.[19] Day wrote on all of these topics in her column, which was often organized around the seasonal rhythms of the farm life in which she had grown up.

The person of Martha Day, the badge of her integrity in her home community, became a badge of her value to the enterprise of farm journalism as it was being practiced at this time. Her conservative farm background, her WASP-ish mores, and her ideological comfort with print as an agent of improvement enabled her to voice the values that the *Mid-Plains Farmer* needed for commercial success. These commercial needs became the vehicle for Day's adult literacy development. This window of opportunity was brief, however. By the time Day retired in the late 1960s, general farm magazines were on the wane, women weren't home anymore to be interviewed for her feature stories, more and more of her published recipes were being provided by large food processing industries, and agribusiness was changing the farm economy from top to bottom. In the interim, though, Day fulfilled her desire to be a writer and had gotten to travel to Chicago and other big cities to gather news, attend conventions, and participate in corporate editorial meetings. All of these opportunities were immensely satisfying to Day from the perspective of the 1990s. At the age of 89, she was still writing and finding her constituency through the newer publishing niche of senior citizen magazines.

It was common to find other European American women among Day's cohort whose early opportunities for education and literacy were freighted with similar responsibilities for upholding agrarian traditions. Rural teaching was one such open opportunity. Industrialization that was under way in the cities at that time relied on steady production of cheap food, so government and business worked programmatically to maintain the farm economy. Rural schools and farm journals were particularly important organs by which the values of agriculture and rural society were reinforced among countryside populations. Ultimately, this effort proved futile, but it was an effort that fell often to women, whether as journalists or grade-school teachers who were recruited to the Country Life Movement at this time.[20] Careers for women engaged them in ideologically conservative work in which their affiliation with rural societies and values became their greatest credential. In other words, conservative gender traditions were exploited for conservative social agendas, with predictable consequences. The work of shoring up a fading way of life that fell to Day and others like her would help to shore up later rounds of economic disadvantage for women as the technological literacy of the male domain came to be much more heavily rewarded later in the century.

In tracing the relationship of Day's literacy development to the economic backdrop in which it occurred, I am not suggesting that hers was the only – or even the most typical – experience of the farm people of her generation. Indeed, among other Midwestern European Americans of her cohort that I interviewed, extreme physical isolation, poor schooling, instability in farm prices, and the catastrophes of the Depression all made access to material and institutional supports for literacy difficult and sometimes impossible. For people bearing the burden of racial discrimination, the conditions usually were much more difficult. However, I did want to show how dynamics of economic competition create the context in which literate resources are pursued, expended, enjoyed, and rewarded. For Day, membership in a cultural majority within a stable – in fact, growing – economy provided both the means and mentality by which her literate interests and skills could pay off. Although Day made a successful transition from agricultural to intellectual labor, the transition depended on being well connected to an older order on whose value she could continue to trade. These social structures provided the forms of sponsorship, invitation, and access by which Day learned and practiced literacy. These structures also provided the ideological constraints that determined what Day wrote, for whom, where, and for how long.

"I Did a Lot with Homelessness": The Case of Barbara Hunt

Barbara Hunt was born in 1971, three years after Martha Day retired from the staff of the *Mid-Plains Farmer*. She was one of three daughters in a family operating a small-acreage dairy farm during some of the most crisis-ridden years in the history of the dairy industry. Lower commodity prices, lower incomes, decreasing farmland values, and difficulty in servicing debt were putting lots of family farms out of business.[21] Wisconsin saw a 50% decline in farms between the 1960s and the 1990s, with the biggest jump between 1987 and 1992, the years that Hunt was attending high school.[22] In ironic contrast to Day's memories, Hunt's keenest memories of the presence of a newspaper in her home were the budget calculations that her father would pencil in the margins.

Like Day, Hunt grew up in a small, ethnically homogenous community founded in the nineteenth century by German Catholic clerics and dairy keepers. At the turn of the twentieth century, it had been one of the main production areas in the state for butter, grain, and tobacco. Now, still characterized as a place where few residents are not related to each other, it is anchored by a stone church, built in the 1850s, which abides as the main social institution. But at the end of the twentieth century, there were neither schools nor much of a commercial base left in this unincorporated community. Hunt was bused 10 miles north across the county line for schooling, and her family drove 20 miles south to find a major shopping district. Passed by when a state highway was built in the 1940s, this community experienced less than a 3% economic growth rate between 1980 and 1990, compared to a 14% economic growth rate in the county overall. Per capita income lagged in relation to the rest of the region as well. On the other hand, dairy herds were still thick, and competition among the farms was quite keen. In the late 1980s, land in the area was changing hands at a record pace as farmers with more capital were buying out their neighbors.

Hunt's residence in a village that had grown little in 90 years was not "typical for its day," and its homogeneity was no longer relevant to the structure of labor, as many residents scattered each morning in their cars for service jobs that had overtaken the urbanizing county.[23] Farm concerns no longer dominated the regional newspapers to which residents of her community subscribed, and the radio, television, and film that infiltrated the Hunt household in the 1970s and 1980s primarily delivered urban-oriented images, information, and perspectives. Hunt recalled with a laugh missing her favorite TV sitcoms because of evening milking chores and then having to watch *The Waltons* and *Little House on the Prairie,* which were on at a later hour. Her school system, answerable to state mandates, typically strained out local culture from its curriculum, so that it would not appear strange, for instance, that in high school, Hunt and her sister studied German as a foreign language, not as the language of the founders of their community. The family purchased used books as well as a used typewriter on trips to a Catholic thrift store. ("We used to go to [the thrift store] and the books were real cheap. They'd be like three cents," Hunt recalled. "So a lot of our books at home were like that. Hey, even if you didn't like them, they were cheap.") Although, as we will see, the teenage Hunt, like Martha Day, was discovering a love of writing and searching for avenues for this drive, she was acquiring literacy as part of a demographic minority, as a member of an unincorporated political unit within the context of late twentieth-century social transformations. Compared with Day's literacy sponsors, Hunt's were more remote and more distributed across geographically and ideologically diverse institutions. Assembling available literacy resources was proving more difficult for Hunt than it had for Day. So was finding employer-sponsors who could enhance her literacy development in her adult years. Her paying jobs were not related to agriculture but rather to low-end retail and government-subsidized services common to areas with stagnant economies. Hired as a home health aide after high school, she charted the weight and pulse of elderly clients on Medicare. ("If anything happened, you had to write," she said, "and I had a lady that everything happened to.") But she was laid off when, during major HMO shuffling in the county, the agency relocated. In the mid-1990s, Hunt's most steady source of income was in day care and private baby-sitting, as farm wives sought off-farm employment to stanch the loss of farm incomes. ("Right now I'm baby-sitting, and I always read to the kids 'cause I think you should. It sinks in," she said.)

To understand how Hunt undertook literacy development during hard times, it will be useful to look at two major sponsors of her writing during late adolescence and early adulthood: the High School Forensic Association to which she belonged for five years and the human resources program of an area two-year college, where she was enrolled part time. Both of these institutions were in some ways helping Hunt to carry her literacy and literate potential into her local economy.

Hunt joined the forensics club in eighth grade. "As soon as I heard about it, I knew I wanted to be in it," she said. For one thing, forensics allowed her to satisfy a lifelong quirk: the love of reading aloud. Early in our interview, she described a familiar living-room scene from her childhood:

> Ever since I was little, I liked to read aloud, and I'd always bug people. I'd be with [my younger sister] and she'd be on the couch and I'd be on the chair, and we'd be reading out loud. We'd get up to a level and it was, "Stop, stop. Stop reading so loud." We'd get louder and louder. She'd stop and I'd go in my room and read out loud anyway. Maybe it was something where I knew, maybe I knew I would like to do my own thing and write on my own.

As a member of the forensic club, Hunt first competed in the category of declamation, reciting published dramatic pieces from memory. But by high school, she was performing in the original speech division, composing and delivering four- and eight-minute speeches.

The forensic club in her high school was part of a statewide consortium of speech, debate, and theater clubs. Interestingly, this association had been founded in 1895 by a school superintendent from the very same district in which Hunt was a student. In fact, this was the first high school forensic association in the United States.[24] In later years it was sustained by the state university extension service and on occasion sponsored joint competitions with Future Farmers of America. By the time Hunt was a member, the forensic association had become an independent organization subsidized by dues from member schools. Headquarters provided handbooks and other instructional guides, trained and certified speech coaches, sponsored regional and statewide competitions, and published a newsletter. This state organization in turn held membership in a national high school forensics association that also sponsored events and provided instructional and promotional print materials.

As a participant in competitions, Hunt wrote speeches on topics of her choice. She picked topics that, in her words, "had real emotion," involving issues that "affected me but kind of affected other people." Her preferred topics included abortion, crack use, racism, and homelessness. "I did a lot with homelessness," she explained. "The homeless problem at the time was my sophomore year, 1986–87. There were three million homeless people in the United States. I wanted to get people to realize what was going on."

To put her speeches together, she used the school library as well as notes she took from TV news and magazine shows. She also was influenced by Hallmark Hall of Fame specials. Song lyrics that she heard on the radio also helped her to reflect on her life and her speech topics. "Songs to me are like some books or some speeches," she said, "when they seem to be exactly what your life is." Hunt also sometimes enhanced her presentations with film clips that she taped on a VCR. She practiced her speeches while doing the chores. "I'd be going along the front of the cows, feeding them with my shovel, and I'd be doing my speech," she recalled. She traveled throughout the region with her speech team, qualifying a couple of times for championships held in the state capital. She also found satisfaction when she developed original introductions that were praised by her coach and sometimes imitated by other students.

Despite its many transformations over a 100-year period, we can say that the forensic association was carrying forward remnants of an oratorical culture that had traditionally sponsored literacy of rural students.[25] The organization trained extracurricular teachers and subsidized public forums in which Hunt usually had more freedom to express herself than in school-assigned or church-assigned writing.[26] That her writing could be performed orally was a powerful incentive for her continuous membership in the organization – one of the few to which she belonged in high school. This format also provided a strong ethical and emotional appeal for her: "When you give a speech, you have to know the material," she said. "I love it when people [in the competitions] know their speeches and are looking right at you as they give them."[27]

For Hunt, high school forensics was sustaining oratorical and ethical values long associated with Midwestern agrarian politics and local self-improvement organizations. Through it, Hunt was able to articulate issues that, as she said, "affected me but kind of affected other people." Like Martha Day, she was voicing the conditions of her time and place but translated through urban equivalents that dominated national media as well as the prepackaged research materials in her high school library. This translation of rural social problems through dominant urban ones was not one with which Day had to contend as a writer. And it was not without tensions – some of which infiltrated into Hunt's relationship with her own parents. For instance, speech practice in the dairy barn was conducted under her breath:

Dad probably got so sick of me. He never knew what I was saying because I would never tell him what I was actually saying. I would say it to the cows so he never knew what I was practicing. I could probably give my homeless speech right now, though, if I really thought about it.

At the time of our interview in 1992, Hunt's forensic experience was finding some resonance in a psychology class that she was taking in a human services program offered at an urban technical college to which she was commuting. In the class, she was being asked to write short essays on contemporary social problems. The course was part of a two-year degree program that had begun in the early 1980s to qualify people as technical assistants in social service programs such as drug rehabilitation and family counseling. This vocational program took shape in response to growing regional demand for professionalization in social work, which was accompanying increased private and public investments in child and family welfare. The program, which focuses mainly on problems of urban poverty, racial discrimination, and substance abuse, had become a popular vocational choice for young, first-generation college women from rural areas. In 1998, six years after our initial interview, Hunt was still trying to finish her two-year degree while continuing to work in area day care centers.

Although it is too soon to predict the full life and literacy trajectory of Hunt, it is clear that many of the local cultural assets that subsidized Day as she made her way into adult literacy either are not available to the younger woman or simply are no longer worth as much in her society. The dairy farm life that Hunt was born to will be hard to parlay directly into economic opportunities – except insofar as it has fine-tuned her sensitivity to human distress. But sensitivity to her rural time and place needs lots of reinterpretation and transformation to operate in the field of social service as it was taught and practiced at the end of the twentieth century. To become a writer in this field, Hunt would need to negotiate abstract academic training, bureaucratized delivery systems, and urban biases that did not confront Day – at least not so centrally – as she broke into agricultural journalism in the 1920s. Hunt's imaginative use of mass media, including songs, news, and TV docudramas, were of some assistance in helping her to develop a more abstract sensibility and identity on which so much contemporary writing relies.

For all of the differences in situation between the two women, it is also worth noticing the similarities in their accounts, particularly the conservative effects of gender. Across the century, gendered divisions of labor constrained options for women, especially those with modest educations.

If Day as journalist was tapped to stabilize traditional farm families for the benefit of an industrializing economy, Hunt as day care worker was tapped to stabilize families in which women and men were being drawn off the farm into wage jobs.[28] At the same time, conservative cultural supports associated with traditional agrarian societies proved vital in encouraging and validating both women's literate skills. Like the figure of the Sunday school teacher/publisher in Day's young adulthood, the state forensic association in Hunt's life delivered traces of older agrarian institutions like the state extension service and self-improvement societies. With its ties to agrarian oratory, speaker integrity, and concern with social issues, the forensic club served as a reservoir of literate practices and values through which Hunt could use her writing to witness for her place – even as she encountered a form of schooling and a larger society that did not make that easy.

Literacy Learning and Economic Change

Literacy learning is conditioned by economic changes and the implications they bring to regions and communities in which students live. Economic changes devalue once-accepted standards of literacy achievement but, more seriously, destabilize the social and cultural trade routes over which families and communities once learned to preserve and pass on literate know-how. As new and powerful forms of literacy emerge, they diminish the reach and possibilities of receding ones. Throughout the 20th century a lopsided competition between corporate agribusiness and family farming altered life for millions of people in the rural Midwest. The accounts of Martha Day and Barbara Hunt can aid speculation about where in the processes of literacy learning economic change has greatest impact. First, we must notice the potential advantages that come with being well connected to dominant economies, whether in periods of stability or change. Dominant economies make their interests visible in social structures and communication systems. Growing up in the heyday of independent agriculture, Day literally could see her way of life reflected everywhere – from the physical arrangement of the institutions sponsoring her literacy learning to the stories and pictures carried in the print media she encountered. Economic typicality as enjoyed by Day seems to remain an advantage even during periods of stressful transition because at least for a while the powerful resources and skills built up in well-developed economies are attractive sites for reappropriation by agents of change. But as family farming receded in economic and cultural dominance, its social structures weakened as an objectified presence in the world around Hunt.[29] With every revolution by which the greater region in which she lived turned to information and service production, the mismatch intensified between the conditions in which her family labored and the conditions in which she was forced to learn and find a living. It is here where literacy disadvantage and economic disadvantage find their relationship.

Hunt's contemporary experience helps to gauge particularly the effects of late twentieth-century economic life on literacy learning. Even in rural areas, the complexity of social organization as well as the proliferating reliance on print means that encounters with literacy are more likely to be spread out across ideologically diverse sources and specialized, often remote institutions. Influences on literacy are simply more diffused. The role of multimedia in Hunt's writing development is perhaps the best illustration of this phenomenon, as she coordinated sources from print, television, radio, and film and transformed them all into the older rhetorical genre of the timed speech. Especially in contrast with Day's experience, Hunt's experience also shows how rapid economic change can interrupt or enervate the social mechanisms that traditionally have supported and sustained literacy. As investments in local education, commerce, and social welfare drain away from a community, the process alters if not erases the institutions by which literacy learning – at least until recent times – has been most broadly sponsored. For these reasons, making literacy, like making money, was proving more complicated for Hunt than for Day, requiring considerable ingenuity, translation, and adaptation. In her early twenties, Hunt was learning to write for an economy she aspired to join while enjoying few of the powerful subsidies that the sponsors of that economy contributed to literacy learning. This is a condition faced by millions of literacy learners of all ages at the beginning of the twenty-first century, learners whose ways of life and labor are undergoing permanent destruction and replacement.

This analysis has tried to get beyond the rhetoric that usually surrounds the topic of literacy and the economic needs of the nation. No teacher or policymaker at any level can ignore the power of the country's economic system, its direction of change in the twentieth century, and the implications that brings, especially now, for literacy and literacy learning. However, we do not need to think only in the terms that government reports suggest. The school's responsibility should not be merely – and perhaps not mainly – to keep raising standards, revising curricula, and multiplying skills to satisfy the restless pursuers of human capital. Efforts must not go only to preparing students for future demands, nor should students' problems with reading or writing be defined solely in terms of rising expectations versus insufficient skills. Economic changes create immediate needs for students to cope with gradual and sometimes dramatic alterations in systems of access and reward for literacy learning that operate beyond the classroom. Downsizing, migrations, welfare cutbacks, commercial development, transportation, consolidation, or technological innovations do not merely form the background buzz of contemporary life. These changes, where they occur, can wipe out as well as open up access to supports for literacy learning. They also can inflate or deflate the value of existing forms of literacy in the lives of students. Any of these changes can have implications for the status of literacy practices in school and for the ways students might interact with literacy lessons.

Increasingly, the ramifications of economic transformation form the history of literacy itself. For these reasons, they deserve a more central role in developing theories of individual literacy development. How do rapid changes in the means and materials of literacy affect the ways that people acquire it or pass it along to others? What enhances or impedes literacy learning under conditions of change? What might we gain by approaching learning disturbances in reading and writing not as individual difficulties but as the perpetual condition in which all of us are forced to function? How can we develop approaches to literacy that are more sensitive to the actual conditions in which people learn to read and write?

The economic conditions of students' lives – although usually the purview of school social workers or financial aid officers – should also be consulted for guidance in curricular thinking. Lessons in reading and writing at any level can bring conscious attention to the origins of texts and their relationship to social context. Learning how to read and write should include developing knowledge about material and technological conditions involved in those practices, as well as the changes that have occurred in reading and writing across time. The problems of literacy as a social issue can and should be incorporated into what counts as basic literacy instruction.[30]

The concept of sponsorship is a concrete analytical tool that can be used toward such projects at various levels. Tracing the sponsors who develop and deliver curricular materials to their schools can heighten students' awareness of who is interested in their reading and writing skills and why. It also can bring attention to the complicated, fast-moving, and far-ranging interrelationships that bear on contemporary reading and writing and may give students useful ways to understand the reasons that school literacy differs from the kinds they engage in elsewhere. Sponsorship is a tool that can clarify for teachers how students in their classrooms are differentially subsidized in their literacy learning outside of school by virtue of the economic histories of their families and regions. Because sponsorship focuses on the many factors that create and deny literacy opportunity, it moves our sights beyond the socioeconomic profiles of individual families toward broad systems of resources for literacy operating in students' worlds. Those who consider public schools an organ of democracy rather than of the marketplace can evaluate how well their schools manage the public resources of literacy under their control to extend the broadest benefit to the most people. As public sponsors of literacy – and not merely teachers, testers, or sorters – schools might include among their measurements of performance how well they redistribute their considerable material powers and intellectual resources to equalize life chances.

Educators at all levels deal with curriculum and performance standards that emanate from governments, regents, district offices, or other centralized agencies. These standards, which usually come in the form of objective aims, goals, requirements, outcome criteria, and so on, usually mask the struggles among competing parties that have gone into their making. They almost always deliver, in unquestioned ways, the prevailing interests of dominant economies. The writing instruction that Barbara Hunt received, the materials she used, the opportunities she was given and not given were all connected, in various ways, to the victories of agents of economic change in her society. New ways of producing wealth invite new forms of social and labor relations, including communicative relations.[31] These presumed relations work their way into the teaching and learning of writing both in and out of school. And they are telegraphed in education standards or policy statements like the one with which this chapter opened. Bourdieu (1998) has observed that

> What appears to us today as self-evident, as beneath consciousness and choice, has quite often been the stake of struggles and instituted only as the result of dogged confrontations between dominant and dominated groups. The major effect of historical evolution is to abolish history by relegating to the past, that is, to the unconscious, the lateral possibilities that it eliminated. (pp. 56–57)

Yet in Hunt's writing, in her efforts to "do a lot with homelessness," we see that histories are not abolished, are not yet submerged in full unconsciousness, even as they undergo transformation. Her experiences speak to the importance of rejecting the amnesia invited by the new imperatives for literacy and reanimating standards with historical awareness. In that way, we can better appreciate the positions of students (or entire schools) in receding economies. To be viable, Hunt, mostly on her own and in the span of a lifetime, must accomplish an abrupt transition from family farm to twenty-first-century postindustrialism – a transition that took the country itself several generations and myriad forms of sponsorship to accomplish. And she must rely heavily on the institution of the school to make that leap. For her and many others, literacy learning entails more than attaining the reading and writing abilities implied by ever-rising standards. It also entails an ability – somehow, some way – to make the transformations and amalgamations that have become embedded, across time, in the history of those standards. Teachers sensitive to the projects of translation and adaptation that underlie students' writing can listen for those moments when students express them and then recognize their value. But, even further, with the right care and insight, the "lateral possibilities" that Hunt's writing remembers and imagines may not be eliminated. Hunt should be able to look to her school for help in articulating the suffering of her community and for realizing her solidarity with those people, urban and rural, who are "kind of affected" by the same issues as she. When we read, write, teach, and learn with historical consciousness, we save from extinction the often inchoate yearnings of voices in change.

2

LITERACY AND ILLITERACY
IN DOCUMENTARY AMERICA

In his fascinating book, *Literacy, Law, and Social Order*, Edward Stevens (1988) explored the difficult relationship between literacy and justice in U.S. legal history. Literacy came to be presumed of the citizen in both political and economic dimensions. Voting, serving on a jury, and seeking entitlements all required access to information that was embodied in writing. Likewise, under the rules of contract, signers were expected to know what they were signing and were bound by it. Although in principle literacy is a foundation of American democracy, it is in practice a troublesome source of inequity and disequilibrium in the administration of justice. Knowing how to read enhances political and economic rights, whereas not knowing how to read diminishes them. In relationship to illiterates, literates enjoy more autonomy and prerogative; in a practical sense, their liberties are worth more. What happens to fairness and equality under the law under such conditions? Stevens explored the crises for individuals and public institutions in a society where justice depends so heavily on the printed word. Drawing on case law, Stevens showed how, at times, U.S. courts tried to protect illiterates from political exclusion and economic exploitation. However, the rights of illiterates gradually lost out to what Stevens called the "ideal of the contract" in American thought – a belief in the unfettered right to pursue private interests by engaging freely in mutual exchanges and obligations. The principle of contract was so powerful that illiteracy eventually came to be treated as a form of irresponsibility.[1]

Connections between literacy and social viability tightened further with what Stevens called the rise of "advanced contractarian society" (p. 25) in the twentieth century. More and more aspects of economic, political, and even social relationships were being conducted through documents – spurred by the development of corporations and the concentrations of power and money that they accrued. Direct market relations between individuals gave way to corporate-style activity – a growth in bureaucratic structures, interdependence, planning, restrictions on the flow of information, and other forms of control, all based largely on written and other symbol-based instruments (p. 185). The industries of insurance and banking grew in size and complexity to handle problems associated with large-scale investment. Governments grew in kind as efforts to regulate commerce and administer justice under these changing conditions required public bureaucracies equal in size and strength to private ones. These developments helped to standardize contracts, rules, and rights, and, in some ways, illiterates and literates alike benefitted from protections built directly into standard language.[2] However, as more political and economic processes were bound up with documents, illiteracy grew more limiting and more punishing. Indeed, these developments strained the basic literacy of all citizens, as staying informed, exercising rights, and claiming a fair share of public resources all involved the negotiation of increasingly complex institutional systems and their thickets of documents. The potential power of one's civil rights rose or fell depending on one's ability to match or surpass a growing standard of sophistication in reading and writing. In an advanced contractarian society, the ability to write has grown as integral as the ability to read; in a world of print, writing is often the only viable way to have voice. At the start of the twenty-first century, the troubled and troubling connections between literacy and justice persist in new form, as society's political and economic relations move increasingly on-line. Unequal access to computer technology introduces new sources of inequality into the processes of staying informed, exercising free speech, and enjoying economic benefits and choices.[3] In a practical way, computer technology amplifies the civil and economic rights of those that have it over those that don't.

Dorothy Smith (1974) explored other ideological dimensions of what she called "documentary reality," a term she used to underscore that in contemporary society, much of what we count as basic features of work and life already has been highly processed through print and other symbolic media. Those who control everything from news reporting to reporting forms structure the ways that people can know the world and determine what counts as fact. Smith called the accounting categories and documentary procedures of any organization its "enforced linguistic resources" (p. 265), the manner and substance in which organizational thinking and action occur. That which is unrepresented or unreported falls away as if it were not there or had not happened. When documents then become the basis of official decision making, their power grows even more profound. Written reports in schools, mental health care facilities, credit bureaus, prisons, hospitals, divorce court, personnel departments, adoption agencies, and Social Security offices – in fact, documents in all modern organizations – control the way that decisions are made, justice is rendered, and resources are distributed. The dominion of documents in very real ways constructs who we are and to what we are and are not entitled. "Our relation to others in our society and beyond," Smith observed, "is mediated by the social organization of its ruling" (p. 267). Again, the growth of computer-based communication will only intensify these trends as more basic social activity will play out in the symbolically arranged world of virtual reality.

Written accounting procedures were a ubiquitous presence in the literacy histories that I collected, and it was clear that learning to write in the twentieth century involved many people in learning how to negotiate – and, at times, circumvent or subvert – various systems of accounting procedures. Henry Schmidt, born in 1908 and a dairy farm inspector for a large milk processing corporation, used to physically carry loan documents and government regulatory booklets into the barns and milk houses that he visited, convincing small-dairy farmers to negotiate loans from his company for modern equipment and helping them to complete government reporting forms that would protect the grade A status of their milk. Independent plumber Sidney Vopat, born in 1913, recalled how he learned to read regulations regarding construction materials and procedures, translating them mentally all the while into cheaper alternatives that still technically met code. "You had to abide by it," he said about plumbing regulations. "But we could always find a cheaper way of doing it. You learned how to be an honest crook." Meat salesman Bill Short, born in 1919, laughingly referred to the expense account he had to keep track of as his "swindle sheet." Animal technician Phil Barnett, born in 1907, recalled increasingly formal accounting procedures at a large public institution that employed him – procedures that required bids for virtually any purchase. In reaction, he and other blue-collar technicians increasingly were called on to make or jury-rig needed equipment as a way to circumvent the lengthy and cumbersome outside contract procedure. Gladys Robinson, born in 1946, served as a home health aide to her ailing mother as a means of supporting both of them as well as an extended family of grandchildren and great-grandchildren. As she documented her mother's condition, she was well aware that the forms also would be scrutinized for judgments about continued funding of her position.[4] Just how much the formal accounting procedures of modern organizations can "rule" inter-personal relations was made clear by Cassandra Hackman born in 1960, who at the time of our interview had just given birth to a son with cerebral palsy. She had been asked by her child's pediatrician to keep an ongoing written record of the baby's sleep patterns, mood, and responses to food and medicine, a log that she took along on all doctor visits. And a young father I interviewed said that a journal that he kept at the request of a mental health counselor during his divorce had become part of the official record during a custody hearing.

These brief illustrations demonstrate the impact of a burgeoning documentary society. Print proliferates in the lives of Americans, as documents form part of the general environment in which the meanings of writing and reading develop. Beyond that, however, we can see how documents become a site on which struggles for rights and resources play out. For individuals, these struggles can both stimulate learning and affect the worth of one's skills. Gladys Robinson's LPN charting skills, for instance, had to craftily keep up with a system that was growing less supportive and more demanding of accountability in medical costs. As her case and those of others show, the struggles of competing interests fought out on the grounds of documents often determine how effective individual literacy skills can be in protecting rights and pursuing well-being. But the competitions that develop in a documentary society reach even further into the history of individual and collective literacy learning, as literacy skills especially over the twentieth century were recruited into the interests of sponsoring agents. The adult writing of dairy inspector Henry Schmidt, for example, developed along with the changing fortunes of the corporation that employed him as it jockeyed for market position and responded to government regulation. With each turn in the contest came new demands on his writing and reading skills. The explosion of information workers over the course of the twentieth century and the rising norms in literacy achievement are both results of the rounds of competition waged on and through the grounds of written instruments. So, to Edward Stevens's concerns about the status of outright illiterates in the rise of documentary society must be added concerns about the role of documentary society itself in making literacy and illiteracy. As documentary activity intensified, the skills of American literates not only got caught up in the struggles but were vulnerable to the outcomes, as fights over valuable access to information or control over accounting procedures would bring inevitable consequences for the status and power of individual literate skill. In document wars (and the technology wars that have evolved from them), rendering an opponent ill-informed or, better yet, illiterate becomes an irresistible and effective strategy.[5] The impact of this process on literacy learning and on the problems of literacy and justice are consequential.

This chapter, then, continues to explore the impact of sponsorship on literacy learning by examining how it functions as part of the growth in "contractarian society." The exploration proceeds again through two extended case studies of literacy development, this time involving two American men. One is Dwayne Lowery, born in 1938, an auto worker turned union representative. He saw the demands on his literacy skills rising precipitously in the 1970s and 1980s as labor and management turned increasingly to document-based struggle to advance their interests. The other man, Johnny Ames, born in 1950 and raised a sharecropper, could barely read or write when he was sent to prison in the late 1970s. Over a period of seven years, he became literate from inside a maximum-security prison during an especially intense period of struggle over the meanings of rehabilitation and the limits of prisoner rights. The analysis of both cases proceeds with several aims. Most generally, the analysis continues to employ the concept of sponsorship to explore how individual literacy development takes shape in synchrony with economic and political developments. The cases also illustrate how struggles among sponsors of literacy create opportunities and barriers for individual literacy learners. Competitions for control or ascendancy inject volatility into the value of people's literacy skills and are most responsible for the unrelenting rise in literacy standards. We will see how intensifying competitions for economic and political edge raise the stakes for literacy for individuals caught up in those contests. The dynamics of these contests affect not only people's economic chances but often their ability to exercise basic rights.

At the same time, the analysis will explore how histories of competition among the sponsors of literacy also provide the resources on which people depend as they cope with escalating demands and shifting definitions of literacy. Residues of past struggles around literacy leave behind critical materials, tools, practices, and values that individuals can amalgamate into new and more adaptive forms of literacy and literacy learning. This accumulating history of literacy grew in ideological density as well as sheer material excess as the twentieth century proceeded. The resultant complexity was both hindrance and help in learning to read and write.

We will see how two men, positioned quite differently by race, region, occupation, and circumstances, are both caught up in the intensifying power of contractarian relations, the thickening context of rules and regulations that came to regulate public and private domains of contemporary society. Contractarian struggles entered labor–management relations and inmate–prison relations during the same 20-year period, bringing dramatic implications for the lives of Dwayne Lowery and Johnny Ames. These struggles both expanded and curtailed the political and economic rights of the two men and, at the same time, expanded and curtailed the power of their literacy. In treating these two case studies in depth, the chapter continues to demonstrate a method for exposing sponsorship patterns in individual literacy learning and also tries to capture the dense and complex character of literacy as it was developing across the latter half of the twentieth century.

Dwayne Lowery, Born 1938

Consider, first, then, the case of Dwayne Lowery, whose transition in the early 1970s from line worker in an automobile manufacturing plant to field representative for a major public employees union exemplified the major transition of the post–World War II economy – from a thing-making, thing-swapping society to an information-making, service-swapping society. In the process, Dwayne Lowery had to learn to read and write in ways that he had never done before. How his experiences with writing developed and how they were sponsored – and distressed – by institutional struggle will unfold in the following narrative.

A man of eastern European ancestry, Dwayne Lowery was born in 1938 and raised in a semirural area in the upper Midwest, the third of five children of a rubber worker father and a homemaker mother. Lowery recalled how, in his childhood home, his father's feisty union publications and left-leaning newspapers and radio shows helped to create a political climate in his household. "I was sixteen years old before I knew that *goddamn Republicans* was two words," he said. Despite this influence, Lowery said he shunned politics and newspaper reading as a young person, except to read the sports page. A diffident student, he graduated near the bottom of his class from a small high school in 1956 and, after a stint in the army, went to work on the assembly line of a major automobile manufacturer. In the late 1960s, bored with the repetition of spraying primer paint on the right door latch of 57 cars an hour, Lowery traded in his night shift at the auto plant for a day job reading water meters in a municipal utility department. It was at that time, Lowery recalled, that he rediscovered newspapers, reading them in the early morning in his department's break room. He said:

At the time I guess I got a little more interested in the state of things within the state. I started to get a little political at that time and got a little more information about local people. So I would buy [a metropolitan paper] and I would read that paper in the morning. It was a pretty conservative paper, but I got some information.

At about the same time, Lowery became active in a rapidly growing public employees union, and, in the early 1970s, he applied for and received a union-sponsored grant that allowed him to take off four months of work and travel to Washington, D.C. for training in union activity. Here is his extended account of that experience:

> When I got to school, then there was a lot of reading. I often felt bad. If I had read more [as a high school student], it wouldn't have been so tough. But they pumped a lot of stuff at us to read. We had extensive homework. We had reading to do and we had to make some presentation on our part of it. What they were trying to teach us, I believe, was regulations, systems, laws. In case anything in court came up along the way, we would know that. We did a lot of work on organizing, you know, learning how to negotiate contracts, contractual language, how to write it. Gross National Product, how that affected the Consumer Price Index. It was pretty much a crash course. It was pretty much crammed in. And I'm not sure we were all that well prepared when we got done, but it was interesting.

After a hands-on experience organizing sanitation workers in the West, Lowery returned home and was offered a full-time job as a field staff representative for the union, handling worker grievances and contract negotiations for a large, active local near his state capital. His initial writing and rhetorical activities corresponded with the heady days of the early 1970s when the union was growing in strength and influence, reflecting in part the exponential expansion in information workers and service providers within all branches of government. With practice, Lowery said he became "good at talking," "good at presenting the union side," "good at slicing chunks off the employer's case." Lowery observed that in those years, the elected officials with whom he was negotiating often lacked the sophistication of their Washington-trained union counterparts. "They were part-time people," he said. "And they didn't know how to calculate. We got things in contracts that didn't cost them much at the time but were going to cost them a ton down the road." In time, though, even small municipal and county governments responded to the public employees' growing power by hiring attorneys to represent them in grievance and contract negotiations. "Pretty soon," Lowery observed, "ninety percent of the people I was dealing with across the table were attorneys."

This move brought dramatic changes in the writing practices of union reps, and, in Lowery's estimation, a simultaneous waning of the power of workers and the power of his own literacy. "It used to be we got our way through muscle or through political connections," he said. "Now we had to get it through legalistic stuff. It was no longer just sit down and talk about it. Can we make a deal?" Instead, all activity became rendered in writing: the exhibit, the brief, the transcript, the letter, the appeal. Because briefs took longer to write, the wheels of justice took longer to turn. Delays in grievance hearings became routine, as lawyers and union reps alike asked hearing judges for extensions on their briefs. Things went, in Lowery's words, "from quick, competent justice to expensive and long-term justice."

In the meantime, Lowery began spending up to 70 hours a week at work, sweating over the writing of briefs, which are typically 15- to 30-page documents laying out precedents, arguments, and evidence for a grievant's case. These documents were being forced by the new environment in which Lowery's union was operating. He explained:

> When employers were represented by an attorney, you were going to have a written brief because the attorney needs to get paid. Well, what do you think if you were a union grievant and the attorney says, "Well, I'm going to write a brief" and Dwayne Lowery says, "Well, I'm not going to"? Does the worker somehow feel that their representation is less now?

To keep up with the new demands, Lowery occasionally traveled to major cities for two- or three-day union-sponsored workshops on arbitration, new legislation, and communication skills. He also took short courses at a historic school for workers at a nearby university. His writing instruction consisted mainly of reading the briefs of other field reps, especially those done by the college graduates who increasingly were being assigned to his district from union headquarters. Lowery said he kept a file drawer filled with other people's briefs from which he would borrow formats and phrasings. At the time of our interview in 1995, Dwayne Lowery had just taken early and somewhat bitter retirement from the union, replaced by a recent graduate from a master's degree program in industrial relations. As a retiree, he was engaged in local Democratic Party politics and was getting informal lessons in word processing at home from his wife.

Over a 20-year period, Lowery's adult writing took its character from a particular juncture in labor relations, when even small units of government began wielding (and, as a consequence, began spreading) a "legalistic" form of literacy to restore political dominance over public workers. This struggle for dominance shaped the kinds of literacy skills required of Lowery, the kinds of genres he learned and used, and the kinds of literate identity he developed. Lowery's rank-and-file experience and his talent for representing that experience around a bargaining table became increasingly peripheral to his ability to prepare documents that could compete in kind with those written by his more highly educated, professional adversaries. Face-to-face meetings became occasions mostly for a ritualistic exchange of texts, as arbitrators generally deferred decisions, reaching them in private, after solitary deliberation over complex sets of documents. What Lowery was up against as a working adult in the second half of the twentieth century was more than just living through a rising standard in literacy expectations or a generalized growth in professionalization, specialization, or documentary power – although certainly all of those things are, generically, true. Rather, these developments should be seen more specifically, as outcomes of ongoing transformations in the history of literacy as it has been wielded as part of economic and political conflict. These transformations become the arenas in which new standards of literacy develop. And for Lowery – as well as many like him since the mid-1970s especially – these are the arenas in which the worth of existing literate skills become degraded. A consummate debater and deal maker, Lowery saw his value to the union bureaucracy subside, as power shifted to younger, university-trained staffers whose literacy credentials better matched the specialized forms of escalating pressure coming from the other side.

In the broadest sense, the sponsorship of Lowery's literacy experiences lies deep within the historical conditions of industrial relations in the twentieth century and, more particularly, within the changing nature of work and labor struggle over the last several decades. Formal relationships of all kinds came to rely on elaborately explicit rules and regulations. For labor, these conditions only intensified in the 1960s and 1970s when a flurry of federal and state civil rights legislation curtailed the previously unregulated hiring and firing power of management. These developments made the appeal to law as central as collective bargaining for extending employee rights.[6] I mention this broader picture first because it relates to the forms of employer backlash that Lowery began experiencing by the early 1980s and, more important, because a history of unionism serves as a guide for a closer look at the sponsors of Lowery's literacy.

These resources begin with the influence of his father, whose member-ship in the United Rubber Workers during the ideologically potent 1930s and 1940s grounded Lowery in class-conscious progressivism and its favorite literate form: the newspaper. On top of that, though, was a prag-matic philosophy of worker education that developed in the United States after the Depression as an anticommunist antidote to left-wing intellectual influences in unions. Lowery's parent union, in fact, had been a central force in refocusing worker education away from an earlier emphasis on broad critical study and toward discrete techniques for organizing and bar-gaining. Workers began to be trained in the discrete bodies of knowledge, written formats, and idioms associated with those strategies. Characteristic of this legacy, Lowery's crash course at the Washington-based training cen-ter in the early 1970s emphasized technical information, problem solving, and union-building skills and methods. The transformation in worker education from critical, humanistic study to problem-solving skills was also lived out at the school for workers where Lowery took short courses in the 1980s. Once a place where factory workers came to write and read about economics, sociology, and labor history, the school is now part of a university extension service offering workshops – often requested by management – on such topics as work restructuring, new technology, health and safety regulations, and joint labor–management cooperation.[7] Finally, in this inventory of Lowery's literacy sponsors, we must add the latest incarnations shaping union practices: the attorneys and college-edu-cated coworkers who carried into Lowery's workplace forms of legal dis-course and "essayist literacy."[8]

What should we notice about this pattern of sponsorship? First, we can see how the course of an ordinary person's literacy learning – its occasions, materials, applications, potentials – follow the transformations going on within sponsoring institutions as those institutions fight for economic and ideological position. As a result of wins, losses, or compromises, institu-tions undergo change, affecting the kinds of literacy they promulgate and the status that such literacy has in the larger society. So where, how, why, when, and what Lowery practiced as a writer – and what he didn't practice – took shape as part of the postindustrial jockeying going on since the 1970s among labor, government, and industry. Yet there is more to be seen in this inventory of literacy sponsors. It exposes the deeply textured history that lies within the literacy practices of institutions and within any individ-ual's literacy experiences. Accumulated layers of sponsoring influences – in families, workplaces, schools, memory – carry forms of literacy that have been shaped out of ideological and economic struggles of the past. This history, on the one hand, is a sustaining resource in the quest for literacy. It enables an older generation to pass its literacy resources onto another. Lowery's exposure to his father's newspaper reading and supper-table political talk kindled his adult passion for news, debate, and language that rendered relief and justice. This history also helps to create infrastructures of opportunity. Lowery found crucial supports for extending his adult literacy in the education networks that unions established during the first half of the twentieth century as they were consolidating into national powers. On the other hand, however, this layered history of sponsorship is also deeply conservative and can be maladaptive because it teaches forms of literacy that oftentimes are in the process of being overtaken by new political realities and by ascendant forms of literacy. The decision to focus worker education on practical strategies of recruiting and bargaining – devised in the thick of Cold War patriotism and rapid expansion in union memberships – became ripe, by the Reagan years, for new forms of management aggression and cooptation.

It is actually this lag or gap in sponsoring forms that we call the rising standard of literacy. The pace of change and the place of literacy in economic competition have both intensified enormously in the recent past. It is as if the history of literacy is in fast-forward. Where once the same sponsoring arrangements could maintain value across a generation or more, forms of literacy and their sponsors can now rise and recede many times within a single life span. Dwayne Lowery experienced profound changes in forms of union-based literacy not only between his father's time and his but also between the time he joined the union and the time he left it, 20-odd years later. This phenomenon is what makes today's literacy feel so advanced and, at the same time, so destabilized.

Johnny Ames, Born 1950

If we can say, in a rough sense, that Dwayne Lowery's literacy was overpowered by late-century competitions between labor and management, we find in Johnny Ames a man whose experience moved him in an opposite direction – from illiteracy to literacy – in approximately the same time period, from the late 1970s to the early 1990s. Ames was an inmate for more than 16 years in maximum- and medium-security prisons in the Midwest during a period of sharp ideological fluctuations in approaches to penal administration, prisoner rights, and rehabilitation. The same civil rights rulings that informed labor–management battles in which Lowery was involved also informed inmate–institution battles during approximately the same time period. In the cross-currents of these competitions,

Ames amalgamated the resources by which he taught himself to read and write, passed a GED test, and completed an associate's degree as a para-legal technician. He wrote an appeal that overturned his conviction and eventually was released from prison. In the early 1990s at the age of 41, he began a career as a legal-aid researcher and part-time counselor of youth offenders.

The case of Johnny Ames is presented here not because it is represen-tative of people sent to prison – for it clearly is not.[9] Nor is this case meant to be representative of how one unusually humane, gifted, and hard-work-ing individual can overcome all odds – although it clearly is. Rather, the aim is to continue to explore the dynamics of literacy sponsorship as they function within current institutional and cultural life – to examine in detail how barriers and opportunities for literacy learning arise out of accumu-lating struggles for economic and political advantage, struggles to which the powers of print increasingly become tied. Out of the dense and often contradictory conglomeration of materials, practices, and personnel con-verging in a penal institution in the late twentieth century, Ames was able to reroute even some of the most oppressive aspects of literacy's power into a project of justice and self-rescue.

Ames, an African American, was born in 1950 in a rural community under oppressive political and economic conditions still bearing the arrange-ments of nineteenth-century slavery and peonage. He grew up in an extended family led by his grandmother, who served as a tenant forewoman on a cotton farm and in later years built her own home and worked as a domestic. Except for an aunt who had migrated to New York, Ames said he knew of no adults in his family who had more than a fourth-grade educa-tion. However, Ames saw his grandmother writing and keeping figures in connection with her work overseeing day workers. He explained:

> My grandmother's job was to hire people to pick cotton, fill out, do all the figures. She had to put the name of the people, how much they worked, how much they picked a day. Every time they picked, she had to weigh the cotton and tally it up at the end of the day, take it to the gin, get it weighed, get the money, pay the people off, and take the money and turn it in. She had to keep books for the person she worked for. We lived in a sharecropper's house. The person my grandmother worked for, the man on the farm, let us live in the house.

Evenings at home were spent around a wood-burning stove or on the porch where adults told stories or his grandmother read from the Bible.

"She would tell me stories about it," he recalled. "She would tell me stories based on nature. Most of her stories were based on the Bible and nature. Mostly proverbs." Other family members, some who were visiting temporarily, also told stories: "The stories were so real," he said. "You could tell that most of the stories came of life experience. Down South it would be real dark, no street lights. So when they'd tell these stories, it'd seem like you could see the things they were talking about. They made the stories humorous. But they'd seen a whole lot of stuff and they were telling us about it."

Despite intense interest in imaginative and didactic stories heard at home and at Sunday school, Ames was a reluctant student who preferred the company of his grandmother over the classroom. "School was not interesting to me," he said. "My focus was mostly on my grandmother. When she'd go clean up, I used to clean up. I'd cook. I'd do everything. Everything she used to do, I used to do." Ames said he attended school only because his grandmother told him she would be arrested if he didn't go. But reading and print were often sources of negative racial messages – messages that he knew enough to repudiate even at a young age. From the prohibitive signs on segregated water fountains and eateries to his teacher's reading aloud of the racist story *Little Black Sambo*, print was a source of confusion and turbulence:

> That story about Little Black Sambo did something to me, I mean it really did. It just didn't make sense. And I guess during that time when you're a kid and you're trying to make sense out of something that don't make no sense, eventually you just resolve in a way that none of this makes sense. That story threw everything out of whack. And then there were the signs [i.e., No Negroes Allowed], and they had to write those signs. In my mind I can see how that association took the drive out of me. It didn't motivate me to write.

By the time he reached eighth grade in the early 1960s, virtually unable to read or write, Ames followed what was then local custom and stopped attending school: "Down South everybody dropped out of school mostly because they worked in the fields. They worked more instead of going to school. Working was our livelihood. It was connected to our supporting ourselves."[10] But that system of tenant farming was fast evaporating, even in the isolated counties of central Missouri where Ames was coming of age. As farm mechanization appeared, so did truant officers. "They were trying to get most people down South to go to school because it was a big political thing," Ames explained.

The "big political thing" was an escalating youth unemployment rate that was of growing concern to government. In addition, at this time, in the early stages of the Vietnam War, up to one third of military recruits were being rejected for a lack of basic skills. In 1964, Lyndon Johnson signed the Economic Opportunity Act, creating, among other antipoverty initiatives, the Job Corps.[11] Under this program, hundreds of residential training facilities were opened, many in remote areas of the country, to provide vocational and educational training to low-income teenagers. Among the first recruits was 14$^1/_2$-year-old Johnny Ames, who was taken from Missouri to Idaho. He described the experience:

> It was on-the-job training in manual labor. Driving heavy equip-
> ment. I guess they had another part of the Job Corps where they
> had a lot of reading and writing. I guess. But at the time, the one I
> was in, we mostly did manual labor. Dig trenches, cut trees, land-
> scaping. Never had too much reading or writing.

Nevertheless, Job Corps field trips sometimes included visits to college campuses.[12] Ames particularly recalled one outing to a college in a small northwestern town:

> It was the first time I saw a real African person. I said, "Hey, there's
> a black person right there." It was the first time I had seen a black
> person in this little town. And they said, "No, that's an African." So
> I went over and started talking to him. He didn't even talk English
> that much. But that was the first time I ever saw anything besides
> the Tarzan program of Africa in my life at that time.

Like many Job Corps enrollees in this period, Ames quickly grew homesick and miserable. He was released after five months and returned home.[13] "I just roamed around, went fishing and stuff like that," he said. When he got older, he found marginal agricultural employment, then married and migrated to the automobile manufacturing areas of the upper Midwest. It was there that he was arrested and convicted of a capital offense. At age 25, he received a life sentence and entered a maximum security prison. Ames said his efforts to learn to read and write began with the urge, eventually realized, to be able to read the transcript of his trial.

> When I went to prison, I knew I was functionally illiterate. I could see
> things but I couldn't understand what I saw. I told the truth [at my
> trial] and they talked over my head. I didn't know what was happen-

ing. I literally did not understand what was going on. I heard the words; I went through the nods and the gestures. But in all actuality, I didn't know what was going on. They were painting a picture of me that I really didn't understand. When I could read and understand what they said about me, [I could see that] they made me out to be something that I was not. And it hurt me real, real bad, in my heart, in my soul. And I said I would never let anyone talk over my head again. I vowed to myself that I would never do that.

Ames's reeducation in prison began with a chance meeting:

Prison was like total repression. We marched in twos, we had to stop talking at seven o'clock, and there was nothing about encouraging people to learn anything. But I ran up on an ex-nun named R_____ E_____ who was there at the prison. She was a schoolteacher and she always read books, Booker T. Washington, *Up from Slavery,* and things like that. At first I didn't know what the word *slavery* was. I thought it was like *self,* the word *self.* So I asked a friend what the word was and he said *slavery.* So I went to her and I said, "Well, you must like what your people did to us." And she said, "I'm going to show you that all white people are not alike." So she made me sit at a desk the days after that and made me read that book. I used to stumble through the words and she used to tell me words. And she kind of encouraged me to continue to read. So I began to like it. I got really interested in books.

Using a dictionary given to him by the nun, Ames continued to work through books by Washington and Frederick Douglass as well as titles on inner growth, also given to him by the nun. He sought additional books through the prison library and began copious copying of passages that appealed to him. "I would go over the words, and the ones I didn't understand, I would get a dictionary or I would ask," he explained. "I had no qualms about asking a person, 'What does this mean?' I do that right today. If I run up on words I can't pronounce, I just say, 'Pronounce this word for me,' 'cause now basically I know the meaning of a lot of words that I may not pronounce well."

Ames was assigned to work in the prison clinical services department, where a staff of psychologists and social workers administered tests, classified inmates, ran group therapy sessions, and controlled and monitored prisoners classified with mental problems. Ames was buying a lot of books by this time and occasionally exchanged them with the psychologists and social workers with whom he was associating. "Because of the nature of my offense, the staff people always liked to give me psychological tests just to see if I could do them. I'd say I was their guinea pig and they were my specimens, because I was studying them, too." Ames also became active in the Lifers' Group, which had been organized in the mid-1970s to gain more opportunities, including education privileges, for prisoners with life sentences. "The policy of the Division of Corrections then was not to educate lifers. They wanted to focus their funds on people who were going to get out," he explained. This group independently began raising money for education programs for themselves and others, helped by some members who already had education. "This was a diverse group of men," he explained. "It was men that could write and could think." They established an anticrime program for teenagers. They sold candy, canned goods, and photographs and applied for grants. The group was able to sponsor master's-level correspondence courses for one of their members to become a psychologist for the group. "Our objective was that we needed our own psychologist," he explained. "A person who had a life sentence could understand the mind of another lifer."

Many petitions and proposals were written through the 1970s and early 1980s, as the group had to win the right to meet and have access to written materials. "That's how other groups in the prison system now get to meet," Ames explained, "because we established a rule for that." Eventually Ames became coordinator of the group, serving for two years, working intensely on a number of grant proposals and petitions, written on a typewriter bought for him by his mother. Although he had enrolled in no formal course work, Ames talked his way into taking the GED and passed it. Soon after, as we will see below, he enrolled in college courses.[14]

At about this time, in North Carolina, inmates won a crucial U.S. Supreme Court case, *Bound v. Smith*, that upheld their Fourteenth Amendment right to represent themselves in court and to have access to legal research facilities from inside prison. The court ruled that state prisons had to help inmates in the filing of legal papers either by providing adequate law libraries or adequate assistance from trained legal personnel. At the time, the law library in the prison that held Ames was underequipped ("nothing more than a three-sided closet," as he recalled, with minimal and out-of-date holdings), and most inmates were not allowed access to it. In the wake of *Bound v. Smith*, a legal aid agency operating at the prison began to expand its presence, helping the inmates and prison staff construct a functioning law library. University professors associated with the legal clinic recruited Westlaw (a major electronic commercial legal database) to donate time to teach legal reading and research techniques to a small group of inmates, who would, in turn, teach other prisoners. Two community colleges were recruited to sponsor a formal associate's degree program in legal assistance.

Ames was among 15 inmates chosen for the formal program. He took courses in research and legal writing and used the law library, helped there by a librarian who took an interest in his well-being (and would eventually serve as proofreader of his legal appeal). Reading was intense during this period. "That's the good thing about this country," Ames remarked. "Everything they do, they write down. If you have enough patience, you can read about how they do it and then you can do it." Ames used his legal education to appeal his original conviction, helped in the process by students and lawyers employed by the legal clinic. His conviction, in fact, was overturned in 1981, but because of bureaucratic delays accomplished by a powerful, tough-on-crime state administration, Ames would remain in the prison system on technicalities for another 11 years.

He was, however, transferred out of the mass, concrete cell blocks of the maximum-security prison to a medium-security prison that had been founded 20 years earlier on progressive principles of rehabilitation. Built on 85 acres, the prison provided dormitory-like facilities with individual rooms and large, open lawns. Every inmate had a job or went to school or both and all were strongly encouraged to participate in clubs or work on projects. Heavily treatment oriented, the prison had a policy that considered everyone on the staff, including guards, as counselors and the entire staff participated in formal counseling sessions. Ames went to work for the legal clinic, teaching other inmates how to do legal research and explaining the law to them. It was at the time of his transfer, according to Ames, that "writing on my own started to kick in."

> For seven years I had only seen the tops of the trees. I'd make jokes about it. The trees don't have bottoms. We'd never see the bottoms. When I got to [the medium-security prison], there was grass and the bottoms of trees. I was talking about how exuberant I was and how I could smell. I wrote all that down.

He also started using writing to record incidents of racial tensions and injustices that he witnessed in the prison. "I'd write my feelings about that and throw them away," he said. "I knew there was trouble to get into for speaking, so I said, well, I'm not going to speak it. I'll just write it down."

Throughout his prison term, Ames also wrote in connection with mandatory participation in therapeutic groups, in which he was frequently chosen leader. This writing ranged from workbooklike questions and answers to a full-blown autobiography. "It was basically done for yourself," he said of this writing, although the writing was reviewed by administrators and sometimes used in the preparation of psychological profiles introduced at parole hearings.

In 1992, Ames was at last paroled and became a full-time researcher in a legal clinic providing assistance to incarcerated people. He researches law and translates legal issues into lay terms, both in speaking and writing. Of the writing he does on his job, he said:

> I basically explain administrative codes, what the statutes are, what the latest rulings of the courts are. I basically do factual writing. It has to be very concise. [The clients] must have no reason to be misled as to whether we are going to represent them when in fact we're not going to represent them or whether they have an issue when in fact they don't have an issue. The work I do is important because the men really need someone to explain to them their particular situation. I learned to write in order to convey that message to them so that they can understand what's going on in their life.

Ames learned how to use a computer on the job, primarily by reading a word processing book. Occasionally, he said, he asked questions of more experienced supervising attorneys or younger law students who worked with him, "little things mostly just to confirm what the book said," he explained. On nights and weekends, Ames also works for a community organization providing programs for youth offenders in presentencing or probation. Counselor and mentor, he loans books to the teenagers and takes them to area lectures. Ames also served on a citizen task force on gang activity in the county in which he lived, attending meetings with elected officials, school authorities, corrections personnel, community organizations, and area policy makers.

Ames said that he continued to go through "great pains" as a result of the gaps in his formal education. "Some things are hard for me to grasp," he said, "but once I grasp something, I got it. So some people can read something once or twice. Maybe I'll have to read it three or four or five times. But I know the value of rereading it four or five times." Reflecting on his literacy development, Ames said that reading and writing gave him a "chance to evaluate what is valuable and what is not. I wouldn't have been able to make those determinations in my life without reading and writing."

Ames's pursuit of literacy took place within a penitentiary system that had grown dense with the products – material and conceptual – of competing philosophies of prison management, rehabilitation, and law. This history, which ebbed and flowed with shifting political and social pressures from the larger society, was embedded in many of the institutional structures on which Ames relied for support. At the same time, Ames was finding ways to scaffold his emerging literacy on a number of important judicial decisions that were emerging from the courts during the very same period in which he was learning to read and write. These rulings, having to do with prisoner rights, as well as the responses of prisons to these judicial pressures, were a crucial part of the context for Ames's literacy learning. A close look at this synchrony of individual development with institutional development will be useful for understanding the deep structures of opportunities and barriers for literacy.

Historians of the American prison system point to a number of pressures that bore down on the corrections systems in the 1940s and 1950s. Autocratic for most of their history, state prisons typically had been administered independently with strong wardens and weak oversight. But by midcentury, prisons, like other burgeoning state institutions, began moving for financial and political reasons toward more bureaucratic and rational models of administration. As modern management theories were adopted, wardens became more professionalized and greater attention was given to communication, planning, public relations, fiscal management, legal awareness, central oversight, and written policies and procedures. These developments brought a flood of documents, forms, schedules, and regulations into the lives of prisoners. With more coordinated management, prisons differentiated into various types and missions, a process that induced an elaborate classification system for inmates, based not only on categories of crime but also increasingly on diagnostic evaluations, psychological and psychiatric testing, and social casework. Prison guards were joined by growing staffs of college-educated psychologists, activity specialists, testing experts, and casework managers, along with teachers and librarians who had had a more long-standing presence in the prison. The documentation that occupied so much of the time of the professional staff came to have increasing influence over the fate of prisoners in terms of treatment programs, work assignments, and, most important, parole. In his case study of one Wisconsin prison over a period of 30 years, Dickey (1991) suggested that the bureaucratizing of the post–World War II prison became a new form of repression. Expanding prison populations, increased paperwork, more government regulation, and increased public scrutiny all favored elaboration of standard procedures and documentation. According to Dickey, "all of these forces push toward rigidity, control, case processing, and no risk-taking," a process he believed reduced chances for human transformation within the prison (p. 7).

Professionals who were hired to control, classify, and monitor inmate populations by document rather than by force also carried with them new, competing philosophies of rehabilitation. These approaches could range at any time period from group therapy to behavior modification to transactional analysis to transcendental meditation (Pollock, 1997, p. 163). Especially in the 1960s and 1970s, when rehabilitation enjoyed lots of public support, inmates and groups of inmates could become engaged in analyzing life scripts or identifying communication patterns or participating in encounter groups. All of these treatments generated certain kinds of reflective discourse and reading and writing assignments for those who could manage them. At the same time, as a literate practice, participation in therapeutic programs in prison was complicated by the potential of having one's words reported and evaluated in other contexts – for instance, in surveillance for illegal or dangerous behavior or in judgments about assignments, privileges, parole, or release. Among the many thick files of his prison writings, Johnny Ames showed me worksheets associated with substance abuse therapy that were used as part of psychological evaluations and parole reports.[15]

Another factor with implications for literacy was a round of important court decisions that gradually, over a series of discrete rulings, articulated citizenship rights of prisoners. Beginning with a U.S. Supreme Court decision in 1941 that acknowledged prisoner access to due process, a spate of decisions in the 1960s and 1970s expanded prisoners' access to legal services and information, banned censorship of correspondence between prisoners and lawyers, gave inmates access to law libraries and photocopiers, allowed prisoners to carry law books and legal papers, and allowed them to loan books and papers to others. These and other rulings also addressed other freedoms, including First Amendment protections. The Office of Economic Opportunity in the 1960s funded legal aid groups that pressured for better prison conditions, and subsequent civil rights legislation gave all citizens, including prisoners, the right to sue public officials. Prison historian James B. Jacobs (1977) described the late 1970s especially as a period when federal and state courts "scrutinized every aspect of the prison regime" and "issued injunctions and declaratory judgments affecting discipline, good time, living conditions, health care, censorship, restrictions on religion and speech, and access to the courts" (p. 9). Occasional high-profile prison riots through the 1950s, 1960s, and 1970s provided added pressures for expanding rights and improving material conditions. Most crucial overall was the broad social and judicial impact of the African American civil rights movement, which was affecting legal philosophy and inmate consciousness simultaneously.[16]

Prison responses to liberalizing judicial rulings – including backlash – also affected the climate for literacy inside prisons. For instance, after U.S. Supreme Court rulings that upheld prisoner rights to access to legal services, many prisons added law libraries to their facilities as an alternative to providing direct legal aid. Cheaper and more politically palatable than assigning lawyers to take up inmates' cases, libraries also made the pursuit of litigation more arduous for the individual, usually poorly educated inmate. Pollack (1997) also reported that throughout the 1970s, especially as racial consciousness and political activism rose, prisons officials were able to use court rulings on the First Amendment to curtail freedom of speech in a variety of areas, to suppress rights of prisoners to organize, and to put more systematic controls on prisoner writings. In some prisons, nonlegal correspondence was censored, writing and publishing for profit were forbidden, and printed material not received directly from publishers was banned.

Nowhere can the ideological vicissitudes of institutional contexts for literacy be better felt than in the history of prison libraries, whose health and mission rose and fell not only with various reform movements but also with shifting social beliefs about literacy itself. According to Coyle (1987), libraries appeared in prisons in the late eighteenth century primarily as a moral force, "as part of the internal discipline aimed at reform."[17] But as reading took on other purposes in the larger society, shifting from a focus on religious and didactic functions to leisure and entertainment, rationales for prison libraries became more tenuous. The twentieth century saw a revival and gradual professionalization of prison libraries but also intensifying arguments about their appropriate mission. As notions of rehabilitation bounced between education and therapy, the kinds of materials and services shifted accordingly. In the 1960s and 1970s with a focus on the prisoner's right to read, there was a growing call for decoupling libraries from prison objectives and adopting the all-purpose service models of regular public libraries. Throughout this period, however, most libraries remained under control of correctional authorities and functioned primarily as adjuncts to education programs. By 1982, federal prison libraries saw their mandate clarified when the Federal Bureau of Prisons made literacy programs mandatory. Inmates with less than a sixth-grade education were required to enroll in adult basic education classes. By 1986, the standard had moved to eighth grade, and, by 1991, GED classes were required for anyone who had not already completed high school.[18]

A return to Johnny Ames's account of his literacy learning in prison demonstrates how his development partook of complex sediments of conceptual and material resources formed of the struggles for ideological control going on in twentieth-century correctional facilities. These included bureaucratic, educational, judicial, and political initiatives whose competing agents, wittingly and not, became the sponsors of Ames's literacy learning. Faced with the need not only to become literate but to build his own framework for doing so, Ames found, within the bureaucratic congestion of a maximum-security prison, the people and materials that he could divert to his effort at literacy learning. Like so many other modern bureaucratic institutions, the prison carried along within its practices, materials, and personnel multiple recessive and ascending literacy traditions.

In Ames's remarkable encounter with the teacher-nun, we see the oldest ideologies of reform, based in spiritual redemption through literacy, still at work in the education apparatus of the prison. Reading books by ex-slaves with dictionary in hand, Ames was reenacting a scene by which many African Americans learned to read in the decades before and after Emancipation.[19] At the same time, his experience in the clinical services department allowed him to reroute resources of the college-educated personnel – their books, outlooks, knowledge, and liberalism – into intellectual stimulation in what was otherwise a repressive environment. His agreement to serve as a "guinea pig" for their scientific methods of classification and analysis gained him experience with the very testing formats that regulated everything from GED certification to parole evaluations. Books on inner growth and healing, which comprised much of his reading during this period, also were present by virtue of philosophies of rehabilitation that had cycled through the prison over the previous decades and had accumulated in the library holdings.[20] This reading was reinforced by writing that was required as part of therapeutic programming. On the bureaucratic side, Ames and his fellow Lifers carved a space for learning out of written policies and procedures that were proliferating in penal institutions in response to public demands for more accountability and to the need to both equalize treatment of prisoners and limit their organizational activism. Most critical to Ames's development were the cultural currents of racial consciousness and political liberation that were being inspired by the contemporary African American civil rights movement. As part of that milieu, activist courts expanded prisoner rights, granting more access to legal discourse and communication and precipitating a period of intense litigation, petition, and appeal that promoted writing among inmates and inmate organizations. We see in Ames's intersection with this history especially how the ability to write develops in relationship with the prerogative to write.

It is clear that the curriculum that Ames put together for his own literacy learning was far more complex and far-reaching than the official offerings in adult basic and technical education programs in which prisoners are typically enrolled.[21] Ames benefitted considerably from formal course work in the legal technician program, especially from the credentials that it gave him. But his schooling was embedded in a much larger sphere of reading and writing that was linked to immediate and palpable changes, both in his mental outlook and in the political and educational conditions in which he and his fellow inmates were living. He put together a reading and writing regimen that spanned the many fields – psychology, law, sociology, racial politics – whose systematic influences bore directly on his immediate conditions. It is here that we see more tangible evidence of relationships between institutional developments and individual literacy development. Ames's success resided not in a simple motivation to stay clean and work hard in the degree program in which he was enrolled but in a complex motivation encompassing personal history, current conditions, and future ambition. The compound interactions among his inventively self-made curriculum, his liberatory motivations, and his corralling of sponsorship forces inside the prison explain not only the complexity of his means of achievement but also the reason such an achievement remains so rare under prison conditions.

Soon after Ames reentered society as a free man in the early 1990s, prison populations in his state reached an all-time high, caused most directly by mandatory sentencing for drug offenses. By the late 1990s, as minority populations inside the prisons were rising at unprecedented rates, the state was appropriating more of its budget to corrections than to higher education. So overcrowded was the system by the late 1990s that some inmates were being rotated to private prisons out of state. In the medium-security prison where Ames served his time, inadequate space and resources put prisoners on waiting lists for access to education programs. Legal aid societies continued to retrench in the absence of public funding. And legislative remedies were being sought to reduce the number of lawsuits initiated by prison inmates.

Conclusion

This chapter has focused on sponsors of literacy as they appeared in the learning accounts of Dwayne Lowery and Johnny Ames. These sponsors included family members, teachers, workplaces, newspapers, unions, libraries, religious organizations, government programs, liberation movements, correctional systems, rehabilitation practices, the judiciary, and other agents as they bore at particular times and places on the lives of these two men. The interests of these agents at their particular moments of contact affected what the two men learned, how, from whom, and for what. Sponsors deliver the material and ideological possibilities for literacy learning, often as a by-product of the struggles for economic or political ascendancy in which they are involved. Sponsors subsidize (or don't) the development of people's literate resources as a way to recruit or coerce those resources to their cause; they also can reject or discard the literate resources of people that no longer serve their interest. Often prolific in assets, sponsors may have their resources diverted to projects of self-interest or self-development by literacy learners under their aegis. Conservative in nature but often ruthlessly demanding of change, sponsors carry within their material and ideological orbits multiple aspects of literacy's past and present, receding and emerging traditions that accumulate as part of a history of contact and competition. Even within single institutions, the uses and networks of literacy crisscross through many domains, potentially exposing people to multiple sources of sponsoring powers – secular, religious, bureaucratic, legal, commercial, technological. It is these characteristics of the sponsors that give contemporary literacy its demanding qualities of complexity, multiplicity, and stratification, its sense of surplus and its volatility. The fast pace of change in communication technologies only intensifies this process.

Dwayne Lowery and Johnny Ames learned to write during a period in American history when standards for literacy achievement were rising higher and faster than ever before, and when the meaning of how much literacy was enough was changing quickly for both of these men. The course of their literacy learning was plotted across fast-moving transformations that were bringing the need for individual writing skills ever more widely and deeply into the conduct of competitions over liberty, money, ideas, and control. The histories of these larger competitions – for them, labor–management relations, correctional philosophies, law, and civil rights – delivered the sponsoring agents through which the two men developed adult literacy. Although positioned differently within it, both of these men were learning to write in times and places in which civil rights and litigation were central to political and economic activity. With capacities for both oppression and liberation, this expanding legal arena implicated writing as increasingly necessary for the representation of one's interests and the exercise and recognition of one's rights. These developments had specific, tangible, and abiding implications in the lives of both Lowery and Ames.

This synchronization among literacy learning, histories of economic and political struggle, and sponsorship suggests a need for definitions of literacy that better incorporate the ways that literacy actually gets made in the lives of people. That is, it is not enough to investigate the component mental or scribal skills that are required to perform reading or writing at a particular level nor even the components of contexts and their opportunities that are available to people for learning those skills. Rather, we must look even further into the origins and makeup of these components themselves. Individual abilities are one with the historical conditions in which they are made and permitted. Opportunities for literacy are not merely the occasions on which people learn to read and write or not; from a biographical perspective, they can be the internalized structures that organize and define individual skills.

This point is most starkly illustrated by the extent to which the reported experiences of Lowery and Ames carry in their details so much of the general history of literacy in America. As we have seen, Lowery's work history moves like the American economy from manufacturing to information, a process that inflated the value of the written word not only in the production of goods and services but in the basic pursuit of labor rights and interests. It was this double change that we saw Lowery working to accomplish in his writing. The principle is even more profound in the life experience of Ames. Born at midcentury into one of the most economically and racially oppressed social systems in the country, he encountered as a child forms of literacy still connected to remnant regimes of slavery and peonage. These included writing embedded in the practical exchanges of local agricultural labor and an oral tradition that, in the absence of real access to schooling and in resistance to harsh racism, transmitted mother wit and survival skills from old to young.[22] As his social system gave way, Ames's exploitable value as an agricultural worker gave out, and the few resources he possessed won little articulation in the world beyond his family economy. Caught in a period of acute mental depression and reckless behavior, he was sentenced to life in prison. Then he gradually diverted the ideologically congested resources of a late-twentieth-century prison to accomplish transformations in his literacy and work that recapitulated – within a span of 16 years – transformations that had taken the country an entire century or more to accomplish.

As we saw also with the case of Barbara Hunt in the previous chapter, traveling that distance, making those transformations, in fact is the daunting challenge for many literacy learners in the nation now, especially those who were left out of economic and political expansions of earlier periods. Literacy learning entails more than attaining the scribal abilities implied by an imposed standard. It also entails an ability, somehow, to make the transformations and amalgamations that have become embedded, across time, in the history of that standard. The farther away one is to start with, the more it takes to become and stay literate. This second kind of ability, this deeper aspect to literacy learning, is what Dwayne Lowery and Johnny Ames worked so hard to develop. It is here, in the second, deeper, sponsor-reliant level of literacy ability – the one so affected by economic and political inequities – that the pressures of the rising standard of literacy are most wrenchingly felt.

3

ACCUMULATING LITERACY

How Four Generations of One American Family Learned to Write

Genna May was born in 1898 on a dairy farm in south central Wisconsin, the eighth of nine children of Norwegian immigrants. She spoke no English when she enrolled at the age of 7 in a one-room schoolhouse built on land donated to the school district by her parents. Although Genna would eventually go on to complete high school by boarding in a town 10 miles from her farm, she started school at a time when Wisconsin required only that young people ages 7 to 15 attend a local grammar school for 12 weeks a year.[1] As a student in "the grades," as she called them, Genna wrote spelling lessons on slates, erasing them with a wet cloth to go on to arithmetic lessons.[2] She remembered a home with few books and little paper, and she said she would have had no reason to write as a girl except to compose an occasional story assigned by her teacher. After high school graduation in 1917, she enrolled for several months in a private business college in the state capital, just long enough to learn typing and shorthand and win a certificate in penmanship before gaining employment in the office of a company manufacturing disinfectants for dairy barns. In the mid-1990s, Genna was using writing to record recipes, balance her checkbook, and send holiday and birthday greetings to family members.

Genna's great-grandson Michael May was born in 1981 in a sprawling suburb built on former farmland east of Wisconsin's state capital. In the early 1990s, he was attending a middle school equipped with computers. The first of four children in his family, Michael remembered that his earliest composing occurred when he was two years old and his parents helped him form simple words with magnetic letters on a metal easel and chalkboard in the family's TV room. As a participant in a grade-school enrichment program called the Future Problem Solving Program (FPSP), he wrote a letter to his principal proposing to correct erosion on the school playground. In the bedroom of his younger sister was a manual typewriter that their father had bought while attending a local technical school, a typewriter that the girl was using recreationally. One weekend, Michael's mother brought home a personal computer from her job as a data processor at a national insurance company so that she could practice a new software program, and, Michael remembered, she allowed him and his sister to type messages back and forth to each other on it. Asked what made writing important to him, Michael responded that it "has a lot do with speaking," with "seeing correct words."

These accounts by two members of the same family capture many of the economic and social transformations of twentieth-century America: population movements from farms to urban centers to suburbs; shifts in the economic base from agriculture to manufacturing to information processing; the rise of big business; a rapid escalation in educational expectations; revolutions in communication technology; and the growth of a print culture so saturating that it has become a principal means by which some children learn to talk. Against that backdrop we see the dramatically different social contexts in which Genna May and her great-grandson learned about literacy and its relationship to the world. In the sparse setting of Genna May's prairie farmhouse, paper, hard to come by, was reserved for her father's church work. In Michael May's print-cluttered suburban ranch home, his parents introduced him to writing and reading amid the background chatter of network television. For members of the community in which Genna May grew up, the ability to write the words of everyday life often marked the end of formal schooling, whereas for Michael May, these same experiences served as a preparation for kindergarten. In the social dynamic of the rural school district of the 1890s, it would not have been unusual for a teacher to board with her students' families while school was in session. Three generations later, in a twenty-five-room middle school, students learned to address their principal by formal letter as a lesson in bureaucratic action.

These accounts complicate the argument that the demand now is simply for more people to achieve a kind of literacy that used to be achieved only by a few. To say merely that social changes dictate that Michael achieve a higher level of literacy and education than his great-grandmother is to miss how the same social changes that demand higher eventual skill are already tangibly present at the scene of his literacy learning – part of the way a two-year-old in the 1980s learned what literacy is. Not even highly educated elites of the past encountered the current contexts in which literacy in its many forms is being practiced and learned.

In fact, these accounts suggest that what is unprecedented about literacy learning in the current climate is not so much a demand for literacy that seems always to exceed supply but rather the challenges faced by all literacy learners in a society whose rapid changes are themselves tied up so centrally with literacy and its enterprises. If Genna carved out a turn-of-the-century literacy amid a scarcity of print, her great-grandson must carve one out amid a material and ideological surplus. The setting in which Michael first encountered the ABCs is layered with discarded and emergent forms of literacy and their histories. With his magnetic slate, he recapitulates in eerie ways a rudimentary ritual of the nineteenth-century schoolhouse at the same time that he must absorb from his parents the meanings that literacy and education have for middle-class families of the late twentieth century.[3]

The piling up and extending out of literacy and its technologies give a complex flavor even to elementary acts of reading and writing today. The history of literacy in the United States has involved constant transformations in the ideological basis of its practices, transformations that gradually co-opt and eclipse earlier versions. However, because changes in the twentieth century have become so much more rapid, the ideological texture of literacy has become more complex as more layers of earlier forms of literacy exist simultaneously within the society and within the experiences of individuals. When Genna and her great-grandson exchanged written greetings at birthdays and holidays, we can appreciate how the complexity of contemporary life derives in part from the fact that so many generations of literacy, so to speak, now occupy the same social space. Contemporary literacy learners – across positions of age, gender, race, class, and language heritage – find themselves having to piece together reading and writing experiences from more and more spheres, creating new and hybrid forms of literacy where once there might have been fewer and more circumscribed forms. They also must understand reading or writing in relationship to other communication options, options that themselves continue to change and expand. What we calculate as a rising standard of basic literacy may be more usefully regarded as the effects of a rapid proliferation and diversification of literacy. This relentless process has forced literate ability to include a capacity to amalgamate new reading and writing practices in response to rapid social change. Developing and maintaining such an ability is not always an easy, fair, or – as we have seen in earlier chapters – a happy endeavor.

This chapter considers the implications of such rapid changes in the meanings and methods of literacy learning from the perspective of one ordinary family. The discussion will focus on four living generations of the Mays, an average, midwestern European American family. In addition to Genna and her great-grandson Michael, the family includes Genna's son, Sam, who was born in 1925 and raised in the same rural community as his mother. Sam served in the army in Europe during World War II, attended college on the GI Bill, and worked the rest of his career as an electronics technician in a science department at a research university. Also included is Sam's son Jack, the father of Michael, who was born in 1958 and raised in a postwar housing division in the state capital. After high school graduation in the late 1970s, Jack earned a two-year business degree at a local technical college. In his mid-thirties, he was working as a courier for a global parcel company and, with his wife, a home day care provider, was raising young children in a suburb near the state capital.

In this family's social and economic history, lived out within the same 25-mile radius in south central Wisconsin, can be read many of the economic changes that affected this part of the country, as it turned from a predominantly agricultural-based rural area into a more densely populated, highly technical, service-oriented area. This is a family that made these basic transitions along with the wider society. In separate interviews conducted in the early 1990s, the four Mays were asked to remember everything they could about how they learned to write and read, focusing on the circumstances, materials, people, and motivations that animated those memories. What will be of particular interest in the analysis of these literacy accounts is how the family coped with changing literacy standards. The analysis will focus on how literate resources that family members accumulated across changing economies moved along with them, getting refurbished, reinterpreted, or abandoned to meet new conditions. It also will consider how their literacy was valued and revalued along with economic change. At times the analysis will be amplified by other life history accounts collected as part of this study.

As suggested earlier, emphasis will be given to how opportunities for individual literacy development are connected to past and present economic competitions going on at particular times and places and the way that various family members are positioned in those competitions. As economic sponsors demand and reward new kinds of literate skills, opportunities for literacy shift in school, workplaces, and in the wider immediate community. These changes in turn bring adjustments in family life and in the ways literate resources are pursued or not. Of key influence in the Mays' history are (1) the heritage of traditional nineteenth-century literacy that hung in the conservative societies of the rural Midwest; (2) transformations in agriculture before and during the Great Depression, including the penetration of commercial activity into small towns and rural areas; (3) the advent of World War II and the sharp appetite for technological and communications skill that it stimulated; and (4) the association between advanced schooling and economic viability, especially as that association tightened in the late twentieth century. What these developments have meant to the May family and the course of their literacy learning will be the focus of the following discussion.

Genna May, Born 1898

One of the most striking qualities of Genna's May earliest memories of writing is how deeply they are embedded in the major formations of nineteenth-century mass literacy. The Protestant church and the common school, two institutions most culturally responsible for creating a literate citizenry in Europe and America through the first three quarters of the nineteenth century, appear still as nearly the sole reservoirs of literate experience for a young, turn-of-the-century farm girl. These institutions – through which Genna's parents learned to read and write in Norway – were still providing the next generation with incentives and material supports for literacy, albeit in a new, American context. Genna's father put his "precise" and "wonderful" handwriting in the service of the local Norwegian-speaking Lutheran church, whereas Genna's mother would show her school-age children how to form letters or, on occasion, check over their homework lessons. Genna could not remember seeing her mother write anything on her own, could not remember many permanent records associated with the business of the dairy farm, and reported few commercial sources for her early literacy experiences, including few, if any, books in her household. Her father's Norwegian newspapers, which began to arrive with rural mail delivery, were some of the very few distant suppliers of the written language she saw at home. In a community where store-bought materials were rare, the same chalk and slate used for repetitive writing and erasing at school were adopted for use at home as well, by all family members, for games and occasional calculations, written and erased. Writing, as Genna encountered it, was ephemeral, evaporating into small, local systems of family finance, religious and civic activity, and school lessons.

As Genna was one of the youngest of nine children, her earliest literacy influences were firmly entrenched in the nineteenth-century outlooks brought forward by parents and older siblings. All of her older siblings left school by the eighth grade. ("My brother had to stay home and work on the farm," she explained, "and the others, in those days, they didn't think about school.") Genna encountered writing and reading principally in connection with the duties that, according to Soltow and Stevens (1981), had formed the moral basis of nineteenth-century literacy. For the children of this household, it meant obeying teachers; for the mother, it meant reinforcing children's rudimentary literacy as part of proper maternal responsibility; for the father, it meant fulfilling civic and religious obligation.

But Genna represented a distinct line of demarcation in her family – the first of the children to enter high school. The decision to pursue more schooling, made in consultation with her parents, reflected important shifts already underway in the rural economy of her time and place. Going to high school was becoming, in Genna's words, "the thing to do." As we saw earlier in the case of Martha Day, the trend toward more schooling was partly a result of the relative agricultural prosperity of this era. (Family prosperity always favored literacy and schooling for children.[4]) But it was also partly a result of the dramatic reductions in family farm ownership that were already beginning in the region. This was a period when compulsory education became more standardized nationally and when high school enrollments began a tenfold increase over a 40-year period.[5] The decision to send Genna and her younger sister to high school also coincided with the gradual Americanization of their parents, whose church services and choice of newspapers, by that time, for instance, had changed over to English.[6]

Genna's memories of this period, along with those of other youths like her, suggest how whole kinship systems began cooperating in the new societal phenomenon of sending young people off to other locales for schooling. Logistical and financial means had to be found. For Genna, the opportunity came through the in-laws of one of her older siblings. They resided in a town with a population at the time of about 1,000 people, where a public high school had been founded in 1908. This family, already boarding some of the teachers who taught in the school, provided Genna with a place to stay in exchange for domestic help in the household. Similarly, Rupert Jackson, born in 1912, also in rural southern Wisconsin, was urged to attend high school by two older sisters who were country schoolteachers. His aunt, who lived in town, offered her home for lodging, and his mother sold eggs to pay for his keep. Max Congers, born later in 1920 in a remote area of northern Wisconsin, took over the work of his grandmother's farm at the age of 14, both to relieve his large family of a mouth to feed and to be in close commuting distance to a high school. And Carrie Parker, born in 1896 in east central Wisconsin, said she and a handful of other students from her area found another solution:

catching a freight train for a five-mile caboose trip to a high school in town. Her memory of the daily ritual reveals how infrastructures that had been built to move farm products to market could be converted by a sympathetic community into a support system for education.

> We called it Mc_____'s train. He was an elderly man who had been
> on the railroad for years and years and years. So he'd come by and
> punch like he was punching a ticket. But he didn't. He let us go free.

It is in these memories of attending high school that associations between schooling and economic activity first appear in the account of Genna May and others like her. Attending high school gave many rural youths their first roles as off-farm wage earners and precipitated new relationships of exchange and cooperation between the country and the town. These memories also reveal how women generally and mothers in particular were reshaping their traditional responsibility for educating children, adding financial finagling to their repertoire of strategies.[7]

After high school, "the thing to do" for Genna was to keep gravitating toward larger population areas. Graduating in 1917 in a class of 13, she enrolled immediately in a proprietary business college in the state capital 20 miles away. The school, founded in the mid-1850s originally as a preparatory school for the state university, had been bought in the early twentieth century by area bankers and other private investors. The school underwent a new direction and major expansion beginning in 1914 to provide the area with a business-oriented workforce, including, especially, female clerical workers.[8] This training helped to sustain manufacturing and commercial enterprises that were proliferating in midsize cities in the Midwest. Young, single farm women whose basic literacy was certified by a high school diploma made popular recruits for crash instruction in stenography, typing, and bookkeeping. Part school, part employment agency, the college found Genna her first job after only a few months of instruction. She worked in an office of a laboratory producing disinfectants for dairy farms. "At that time, they sent you out when they thought you were able to get a job," she explained. "They always found jobs for you." Within a year, she had transferred to a title company, where, sometimes by typewriter and sometimes by hand, she recorded abstracts of land sales. She recalled the job this way:

> We had descriptions of all the property, you know, and we had to
> write the description on the abstract, and if there were any mortgages
> or deeds or things against the property, we had to put that, too.

As with many of her station in the early 1920s, Genna's writing skills served as a conduit for corporations reorganizing the Midwest farm economy. New products designed to increase productivity were developing in commercial laboratories. Aggressive corporate acquisitions of farm land as well as local buyouts and secondary leasing stepped up real estate sales. In the mean time, the number of people directly involved in agricultural work continued to decline dramatically. Surplus farm labor was rerouted into work in transportation, sales, and clerical support, new needs emerging from the consolidation and integration of agricultural markets. This development created a tier of new products and services that required intensive recordkeeping. Young farm men of Genna's cohort found themselves driving trucks, delivering milk, and working as supply clerks for agricultural distributors as many family farms were liquidated, lost in the Depression, or came to earn too little to support extended families.[9] Those involved in local commerce were likewise affected. Writing on the job was becoming part of "a growing systemness"[10] that was reorganizing the national economy, especially agriculture. These transformations connected young high school graduates to information channels more elaborate, abstract, and much more centrally integrated than the ones they encountered in childhood. Whereas farm-based writing might have been used to keep records of a family's work and monetary dealings, keeping records – other people's records – now became the work itself. It was a kind of writing that required speed, regularity, and predictability of information flow. As Beniger (1986) observed, "the use of human beings not for their strength or agility nor for their knowledge or intelligence, but for the more objective capacity of their brains to store and process information would become over the next century a dominant feature of employment" (p. 225). For the first time in the May family's work history, literacy and labor were linked.

As things would turn out, this brief period of business learning and employment would engage Genna in the most intense use of written language of her life. When she returned to the full-time workforce after her children were raised, it was not into office work, which by then had undergone much change, but to housekeeping, which involved little or no writing. Neither did Genna write much in her private life, except for an occasional letter or recipe. "It just wasn't my line," she explained.

Neither did she remain an urban dweller. As the Depression sparked financial tensions that led to the breakup of her marriage, Genna returned to the family farm in the early 1930s. Her husband, a railroad conductor, moved on to industrial areas of the upper Midwest after the railroad he worked for went bankrupt. As a divorced mother of three small children,

Genna went back home to care for a sickly sister-in-law (her brother was now operating the original family farm) as well as her widowed mother, who had retired to the village where Genna had attended high school. For the next several years, Genna and her children moved between farm and village to live among an extended family that by then – a generation away from immigration – had grown more prosperous. With more property (including more books), more resources consolidated through inheritance and marriage, more leisure, and more commercial enticements, the household was sustaining a literacy of rural gentility upon which Genna's son, Sam, would be raised in the years between the two world wars.

It is in Sam's memories of his earliest literacy learning that we will see how the family by that time was drawing on somewhat different aspects of nineteenth-century literacy traditions – particularly those associated with gentility and self-improvement – made possible by a livelier commercial life that had penetrated by then into remoter rural areas. Commercially available literacy products helped to compensate for a lack of formal education, and growing prosperity allowed some members of the May family to turn their attention to social and political activities that further stimulated uses of reading and writing. As we will see, this genteel literacy stressing manners and decorum, but also self-learning and community involvement, would have a lifelong influence on Sam's orientations to literacy learning. Yet the unstoppable agents of commercialism (and their media accomplices) would also cultivate in Sam distinctly new twentieth-century orientations, spurred on especially by the continued economic pressure for faster and better communication. By the end of the 1940s, Sam's writing development would be thoroughly fused with the technological developments ignited by World War II.

Sam May, Born 1925

If Genna's recollections of young childhood evoked a literacy of immigrant frontier spareness, Sam's early memories included the presence of quite a few books, attention to handwriting, and the use of writing for civic and political participation. These values were promoted especially by an older aunt, an invalid and autodidact, with whom Sam's family sometimes shared a residence. This aunt was "famous for her fancy hand," with which she addressed notes and party invitations. She also wrote frequent letters to the editors of a statewide newspaper, engaged in petition drives, and participated in local political campaigns, into which the children in the household would sometimes be drawn. Occasionally, she would give

Sam and his two siblings penmanship lessons on rainy Saturday afternoons, using Palmer method handbooks that were among the books she
kept in locked cases.[11] "My mother's sister was always chiding us to read
better books and practice more writing," he explained. "When we were a
little bit older and knew how to handle them, she would lend us books and
let us keep them for a week or two. Not children's books." Literacy learning also was part of acquiring manners. "We had to have manners," Sam
explained. "If the minister was going to be at the table on Sunday, we all
were supposed to be able to talk a little bit to anyone who was there, or if
someone important was there." Sam recalled emulating a language style
that he associated with wealthier and more worldly members of his village,
for whom he would do occasional yard work:

> They used proper grammar in their talking, their speech, and their
> actions were geared such that you felt comfortable with them. It all
> had to do with words. If they wrote a note for you, it was beautiful
> handwriting and, gosh, I wish I could have done that. [They] had a
> cultured way about them which we little farm boys would try to
> emulate. At the time. I've since given it up!

Although early school experiences seemed to reinforce many of these values ("spelling and neatness were very important to the teachers"), other
influences pressed in – and were brought in by new technologies. Sam
recalled frequent writing in connection with outdoor boyhood play, such
as leaving messages for his friends of the sides of their forts and developing a "code machine" ("two papers that slid around"), inspired by the
decoder rings promoted on the radio show *Little Orphan Annie*.[12] He also
recalled collaborating with large groups of children on "sideshows" that
they wrote and performed in connection with weekly outdoor movie
nights that local businesses were sponsoring during the warm months as a
way to draw people into town to shop. The children would charge people
a few cents each to watch their skits, which were organized in circuslike or
vaudeville fashion yet also were inspired by the action on the screen:

> When I was from the age of ten on, they had weekly outdoor
> movies. On Thursday night, five hundred people would come into
> this little town, sit down on the grass, and watch a western. So it
> was like carnival night. ... Well, there weren't any live people up
> there [on the screen], so we figured let's make a sideshow. We had
> to write these flyers, and we would have to write these scripts, and
> there had to be a master of ceremonies [who would] have to orga-
> nize this thing, and maybe even write down what he had to say, at

least the order in which the show was going to come off. Then we'd have a little dance and there would be someone singing. It was all fun. It was great.

As Sam explained, with the Depression, large families were moving to rural communities like his, where vegetable gardens could be grown and barter was more acceptable. Composing skits, plays, circus routines, and secret messages was a way for children to build and maintain community during this transient time. Collaborative writing developed as a necessity. ("If you had a neighborhood play and there was only one person organizing it all," he explained, "the rest of the kids would quit.")

Sam's memories directly address how intrusions of new technologies of film and radio stimulated writing and altered recreational literacy. The converging of farm families to watch westerns on Thursday nights created a new, public audience and a new economic niche in which children could write and perform for money. The emerging visual genres of film helped to fuel their imaginations, even as the children borrowed from older, oral traditions of vaudeville and circus to organize their live performances.

New technology stimulated writing in other ways, too. Radio shows such as *Little Orphan Annie* and *Jack Armstrong* encouraged Sam and his siblings to write letters to distant radio stations to acquire promotional items – letters they knew how to address properly because of the modeling provided at home. And the radio became an additional forum for communicating standards of correct or finer speech – a matter that continued to draw Sam's attention:

> So to listen to those stories of *The Shadow* or *Orson Welles Theater* or *Mercury Theater* – God, you could get right in. I mean, you could picture this whole thing going on, and it was all done with words. In our neighborhood plays, we would try to reconstruct that, or if you were entertaining some relatives or a friend. Or if you got a little poem that your mother wants you to read in front of them, a dozen relatives, because they think it's good and you want to show off. And you read this dumb thing and you realize how really limited you are compared to Orson Welles. You were always comparing yourself to Orson Welles.

Sam's recollections of his childhood suggest a more complicated, even contradictory set of literacy sponsors in comparison to what his mother remembered. Among his extended family, a literacy of duty had developed into a fuller, commercialized literacy of civic participation and upward striving, a literacy that bespoke a wider world yet still could be interpreted in terms of family character. Interestingly, the Palmer Method of handwriting, more an instigation of the twentieth-century business school than the nineteenth-century finishing school, was nevertheless adapted via its ubiquitous handbooks and training outreach of the time into projects of self-improvement and social pasttimes, spurred on by Sam's aunt. However, whereas Sam's earliest literacy influences drew heavily from nineteenth-century traditions embodied and communicated by members of the older generation, they also reflected a rapid penetration of commercialism and new technologies into the rural countryside. Radio became an important instrument in constituting a national consumer society, both by providing nationally based, privatized forms of entertainment and by promoting commercial products through advertising and program sponsorship. Radio helped to teach people how to be secular consumers. When radio spurred writing for Sam and others like him, writing took the form of product requests or involved communications designed to encourage listener loyalty.[13]

Although commercial radio competed with reading for families' leisure hours, it also enhanced many of the qualities associated with literacy. Radio delivered into homes an array of scripted narratives and musical performances that arrived by disembodied sound, from outside local communities. For many people like Sam, these voices from somewhere else heightened consciousness about the shaping powers of language and allowed them to set up comparisons between radio versions, print versions, and sometimes real-life versions of dramatic performances. After-school or bedtime stories were read to children not only by adult family members but also by disembodied strangers.[14] For the first time, learning to read and write was occurring simultaneously with learning to listen to the radio, providing a relativity of outlook toward literacy that had not been technologically possible before.

On the eve of World War II, radio was taking on other meanings for Sam. Like other men of his cohort and earlier, he built crystal radio sets as a teenager in a "little workshop" he set up in the barn. There, in a junked car seat, he also would record ideas for inventions in a little notebook that he carried with him constantly. Attending the same high school as his mother, this time commuting the 10 miles by car, he graduated in 1942 – the same year that Congress dropped the draft age from 20 to 18. Knowing he was bound for war, Sam enrolled in a radio repair course, one of many hastily arranged at the state university by the War Management Board to upgrade civilian skills prior to military induction. There he received brief instruction in technical writing before being assigned to the Army Signal Corps for training in radar maintenance. He was assigned to learn the newest radar equipment that was going straight off the assembly lines to the European front. So new were these products that once he arrived in the field, Sam found himself writing service manuals nearly simultaneously with learning about the equipment itself. He also was required to prepare weekly reports back to the factory where the equipment was being made to alert designers to potential problems. "Once we got out into the field, we were allowed to make any changes we wanted to and we had to write up reports on what we changed and why. We were engineering out the mistakes. We had to make full reports on exactly what we were doing every week."[15]

Although confident of his technical ability, Sam said he was less satisfied with his ability to write reports, describing his efforts as "perfunctory." "I'd say, 'I changed this resistor to that' and [the report form] would ask, 'What was the reason for the change?' and I'd write, 'Because this other one here is a mistake.'" Sam then went on to describe a strategy he developed for acquiring a new kind of technical literacy that his position was demanding. Just as he often had to improvise to keep the radar equipment working, Sam improvised a method of learning report writing, modeled in fact on his earlier ways of appropriating worldly language circulating in his boyhood village:

> Other people used to ask my advice a lot, people who were better at phrasing things than I was, and I'd listen to them – especially the officers – I'd listen to them. Or I'd have to discuss what I wanted to do with, say, a lieutenant or a captain. I was just a mere sergeant. These were all college guys and I was, of course, just a high school brat. So I'd listen to how they'd talk with each other and how they would talk to their peers and their minions. So you could sense the correctness of how they phrased things and how they put things. They always knew how to stay on the subject, not get sidetracked. That had something to do with writing.

This account shows in very particular ways how transformations in literacy accompany transformations in the sponsorship of literacy. This change registers in the two episodes in which Sam recalls emulating the language of the elite: the first, as a farm boy in a socially stratified rural village of the 1930s; the second, as a subordinate army officer in an emerging military-industrial context beginning to require even of "mere sergeants" an ability to render technical know-how in professional prose. These scenes predict the emerging power of a highly educated, technocratic elite after the war. By midcentury, the meaning of education and educated language had begun to shift from the cultivated talk of the well-bred to the efficient professional prose of the technocrat. This shift altered the paths of economic opportunity for people like Sam.

In a book that argues that the military shaped the modern industrial era to an extent not normally acknowledged, Merritt Roe Smith (1985) recounted the spate of inventions brought forth by the pressures of the Second World War. These inventions ranged from computers to sonar to radar to jet engines to insecticides and nuclear power. Not only did military needs influence the design, speed of development, and availability and worth of new technologies but also the military was the key institution in developing management systems for these technologies – including management of personnel to run them. Uniformity, order, centralization, instrumentation, quality control, the systematic testing of employees, and the politics of bureaucracy all grew up, Smith wrote, around military enterprises.[16] So, too, did some of the largest campaigns of adult education in the history of the country. According to Goldberg (1951), in mid-1942, "sixty-three of every hundred men inducted into the Army were assigned to duties requiring specialized training. By mid-1943, ninety of every hundred inducted were assigned to specialized jobs" (p. 25). The education of military inductees in Sam May's generation – no matter what their public school background – became of acute interest to military sponsors.

All of the veterans whom I interviewed described their military service as a period of intensified instruction – ranging from basic reading instruction for a man who had left school in the fifth grade to spherical trigonometry for a college-educated man picked for Officer Candidate School. Almost all of the veterans I interviewed also reported doing writing while serving abroad, not only letters to loved ones but also contributions to bureaucratic operations. These duties ranged from keeping attendance and writing court-martial reports to writing shell reports, keeping personnel files, recording medicines administered, registering soldiers for correspondence courses, writing public information bulletins, censoring the personal correspondence of soldiers, and reading aloud the latest war developments from copies of the *Stars and Stripes*.

In an essay about the Signal Corps in World War II, George Raynor Thompson (1965) recounted how the chief of army communications services at the time "enjoyed reminding the Army that the commodity sent overseas in World War II was words, not bullets. He figured the proportion at eight words to every bullet" (p. 170). If the military was conditioning civilian technology in the aftermath of World War II, it was also, through the same channels, conditioning civilian literacy in the aftermath of World War II.

Sam May remained in Europe briefly after the armistice, earning the necessary points to come home by teaching technical courses and continuing to operate 17 radar sets in France and Germany.[17] On release, he became "a college guy," one of the 2.25 million veterans who enrolled in higher education under the GI Bill. Sam studied engineering at the state university, leaving college just short of a degree. He became an electronics technician at the university, where, he said, he devotes about 30% of his workday to writing, mostly making circuit diagrams (often on blackboards) and composing captions, graphs, and other illustrations for science reports produced in the laboratories to which he is assigned. At the time of our interview, 67-year-old Sam indicated he did not use a computer available to him at work. "I haven't had time to learn, but I plan to," he said, "because it is very useful – saves a lot of drafting time."

Before I examine the experiences of the next two generations of the Mays, it is worth stopping here to consider more broadly what shifts in the sponsorship of literacy can mean for ordinary people and how such changes are felt as part of family, school, and social relations. What constituted Genna and Sam May's literacy, and what pressured it to change? Answers to these questions come from two overlapping spheres: a family economy, which includes a family's work history as well as enduring values and practices that are passed, as resources, to the young; and a wider regional economy, which carries broader histories of economic competitions, past and emerging, that influence opportunity for literacy in each generation. Genna's early encounters with writing and reading were constituted within long-standing patterns of sponsorship that reached back to the original dissemination of mass literacy begun centuries earlier in Euro-Protestant societies. This was a literacy principally for moral training transmitted by families with the regulatory influence of church and school. It was meant to reinforce social conformity and integration into accepted ways of life. The different ways that Genna's father and mother used literacy communicated histories of gender expectations associated with this legacy, by which men wrote as part of leadership privileges, in the family and the wider community, whereas subordinate women taught the written alphabet as part of child-rearing duties. It was a literacy held in place by an agrarian social structure in which members were expected to stay and inherit traditional roles organized around the production of food.

This family economy was nested within a regional economy that affected the material base of Genna's early literacy learning and opportunity. The lack of reading and writing implements that she recalled in her childhood represented not merely the ruptures – linguistic and material – that immigrants made with their homelands but also the still thin infrastructure of capital and trade within this farming region at the turn of the century. Although the moral economy of early literacy was transmitted principally through family expectations, its material economy was expressed most profoundly in regional disparities. Mass literacy had flourished first in densely populated urban hubs and seaports where commercial pressures retrofitted a basic Bible literacy to meet the needs of secular exchange.[18] Early literacy levels also were relatively high in villages with landed gentry in which tradition helped to draw and stabilize local education. Literacy spread last and always less well to remote rural areas and newer, poorer industrial areas – a geographic and political legacy that, even today, in the United States, helps to exacerbate inequalities by race, region, and occupation.[19]

This geography of disparity was tangibly in the consciousness of people I interviewed within Genna's birth cohort. The presence or absence of literacy merged in their accounts with the presence or absence of economic and political power in their regions. For example, Belle Mae Bailey, born in 1915 and raised on tenant farms in rural Georgia, described the unlevel geography of material opportunity in which she participated:

> No, there were no books in the house and none in the town. This one little town from us, there might have been some books there because that was the courthouse seat, so there might have been some there.

Stratifications of opportunity and expectation were communicated most literally to members of Genna's cohort through the size and condition of surrounding school buildings. Where, as in the case of Herman Tarklin, born in 1896 in deep rural Wisconsin, all the schools for miles and miles stopped at the elementary level, it was generally expected that students would stop there, too. Where, as in the case of sharecroppers' daughter Anita Taylor, born in rural Mississippi in 1917, makeshift lessons took place in a country church, schooling taught black children, among other things, the depth of their government's indifference toward them. Where high schools were available and a state's compulsory schooling laws were inviting, opportunity tended to come more easily. Eventual college graduate Hope Moore, born in a midsize Connecticut town in 1909 to a grocer and milliner, said of herself and three siblings:

> I guess my parents just assumed that we would go to high school. We were in a city where there was a good one and we didn't have to pay anything. The laws in Connecticut allowed you to stop when you finished elementary school. Now after I got through [in 1926],

there was a law that said you had to stay in school until you were sixteen. And at that point I think that most people who stayed until they were sixteen probably finished high school.

This geographical stratification, an inheritance of nineteenth-century economic and racial arrangements, was still in place when Sam May began his schooling in south central Wisconsin in the early 1930s. As the Depression broke his family apart and put it in movement, he transferred among metropolitan, township, and village school districts, seeing the wide disparities in resources and literacy expectations associated with three economically distinct areas. Sam attended kindergarten and first grade in city schools, which, although overcrowded, engaged him in writing stories, making models, using musical instruments, and "playing store." Then he transferred in 1931 to the school that his grandfather had helped to build. He recalled:

> The rural school had almost zero equipment. Eight grades in one room. Second-grade math class consisted of one set of flash cards, which of course I could memorize in no time. And that was the same set of cards they were using for third grade. That's why I skipped third grade. The teacher said, "Well, he's gone through all the third-grade cards by now, so there's no point in him going to third. We might as well advance him to fourth." By that time, though, I moved to the village, and that school was quite a bit better.

The regional stratifications that Sam encountered in the 1930s and 1940s underscore how conservative the bedrock economies of literacy can be – how they can reach back into the struggles and ways of life of past generations even as those arrangements grow less and less consonant with demands of new times. Genna and her son experienced the most dramatic change not in the bedrock particulars of the regional economies of their early literacy development but in the meaning those particulars were taking on in light of new conditions in a wider society. It was, of course, out of this uneven geography of opportunity – based largely on an order that was fast disappearing – that the "literacy crisis" of World War II emerged. The modern military required more literate manpower than the nation's school systems could supply. In *The Uneducated*, a study of the impact of race and region on preparedness levels before and after the war, Ginzberg and Bray (1953) observed:

> Although the experts in education had been aware of the existence of large numbers of individuals in the population whose ability to

read, write, and reckon was totally nonexistent or minimal, there had been no widespread concern with the problem of illiteracy in the pre-war years. ... It was the large-scale screening of the younger male population consequent to the passage of the Selective Service Act of 1940 that turned a local and isolated fact into a national problem. (p. 39)

Genna May experienced a primarily serial change in the sponsorship of her early literacy learning – moving, quite literally, from an agrarian context in childhood to an urban-commercial context in young adulthood. But Sam May experienced these sets of sponsors in a much more simultaneous and overlapping way (a dynamic that, as we saw in an earlier chapter, only intensified for young people as the century proceeded). Like his mother, he experienced early literacy primarily as part of local identity and community relations, still primarily embedded in face-to-face encounters. Local schooling was part of a more general regulatory system, the responsibility for which was broadly distributed. In Sam's view, he had many early language teachers, all of them local, whether older children in organized play or a fireman who used to tell didactic stories to students as they walked past the firehouse on their way to school. Resources, including books, were shared within the community. Sam recalled visiting a more affluent friend to use his dictionary and occasionally sharing adventure books with other friends.[20] Asked to name anyone he could think of who had helped him to learn to write, Sam answered:

> To tell you the truth, I can't think of anybody who would have discouraged us kids from trying to learn how to write. I can point out some families that didn't care. But their kids would want us to teach them. Your primary purpose for writing was that they made you. Your parents made you. Your friends giggled and laughed at you if you couldn't. Your teachers definitely made you.

Perhaps the most vivid representative of tradition in Sam's background was his autodidactic aunt, who engaged in a form of self-improvement and social activism common for women still barred from full participation in public society. This artistic book collector, whose formal learning ended in grade school, in fact belonged to the last generation of white Americans for whom literacy would not necessarily be synonymous with formal education. In the May childhood community, at a time that began for many groups a dramatic leap in educational attainment from one generation to the next, literacy and formal education could still mean separate things. Literacy was one (of many) potential signs of character or intelligence, whereas education was a sign of wealth, opportunity, luck, or generational change.[21]

Yet although the family economy that supported Sam's early literacy learning was primarily agrarian, traditional, and backward glancing, it did carry more recent traces of the family's sojourn in America – particularly adding advanced schooling to the repertoire of family economic strategies. Scarcity of land and family capital in Norway had encouraged Sam's grandparents to immigrate to America to reestablish a farming life where land was affordable and plentiful. For these immigrants, the scene changed but family work practices did not. It was different, however, for the next generations. Changes to the regional economy set in motion by growing corporate presence and stepped up commercialism brought new products and technologies to bear on Sam's literate encounters and literate consciousness. Radio particularly delivered information and news from distant places in the voices of distant strangers and helped to make Sam part of a national audience and a national demographic target for programming and advertising. Automobiles and the beginning of a commuting work culture in his village also made Sam a more simultaneous habitué of rural and urban places. He commuted regularly to the state capital to shop for paperback adventure books and radio parts, and, most significant, connected readily with the emerging network of military-sponsored education that moved into existing university facilities in the early 1940s. The siting in the state capital of the War Management Board as well as the Army Institute, a college correspondence school opened just 17 days after the attack on Pearl Harbor, illustrates how new literacy formations take over older infrastructures – keeping opportunity more heavily weighted to the geography of past power. In any case, as the voracious human resource needs of the military democratized education (mostly for men), opportunities for literacy linked to economic transitions came along for Sam and others similarly situated.

If the sponsoring sources of Sam's literacy were more hybrid, dynamic, and contemporary than his mother's, so were the strategies he developed for coping with escalating demands on his writing skills. Strategies for literacy learning developed in the social hierarchy of his rural village were reinterpreted for use in military hierarchy as the language of grace and worldliness was replaced by the language of technocracy. Exposure to his aunt's modeling of self-instruction – rigged out of materials available from the rural mass market – could not have hurt on the European front as Sam May rigged both equipment and reports with technical knowledge too new to be codified.

These are the basic formations of literacy learning and opportunity that the subsequent analysis will continue to watch: a family economy as the repository of literate resources and strategies, a regional economy as the conditioner of opportunity and change, an intensifying hybridity of literacy sponsorship, and a volatile economic value of individual literacy caught in the interplay.

Jack May, Born 1958

At midcentury, the May family economy blended with the regional mainstream into which it was fitting. By the time Jack May was born in 1958, his family's turn from agrarianism – like society on the whole – was complete. His parents were participants in a fast-paced, information-based urban society. Jack's father designed and made equipment for a physics laboratory in a research university. His mother, also a rural émigré to the state capital, was a college trained x-ray technician. She worked in a modern metropolitan hospital before turning full time to raising children.

The context for Jack's early literacy learning seemed remarkably contemporary – built out of stuff as new as postwar middle-American suburban culture. He grew up in a housing development of new, modest, single-family homes. He lived within walking distance of three schools, all built in the 1960s. Jack May remembered "lots" of books in a room of the house called "the library," most of them associated with his parents' postsecondary educations. ("Some were Mom's, some were Dad's. Some just ended up. They had a lot of their college manuals left over, technical manuals. Mom had her x-ray books and a few of the classics.")

Jack saw both of his parents writing and typing regularly, including letters to relatives and occasional newsletter items in connection with their participation in a neighborhood association. Like many other children of the suburban middle class, he was read to each night by his mother from books purchased especially for that purpose. ("We'd all sit on the couch," he recalled, "and go through a book a chapter a night or read an easy book one night.") In grade school, he read from the postwar basal series, Dick and Jane, learning to structure sentences by answering questions about the stories. As part of a language arts assignment, he composed a fan letter to his favorite contemporary children's book author, who thrilled him by writing back. The family received multiple magazines by subscription, including *Life, National Geographic, Scientific American,* and *Highlights for Children.* Jack's older sister bought Hardy Boys books and other serial hardbacks, which Jack would borrow. As a kid, he had his own AM radio that he used "to pull in talk radio," and the family had a black-and-white television set, although "it wasn't on very much." Jack said he preferred to spend his free time outside, playing in a nearby nature conservancy, sometimes painting graffiti on exposed drainage pipes in a nearby park, and tinkering with cars and carpentry projects, frequently with his father.

The Mays' transition from farm to town, from extended family to nuclear family, from self-employment to salary kept the family generally moving with an American mainstream, an asset hard to underestimate when it came to the contours of Jack's literacy learning. Demographically, ideologically, the Mays' position was broadly compatible with educational and cultural currents on which prevailing midcentury child literacy was being carried. These currents included child-centered, secularized philosophies of education, enhanced by trends toward decreased child labor, rising education levels of parents, smaller family size, more discretionary income, and an expanding children's literature industry ready to appeal to every demographic niche. *Highlights for Children,* a magazine founded in the 1940s for young people aged 2 to 12, boasted an editorial aim of "fun with a purpose." With puzzles, riddles, jokes, cartoons, poetry, science articles, and short stories, the magazine did not "teach or preach" but encouraged children by "positive suggesting." So strong was the commercial presence of juvenile literature becoming that in many locales book fairs and "meet the author" events became routine school-sponsored events.[22]

Children's literature in school and out also was influenced by growing reliance on scientific principles of applied psychology. As his parents labored using military-inspired technologies recently entrenched in civilian economies, Jack May was introduced to Dick and Jane, a basal reading series that systematized reading instruction by controlling linguistic and syntactic form. This series, which gained nearly monopolistic status in postwar American classrooms, used scientific approaches not unlike ones by which military personnel had been taught and tested.[23] It offered simple stories set within the ordinary life of a white, suburban, contemporary American family. For Jack, the cultural fit seemed close. He recalled starting each year of grade school with the assignment to write about what he had done on his summer vacation. ("That was pretty much a given," he said. "It was like watching *Peter and the Wolf.* You knew it was going to happen.") The essays he wrote about what he did could have been written by Dick of Dick and Jane: "You'd say something like 'We walked to the store for candy twelve days and played in the drainage ditch and helped Dad build something on the house.'"

So at one level, Jack's early literacy learning seemed to arise out of contemporary materials and ideologies with which a changing May family economy was apparently keeping up. In three generations, the family had made significant social, technological, and economic transitions and was participating successfully in a culture considerably more complex, almost unrecognizably so, than the one that Genna May's parents entered as Norwegian immigrants in the nineteenth century. The sorts of knowledge that the May family used to work, access information, raise children, and participate in civic life was made up of many innovations from just the previous few decades. Of course, the adaptations on which Jack's childhood was nested reached back to certain turns in the family history, especially the leaps in education attainment achieved by Jack's grandmother and parents in relationship to the previous generations. Their schooling made them available for roles in nonagrarian and increasingly education-reliant enterprises.

In fact, a closer look at the details of Jack's literacy memories in some way disrupts the contemporary look and compatible feel of his midcentury experience. The presence of the past was everywhere in his experience, posing both help and hindrance in his literacy development. Even more than in his father's case, Jack's encounters with reading and writing were ideologically complex as layers of literacy campaigns of the past piled up in the materials and practices to which he was exposed and distributed themselves differently across social institutions with which he had contact. For instance, a literacy of manners and civic connection that came to Sam May at the dinner table of his farmhouse came to Jack through a two-year membership in the Cub Scouts: "We did a lot of letter writing to various people, and thank-you notes, things they tried to develop," he remembered. Autodidactism, represented in Sam's childhood home by his aunt's cabinets filled with instructional books, carried on in Jack's home in copies of *Scientific American* scattered on living-room end tables.

Handwriting was an especially ideologically congested site for Jack, carrying connotations and burdens of previous generations. The distinctive hand of Jack's great-grandfather was used to glorify God, whereas Sam's aunt became "famous for her fancy hand" through the writing of notes and invitations to neighbors. Genna's certificate in penmanship from a proprietary business college certified her as ready for employment in area offices. Sam regarded his handwriting lessons in school as a nuisance. ("I never got good grades in that. It was kind of a forced exercise.")[24] By midcentury, proper handwriting was a site of accumulating meanings, potentially indicating anything from moral character to social-class mettle, from clerical aptitude to scholastic fortitude. Perhaps because of this loaded inheritance, handwriting remained a source of pressure and anxiety for many children, including Jack, even while its cultural and economic relevance was fading. Jack's memories of handwriting instruction were vivid and unpleasant:

> I remember the two- or three-lined pieces of paper, and they would have a letter written on it and you'd have to try to match that letter. They'd do the same with cursive letters. Back then, it was before the D'Nealian method came in, so you would do your cursive letters

without making words out of them. I think it was in third grade –
you already knew how to write – but my writing must have been
really sloppy. I mean, it must have been really bad, because I can
remember them suggesting that I go to additional writing courses
and getting a fair amount of writing to take home. I don't think it
worked, 'cause 'til this day, I have fairly scrawly handwriting.

Jack was not alone in attributing a lifelong aversion to writing to the
opprobrium that was heaped on his grade-school scrawl. The criticism
didn't make him feel like a bad person, just a bad writer. Even as instructional techniques in penmanship were going, like reading, the way of scientific efficiency, moral overtones still clung to handwriting in the minds
and experiences of many.[25]

Nineteenth- and twentieth-century education philosophies also
jammed up together in the eclectic set of reading materials that Jack
encountered at home and at school. Among the books Jack remembered
his mother reading to him were classic fairy tales and fables, which kept
alive a didactic heritage of reading that communicated traditional moral
and cultural lessons. (These also were being translated into filmstrips of
the period, like the perennial *Peter and the Wolf.*) At the same time, juvenile
novels by contemporary authors mixed with adventure stories linked to
radio and television shows of the period and with easy-to-read books and
"fun with a purpose" magazines based on yet more recent scientific theories of language. The ideological swirl in which Jack learned reading as a
child was an inevitable feature of rapid social change, commercial competition, a maturing mass literacy, and growing influence of specialized
knowledge at all levels in the twentieth century. His was not the first generation, certainly, to encounter such proliferating traditions in early reading material. But his generation did experience an unprecedented pace of
proliferation. Among other things, this condition helped to create a kind
of free-floating omni-imperative for reading, a value no longer anchored
in the particular missions of particular institutions. "It's just part of the
culture," Jack observed about his process of literacy learning. "It was just
part of what I grew up in. You will learn how to write and read and try to
fit into society eventually."

These memories of particular literacy encounters show how ideological legacies are preserved and can be present as interpretive puzzles for
contemporary learners. These legacies obviously serve as important
resources by which literate skills are passed across generations, yet they
also can be sources of opacity and surplus at the scenes of contemporary
literacy learning. In their conservative nature, they can both help and hurt
the process of literacy learning.

Perhaps even more dramatically, accumulated histories of literacy make themselves felt in the broader cultural and economic contexts in which reading and writing must be pursued. These effects are most pronounced in the shape of Jack's later literacy learning. This process took place amid the implications spinning out of regional restructuring in south central Wisconsin in the second half of the twentieth century. Ironically, as we will see, the rapid expansion of higher education after the war, which helped Jack's parents parlay their technology-driven literacy into economic security, became, by the late 1970s, a rising hurdle for their son. The rapid takeover of the local economy by what Smith and Parr (1989) called "brain intensive activities" (p. 42) attracted a growing professional class to the dairyland. With an expanding university, state government, health care industry and other information-based enterprises, highly educated, well-paid people continued to migrate to the area.

This group began to put its political mark on the public school district in which Jack was enrolled, increasing the competitive climate in which he pursued his studies. By the time he entered high school in the mid-1970s, the district boasted one of the highest per capita student spending rates in the state. The education levels and incomes of parents as well as student scores on standardized tests were higher than national averages. Close to 90% of students in his high school went on to four-year colleges and universities, helped by a rigorous college preparatory curriculum. Jack's grandmother had come of age when young people she knew "didn't think about school." His father came of age when college educations were linked primarily to rank and wealth. Jack found himself in a climate where being college bound was considered the norm and where most of the school revolved around that expectation.

Part of that expectation was increased attention to writing – an inevitable escalation for children of professionals who would need to use ever-advancing schooling to maintain if not surpass their parents' economic station. In that environment, Jack remained a diffident student, someone who, as he put it, "picked up a hammer, not a pen." Although always an able reader, he avoided classes that he knew required a good amount of writing. "I tried to avoid writing as much as possible, I really did," he said. "If I would have had to choose between six courses in calculus and one in writing, I'd take the math." As part of a "path of least resistance," Jack earned graduation credits in the marketing curriculum of his high school, part of a vocational education track in which approximately 10% of the student population enrolled. Occasionally assigned to write essays on the philosophy of capitalism, Jack more often wrote problem solutions on business-related topics (for instance, how to handle a shoplifting incident). He also studied advertising, made oral presentations, and learned how to write applications, résumés, sales letters, and follow-up letters. He was a peripheral member of the school's chapter of the Distributive Education Clubs of America (DECA), a national organization founded in the 1940s to improve education and career opportunities in retail and marketing. Jack joined so he would be eligible for the apprenticeship program, by which he could earn credits (as well as pocket money) by leaving school in the early afternoons to work in part-time jobs. He caddied, delivered pizzas, and clerked at a bicycle store. After high school graduation, Jack earned an associate degree in marketing from a local, open-admissions technical college, where it was decidedly harder to avoid writing. He explained:

> Just about every class had some kind of report due at least two or three times a semester. There was a class in writing and communication skills. Salesmanship class had a fair amount of writing. There was another class that taught you how to write business letters and résumés. So there was plenty to do there.

Jack said he managed the curriculum because "most things were pretty much off a form. If you can read, you can follow that. There wasn't much creative writing, so far as freelancing and getting a great sentence or paragraph out. I don't think I had to do much of that." At the time of our interview in the early 1990s, Jack worked as a short-distance courier for an international parcel company. "I write mostly numbers because I'm recording numbers all day long," he explained. "I type into the computer all day long, people's names and numbers. I still don't write sentences. [The work] doesn't give me any trouble." While an employee of this company, Jack received on-the-job instruction in customer relations (a repeat from college, he said) as well as an electronics short course on installing and maintaining radios in delivery trucks. Occasionally in the evenings, he attended sales seminars sponsored by other area companies recruiting employees.

These memories help to disclose the impact on ordinary people of escalating standards for literacy and education as well as the complicated cultural, economic, and family relationships in which these changes take place. There is no more intriguing demonstration of these themes than the image of Jack May as a courier typing names and numbers on a hand-held, globally networked computer while operating a two-way radio in his delivery truck. The scene measures the tangible extensions of the economic and technological transformations on which his grandmother's and father's literacy had developed. In his recordkeeping, Jack performed tasks not unlike those his grandmother performed as a recorder of land abstracts in the early decades of the twentieth century (although now the business was swapping information instead of land). And he performed these tasks while sitting amid some of the same communication technologies that his father's generation had worked to develop during World War II – technologies now turned to civilian profit making.

At the same time, despite business-oriented literacy training far more elaborate than what his grandmother had received, the status and value of that education were unextraordinary in the economy in which Jack competed and in fact exceeded the actual literacy demands of his job. In a place in which education and material prosperity were improving dramatically for some groups, there was growing pressure for stratification within an expanding middle class. Literacy – particularly writing – was central to these intensifying processes of occupational stratification after World War II. Writing – which never was much of the May "line" – was gaining greater economic importance and social prestige in a society growing more abstract, bureaucratized, symbol-driven, and networked. This shift was raising the education stakes for the May family.

Jack's experience with distributive education is useful for appreciating how infrastructures for both opportunity and stratification build up out of the economic histories of a region, as well as the role of literacy in those histories. A consumer society that spilled beyond big cities by the turn of the twentieth century gradually brought more curricular attention and government subsidy to distributive education through the 1930s and 1940s. Distributive education became a kind of third wing, with agriculture and industrialism, in high school and technical-college curriculums throughout the Midwest, teaching the practices, genres, and values that underlay entrepreneurship, management, sales, and business communication. Clubs organized to promote competitions among students. These groups also were conduits for businesses and corporations who sponsored events and provided employment for students.[26] In the city where Jack was schooled, services catered to the work and leisure needs of the professional class. This created an ongoing need for low-wage, part-time workers – a niche that high school students helped to fill. The vocational school that Jack attended also had absorbed into its curriculum the shape of mid-century economic life in the region that it served – including an expanding array of credentials in marketing tailored to food, insurance, retail, travel, and agribusiness. What were occupational and technological frontiers for Jack's forbears (and sites of difficult economic struggle) show up as "pretty much givens" and "paths of least resistance" in the curricular arrangements of Jack's schools.[27] These are the ways that recessive and emerging economies circulate through the literacy learning processes of each new generation, assigning changing measures of value to the reading and writing skills associated with them. By the 1990s, enrollment in distributive education in Jack's high school had fallen from 10% to 5% of the student population. In recent years, it has become a popular choice of study for the children of working-class and poor African American and Latino families who are migrating to the area from big cities in search of better employment and better schools.

Michael May, Born 1981

In the early 1990s, Michael May was growing up about 25 miles from where his great-grandmother had been born. His family owned a home in one of several suburbanizing areas that ringed the state capital. These districts, which even into the late 1950s had been rural townships and villages, were now dotted with housing tracts, service stations, office parks, and strip malls. In the town where Michael lived, a majority of the adult population had taken some form of post-secondary education and was engaged in white-collar work. Residents were attracted to the suburbs by lower housing costs, spacious streets, newer schools, and expansive highways that supported easy commutes to capital jobs. Apartment and townhouse complexes also attracted single workers and, more recently, lower-income families stretching the value of their federal housing subsidies. A major shopping mall, consisting mostly of national chains, as well as lakefront businesses spurred a new round of development in the 1970s and 1980s. This was a town of fewer than 9,000 people – set in a contiguous metropolitan area of close to 400,000.

At 11 years old, Michael attended fifth grade at a large, well-furnished middle school that promised in public documents to prepare learners to "think critically and creatively in order to function successfully in a complex and changing world." The oldest of four children, Michael played soccer, belonged to the Cub Scouts, and sometimes wrote video game–inspired adventure stories with his friends. (Unlike his father as a child, he played and socialized indoors most of the time.) With even more intensity than his predecessors, his early reading and writing took shape amid the simultaneous traces of receding and emerging ideologies of literacy. That was most obvious in the multiple technologies that he had encountered. By the age of 11, he had composed using chalk, magnetic letters, pencils and pens, a typewriter, and a computer. He had written journal entries, fictional stories, book reports, essays, a memo, a research report, and letters. Audiences for his original writing included his teachers, his family, his principal, the local community [in a letter to the editor from his scout troop], and one of the clients of his mother's day care service. He also was keeping a diary, modeled after one he recently had been asked to keep in school. "I like to look back on what happens in my life," he explained. As a reader, he identified with the works of particular authors, including Laura Ingalls Wilder.

Among the many sponsors of Michael's childhood literacy was the Future Problem Solving Program. Founded in 1974, FPSP was designed by a university professor in Georgia as a curriculum enrichment project for a program for talented and gifted students. By the 1990s, it had affiliates in most U.S. states, serving students from grade school through high school. In both competitive and noncompetitive events, the organization teaches a six-step thinking process that stresses brainstorming, critical reflection, and verbal presentation, all done within small-group settings. FPSP holds competitions for problem-solving teams addressing such topics as "homes of the future," "extraterrestrial life," "cashless society," "competition," and "increasing the life span." FPSP activities are frequently organized around scenario writing. Guidebooks for teachers provide writing assignments in some 30 genres, including science fiction, historical fiction, poetry, and legends.[28] As noted in the introduction to this chapter, during the year that he participated in FPSP, Michael worked on environmental issues. His class presented a written plan to the principal for relandscaping a muddy hill on the school playground.

Another key sponsor for Michael's writing was his mother, for whom writing did seem to be her "line," to echo Genna May. Michael recounted that he tried to write a poem after finding out that his mother had written poetry when she was young. Further, his mother was so proud of a story that Michael wrote on his own when he was six years old that she showed it to a teacher for whom she was doing child care. Michael's younger sister enjoyed typing as part of her play and as a preschooler had typed out the complete script of one of her favorite children's books (minus spaces and punctuation). In addition, Michael's mother introduced computers and word processing skills into the household, initially when she worked for an insurance company and then, in the late 1990s, when all of her children were in school and she began working as a reporter for a local newspaper. Jack May indicated that his wife "compensated for my weaknesses," when it came to family writing needs and to helping children with language-based school assignments.

It is impossible to tell what course Michael's literacy development will take through his young adulthood and beyond, or to tell, for that matter, what economic transformations will continue to affect opportunity and reward for his generation of learners. It is possible, however, to calculate the contrasts between his childhood literacy experiences and his great-grandmother's. Like a delta, Michael's environment for reading and writing was a repository of accumulating material and ideological complexity that carried the history of economic transformation within his region and his family. This complexity was most tangible in the number of writing instruments that he had used by the age of 11 in contrast to his great-grandmother as well as to the number of literacy traditions that were operating in the materials and experiences in his home and school. These traditions were only multiplying with the work changes that his parents were going through.[29] As part of this complexity, the centrality of writing – specifically, the centrality of authoring texts – was making its way into Michael's young life earlier and more insistently than it had for his forbears. By the age of 11, he had written in many more genres than the others had reported at that age. Although all of the Mays I interviewed had identities as able readers, he was the only one I met who had an identity as a writer. There was a high degree of convergence in the kinds of writing he was doing for school, recreation, social interaction, and personal reflection. Like other members of the youngest cohort I interviewed, he was being invited by the language arts curriculum in his district not merely to read popular literature, especially youth literature, but to write it as well. He and others of this age also were invited by the official curriculum to turn encounters with television and other media into imaginative compositions, including horror stories, teen romances, and television scripts.[30] And programs like FPSP were introducing him and children as young as 7 into the kind of open-ended, generic, collaborative problem solving, verbally rendered, that is in growing demand in late-century workplaces.[31] In any case, many kinds of writing that Michael was doing by his eleventh year never entered the writing experience of his great-grandmother throughout her entire life. Yet what enabled his writing was being carried in a family stock of literacy, work, and learning experience that reached back at least four generations.

Conclusion

Each of the Mays developed literacy within key moments of economic transition in their region. These transitions routed opportunities for reading and writing, defined the shifting value of their skills, and in turn affected the way they practiced and passed on literacy to the next generation. The daughter of immigrant dairy farmers, Genna May came of age when expectations for schooling were rising as prospects for farming were shrinking. Farm communities in the Midwest were more consciously organizing to extend high school education to more of their young residents, most of whom would need to find work in town. Many like Genna who acquired more formal schooling and more literate skill, were recruited into the business-based, consumer-based activities that were transforming the countryside. For Sam May, World War II proved the defining moment, as his high school education and mechanical aptitude were shoveled into the production of America's military dominance. Both before and after the war, resources of a nearby public university, put in place initially to support the progress of farming and entrepreneurship, were reappropriated for the needs of an emerging technocracy. These events made opportunities for higher education abruptly available to veterans like Sam. Through schooling and subsequent employment, his specialized electronic abilities were wedded to heightened requirements for documentation, communication, and representation. Although a beneficiary of the education opportunities of earlier generations, son Jack May was caught up at the same time in the intensifying stratification building up around literacy and schooling in the second half of the twentieth century. Literacy and its derivatives were not merely fundamental to a wider array of learning but were coming to function as both raw material and principle output of an information economy. Opportunity for advantage centered around increasingly sophisticated skills of abstraction and communication in an increasingly competitive and noisy market. For the very youngest May, these aspects of regional restructuring were solidly, mundanely embedded in the material environment and social relations in which he encountered literacy, and the preparation of his cognitive skills for word work reached down into his earliest years. Michael May also was positioned to endure even more cycles of change and proliferation in the communication bases of his society than did his immediate predecessors.

One of the most dramatic effects on this family pertains to a changing relationship between literacy and the metropolis. When Genna was born in the 1890s, people migrated toward cities as centers of literacy, as places for advanced schooling and nonagrarian employment. Those people who moved adjusted their skills to a change of location. By Michael's birth in 1981, advanced forms of literacy were migrating to the metropolis and spilling broadly beyond city limits – in channels of school, commerce, work, and media that were applying continuous pressure on whole metropolitan regions. People living where Michael lived had to keep adjusting their skills to changes within their location. There was no other choice. Where once national companies sent their goods and services to the countryside to be sold, these national and often multinational corporations were now as often showing up in the former countryside as employers. Where once there were standard, integrated markets, there were now standard, integrated workforces, with all of the adjustments to new technologies and work practices implied by that change. School systems large and small were also now under the organization of more widely standardized goals and curricula. For Michael, this migration of literacy was felt most explicitly in the proliferating reading and writing materials that were entering his household through his parents' educations and means of employment as well as the reading and writing ideologies that his school district was embracing. In any case, if it was people's movement toward literacy that affected the value of skills in this region in the first half of the century, it was the unrelenting arrival of literacy change that affected the value of skills in the second half of the century.[32]

It is no wonder that increased stratification around literacy would become an inevitable phenomenon in such conditions. As chances for schooling and literacy development grew more broadly and diversely available in the social structures in which the Mays lived, tightening competition and steeper hierarchies installed themselves as well. Both Genna and Sam recounted significant household stratification by status and age. Genna's father, who was in charge of the significant writing in the family, was entitled to use costly paper, whereas the others used chalk and slate. Sam's aunt kept her books in locked cabinets, meted out carefully to younger relatives who were expected to learn to appreciate adult tastes. By Jack's childhood, literate skills were more democratized in the society and in the household; Jack's parent's books were on open shelves. Stratification more often showed up in the household as consumer categories, as children received their own age-based magazine subscriptions and were taught to read through youth and young adult literature. At a regional level, education stratification had shifted from geography to curriculum, as competition for college entrance and prestigious forms of literacy magnified the implications of particular courses of study in Jack's high school. In fact, we can see how literacy grows more democratic between adults and children in the May family in response to the repercussions of stratification in the regional economy. In Michael's home, writing instruments like typewriters and computers were shared with very young children, and their full-fledged identities as readers, writers, and problem solvers were encouraged through everyday interactions with adults. (Whereas Genna's compositions were erased to make room for arithmetic lessons, Michael's journals were saved and his stories circulated to admiring audiences.) This democracy can flow both ways as parents invest more time and skill in helping their children to succeed in school. Trying, at one point in his interview, to remember how he learned to write reports, 34-year-old Jack responded that "I think I'm learning more now with my own children going through school."

This analysis of literacy across the lives of the four Mays underscores how histories of economic competition and change of earlier generations become the deep infrastructures for literacy encounters by later generations.

This dynamic serves as the chief source of both opportunity and constraint by which literacy skill is practiced and passed along. This accumulation of literacy – shaped out of economic struggles, victories, and losses of the past – provides an increasingly intricate set of incentives, sources, and barriers for learning to read and writing. The contexts of contemporary literacy learning grow ideologically dense, rife with latent forms of older literacy at play alongside emerging forms, much as the children in Sam's village in the 1930s performed their vaudevillian skits beside the outdoor movie screens. Rapid changes in literacy and education may not so much bring rupture from the past as they bring an accumulation of different and proliferating pasts, a piling up of literate artifacts and signifying practices that can haunt the sites of literacy learning. These complicated amalgamations of literacy's past, present, and future formulate the interpretive puzzles faced by current generations of literacy learners.

Especially potent in this process are the literacy materials that come into people's lives and into the scenes of their learning. Materials to some degree always will reflect how individuals are intersecting at a certain time and place with the history of mass literacy and the sponsors who have controlled it. Literacy is always in flux. Learning to read and write necessitates an engagement with this flux, with the layers of literacy embodied in materials, tools, sponsorship patterns, and the social relationships we have with the people who are teaching us to read and write. Indeed, as changes in literacy have speeded up over the course of the twentieth century, literate ability has become more and more defined as an ability to position and reposition oneself amid the flux.

This dynamic also measures the limits of intergenerational strategies for literacy transmission. On the one hand, each new member of the May family inherited higher and higher piles of literacy resources. But on the other hand, the reliability of their value was becoming shorter and shorter lived. Jack May's pursuit of a business degree in a open-admission technical college, for instance, was quite literally built on top of the economic and cultural transformations that his grandmother and father helped to put in place in south central Wisconsin. But their status and relevance within unrelenting, globalizing competition and technological change were dramatically lower than they would have been two generations before. It is in this inflationary cycle that ordinary American literacy is caught.

4

"THE POWER OF IT"

Sponsors of Literacy in African American Lives

Earlier chapters have suggested that competitions in America's emerging information economy in the twentieth century stimulated and claimed the skills of an increasingly literate population. The deepening involvement of reading and, most recently, writing in the production of wealth has conditioned opportunities for literacy, shaping the ways that resources and incentives for literacy learning arrive to people in particular times and places. It also accounts for inequities in opportunity, shaping the ways that the resources, chances, and rewards for literacy learning are distributed unevenly. Patterns of past economic competition install themselves in the makeup of reading and writing and linger in the foundations on which succeeding generations of learners encounter the puzzles of literacy. These patterns also regulate the pace at which forms and standards of literacy fall and rise.

This argument is further scrutinized here through life history accounts involving 16 African Americans.[1] Where the skills of reading and writing have developed among African Americans, it has rarely been at the vigorous invitation of economic sponsors. Relegated for centuries to mostly physical labor and domestic service, African Americans have rarely seen their literacy development figured into the needs of the nation – except in periods of temporary crisis. One such crisis was World War II, when a high rate of illiteracy among Southern men and black Southern men in particular created human resource problems for the U.S. military. The government embarked on a crash effort to teach basic reading skills to military recruits who lacked them. Perhaps another such period of crisis is the beginning of the twenty-first century, as anxieties about global competitiveness are bringing sudden interest in the reading scores of minority school populations.[2] Over most of the twentieth century, however, few of the channels by which literacy was being stimulated and subsidized were equally open to African Americans. Further, because of entrenched racial discrimination in employment, African Americans who attained high-level literacy and advanced education often found that their skills did not have the same status and tradable value as those of the white population. The full worth of their literacy usually was honored only within the African American community itself. Unenlisted in the call-ups for literate skills needed for transitions to an information economy, African Americans more often saw literacy turned as a weapon against their liberties – whether through capricious uses of literacy tests to deter voting or ill-conceived standardized reading tests to stratify academic opportunity.[3] Throughout recent history, literacy has often served as a stand-in for skin color in the ongoing attempts to subordinate African Americans.

The history of African American literacy in some ways confirms the thesis of this study but in other ways complicates it. On the one hand, gaps between white and black literacy have been as persistent a social fact in the twentieth century as gaps between white and black income. These facts favor the claim that in twentieth-century America, opportunities for literacy became increasingly reliant on economic sponsorship and increasingly vulnerable to the lack of it. The thesis also can explain how some of the ideological affordances of literacy could abet racism.[4] Other cases in this study have shown how meanings of literacy become volatile and ever shifting as they link with political competitions and economic change. With its tenacious capacity to preserve within its practices dense and disparate ideologies, the protean character of literacy has always made it a useful tool in political control, ready to take on whatever connotation might be needed at the time. As literacy grew more useful for gaining economic advantage, it developed new ideological uses for preserving white skin advantage.

On the other hand, however, there are parts of the story of African American literacy that elude the argument of this book so far. For despite rather wholesale exclusion from economic and education opportunity through most of the twentieth century, basic literacy rates among African Americans rose from 30% in 1910 to more than 80% by 1930 to over 95% by 1970.[5] Contemporary mass literacy was achieved in a period that preceded landmark civil rights legislation and the end of legal segregation in schools. In fact, this period of literacy growth coincided with a time of heightened backlash against the political and education gains that had been made during and following Reconstruction. In the opening decades of the twentieth century, segregation hardened, voting rights of African

Americans plummeted, violence against African Americans increased, and mandatory education laws were offset by vast racial disparities in spending for schools, especially high schools.[6] How, then, was literacy sustained in the absence of broad-based economic and political subsidy and the presence of so much social hostility?

Although this chapter cannot address this large historical question comprehensively, it does explore the implications of the case of African American literacy as it bore on the lives of individuals who grew up between the 1910s and the 1970s in regions including the rural and urban South, the industrial upper Midwest, and the West. Most of those interviewed lived their childhoods in the South and most bore the brunt of Jim Crow laws and customs, including official segregation in school, military, and public areas; limited occupational opportunities regardless of qualifications; and interference with citizenship rights, including the use of public libraries. All but two people migrated to south central Wisconsin from birthplaces elsewhere, some as part of the Great Northern Migration through the 1940s, others to take jobs in the expanding public sector in the 1960s and 1970s, and still others in the 1980s, often as part of an exodus from deteriorating urban areas nearby. Education attainment ranged from fifth grade to graduate level. Their occupations included bus driving, home health, social service, public utilities, education, civil service, domestic service, medicine, computer programming, small business, and legal aid. Eight were members of one African Methodist Episcopal (AME) church.

My analysis of their life history accounts went in search of the presence of a system for human development long identified with African American society, sets of sponsorship networks that provided political and cultural support to members. The framework of this chapter borrows from a body of sociological literature, particularly work by V. P. Franklin (1984) and C. Eric Lincoln and Lawrence Mamiya (1990), who have identified a core set of cultural agents within African American society who have been most responsible for racial survival since the days of slavery. In the face of economic and political exclusion, these agents circulated resources and nurtured skills, including literacy, all within what several sociologists have identified as a core set of cultural values. These values include self-determination, freedom, education, advancement, and, often, a unity between religious and secular existence. Within circumscribed economic and political conditions, these concentrated sites of sponsorship were the deep wells that fed a steady rise in literacy and education rates among African Americans in the first half of the twentieth century. In many cases, these sponsors remained intact and central to literacy development even as political and economic opportunity expanded in the century's second half.

From various perspectives, scholars have drawn attention to the meanings that literacy acquired for African Americans during slavery and its aftermath, particularly its strong association with resistance, freedom, self-determination, and collective uplift. These values influenced the purposes to which literacy, once obtained, could most responsibly be put. Yet they also often characterized the contexts in which significant experiences with literacy took place. From the eighteenth century on, African Americans organized to provide education for themselves as part of their claim to personhood, through networks of Sunday schools, Freedman schools, as well as clandestine arrangements required in slave conditions. Following the Civil War, Southern blacks were at the forefront of political agitation for universal public education – an effort that would be undercut by the retaliation of segregation. In the twentieth century, thousands of black adults in rural and urban communities learned literacy under the auspices of Freedom Schools and later, civil rights–era liberation projects aimed at expanding voting rights and economic power. And until quite recently, most African Americans who achieved higher education did so within the system of historically black colleges, in whose continued existence are carried the oldest legacies of self-determination and education designed as service to the race.[7]

Placing literacy within a constellation of cultural values developing together out of Africans' experiences in North America, V. P. Franklin observed: "At the core of racial consciousness ... was the cultural objective of black self-determination, which operated in a dialectical relationship with white supremacy" (p. 6). Drawing on an array of testimonies and artifacts expressive of African American culture, Franklin found that "freedom, resistance, education, as well as self-determination were defined over and over again as 'good' and things to be valued" (p. 8). In a book on literacy and rhetoric among nineteenth-century African American female writers, Royster (2000) underscored how the contexts in which the women she studied acquired literacy molded it with the values of "activism, advocacy, and action" (p. 110). As Royster showed, these circumstances of acquisition worked their way into the women's rhetorical orientations, in terms of preferred genres, topics, styles, and occasions for writing.[8]

Most historical accounts of African American literacy and education focus on lives and doings of famous leaders, teachers, and authors as providers of the philosophies and movements responsible for growth in literacy and education. The following analysis, in contrast, continues to treat the lives of ordinary people and focuses principally on the means and material conditions of their literacy learning – how it was that they came in contact with sponsors and, in fact, how their literacy was recruited to the causes of those sponsors. The aim is to examine through the accounts of particular individuals how long-standing forms of African

American self-help provided avenues for literacy learning, especially when other ways were closed off.

Before proceeding, some limitations in the presentation must be acknowledged. First, as mentioned before, by virtue of migration histories in the area in which I conducted my study, experiences reported here heavily represent southern contexts over northern ones, rural and small-town experiences over urban ones, as well as the ways that formative experiences in those contexts were translated into the social and economic conditions of south central Wisconsin. Second, this treatment will not do justice to the full histories of the sponsors that surface in these accounts – particularly African American churches, the African American press, and the modern civil rights movement – and to the very complicated and fast-moving transformations they underwent through the twentieth century. Nor will emphasis be placed on the histories of competition that lie behind African American religious denominations and civil rights organizations.[9]

Rather, the aim continues to be an exploration of sponsorship as a useful lens for approaching processes of literacy learning and an interest in understanding the economies of literacy sponsorship broadly construed. Previous chapters have called attention to the twentieth century's rapid proliferation of literacy sponsors, the array of new interests that became involved in developing and recruiting people's literate skills. These multiplying sponsors, I have suggested, created atmospheres of material and ideological excess, lending increasing complexity to encounters with literacy. In this chapter, we will see how another kind of complex literacy develops from inverse forces: a complexity produced by material and ideological efficiency. As we will see, within black communities, forms of literacy and literacy learning have tended to be held onto, stretched, circulated and recirculated, altered and realtered to meet and make changing conditions. This efficiency has been forced, first, by a shortage of sponsors, and second, by the unique political history of a formerly enslaved people. Like other Americans, African Americans have been under the pressures of waves of social, economic, and communication changes associated with migrations from farms to cities and shifts from industrial manufacturing to information-based work. Yet they have had to cope with these transformations without the kinds of broad education and occupational subsidies that were gradually building across generations in the white population. These discrepancies were evident in the biographies of the African Americans I interviewed. For instance, although their birth dates were distributed evenly across six decades, their families had remained tied to subsistence agriculture much longer than was typical of white interviewees. Half of the African Americans who participated in this study, in fact, were born to poor, rural Southern farmers. Three quarters had parents who did not complete high

school. And although 10 of the 16 people I interviewed performed intellectual labor as adults, only one had parents who did. Further, in black life,
when regional, economic, and education leaps occurred, they were often
accomplished within the context of political struggle. That is, African
Americans were responding to changes in education and economic expectations even as they were working to secure their basic rights to participate
fully in education and economic systems. This double duty, in a sense, put
literacy achievement in a distinctly political perspective for many members
of this group and kept it rooted in values of self-determination and social
activism that have been present at the scene of African American literacy
learning from the beginning.

Further, the complexity and ideological density of African American–sponsored literacy derives from the practices, including literacy practices, of institutions that have supported African Americans throughout
time. Small in number, long in history, these agents of racial preservation
have had to perform multiple and simultaneous functions within African
American society. By necessity, African American self-help institutions
absorbed into their purview as many politically, socially, and culturally
affirming functions as they possibly could. The more uses to which a
resource (including the resource of literacy) could be put, the more value
it would have. Further, although sometimes in competition with each
other, core institutions more often collaborated, converged, and consolidated in efforts to advance African American well-being. As is often
observed, the modern civil rights movement was successful in part
because of the unique orchestration of religious, educational, political,
and media groups that organized around shared goals. As we will see, the
traditions of consolidation and multiplicity affected habits of reading and
writing among people in contact with core cultural sponsors, sometimes
in long-lasting ways. And, finally, the complexity of African Americans'
literacy derives in no small part from the subtleties demanded when they
integrate as readers and writers into white-controlled schools, work, and
social settings, where African American values, experiences, and skills are
so often misunderstood or under challenge. The following discussion,
then, looks, in short, at literacy learning among people who had to keep
up even while they were being kept down.

The Church

Many observers point to the African American Protestant church as the
most essential cultural institution for the well-being of African Americans

since their forced arrival on this continent. W. E. B. Du Bois (1903) explored the role of the black church as a bedrock of education and cultural enhancement. And Lincoln and Mamiya in 1990 asserted that "the Black Church has no challenger as the cultural womb of the black community" (p. 8.) The church's unique role in African American life can be traced to antebellum society where contradictory ideologies of Christianity and racial segregation made religious services the only tolerated site for congregation, education, and literacy among African Americans, whether enslaved or free. In Old Testament and New Testament teachings, especially in the principle of personal salvation, many African Americans found a way to withstand slavery and express their spirituality and faith. At the same time, black churches were the only institutions in America that were free from white domination. Consequently, black churches provided not only a space for the development of theological views but also an opportunity for black people's leadership skills to develop and for frank expression to be exchanged. In the absence of competing institutions, African American churches typically took on many more worldly social functions and responsibilities than did mainstream religious institutions. Chief among their social functions, both before and after emancipation, were the teaching of literacy and the building and staffing of schools.[10] Members of African American churches also organized to provide housing, health care, capital investment, and insurance.[11] In African American sharecropping communities of the late nineteenth and early twentieth centuries, pastors were often the single most important community leaders, and churches were the first buildings to be erected in settlements. Ownership of the church, its education facilities, and its publishing houses had both practical and symbolic significance. Further, in the days of Jim Crow especially, elections of church leaders gave African Americans some of their few opportunities to exercise democracy and political power. Preachers and lay leaders often learned to be effective, creative organizers, strategists, and fund-raisers – particularly given the tenuous financial conditions of many churches. Lincoln and Mamiya (1990) summed up the way that African American churches have operated as multipurpose sponsors for the human development of their members. For African Americans, they wrote, the church "was their school, their forum, their political arena, their social club, their art gallery, their conservatory of music. It was lyceum and gymnasium as well as sanctum sanctorum" (p. 93). Inevitably, churches became the organizational base of the civil rights movement as it grew to unprecedented strength in midcentury, and churches continue to serve as incubators for black elected officials and community organizers in society today.[12]

The AME church has had a distinctive history in this general movement. More strongly than other denominations, it is known for blending spiritual salvation with worldly involvement. In his history of the *Christian Recorder,* the newspaper of the AME church, Gilbert Anthony Williams (1996) described how elements of Christian belief fused with resistance to oppression to shape foundations of AME religious practice:

> The AME Church appropriated religious doctrines of other Christian denominations and adapted them so they became unique to the AME faith and unlike practices in predominantly white churches. Those appropriated customs, ideals, and rituals became identified with what it meant to be an AME member. Moreover, that same set of doctrinal customs and rituals became part and parcel of AME ministerial training. For example, racial solidarity and abolitionist activity were traditions in that church from its founding, and they became institutionalized within the church teachings. From Methodist religious philosophy the AME Church took the concept of social concern and transformed it into a unique social consciousness that promoted racial equality and a focus on educational achievement. Moreover, the AME Church appropriated the general Christian direction to be an open and fearless advocate of liberty, justice, and all righteousness and used it as a kind of guiding AME conviction. (p. 54)

The unique status of black churches changed somewhat as African Americans migrated in greater numbers from the rural South to the urban North, especially between World War I and World War II. Increased social complexity favored the emergence of secular organizations like the National Association for the Advancement of Colored People (NAACP) and the National Urban League, which dedicated themselves to political, educational, and economic advocacy. However, as Lincoln and Mamiya (1990) noted, African American churches continued to assume "complex roles" and "comprehensive burdens" as one of the few friendly institutions African Americans could count upon for cultural support and uplift (p. 18).

The holistic sensibilities of the African American church helped to hold intact a powerful, multiply performing sponsor that promoted integration over fragmentation, persistence over change, remembering over forgetting. As a by-product of helping members to keep body and soul together (often against the harshest conditions), the church also held together unique and enduring orientations to the written word that partook of this tradition.

Evidence of this influence emerged in literacy accounts of eight current members of the Metropolitan AME Church. This group, representing a spectrum of generational, regional, education, and class backgrounds, was united by a dynamic pastor who created the impetus for writing, reading, and teaching among the church membership. Seven of the eight members were reading, writing, learning, and teaching in connection with church worship and administration. Evening and special Sunday services were organized around talks composed and delivered by individual lay members, and five of the eight people I interviewed in 1993 had recently given such talks. In addition, adult Sunday school classes, led by the pastor, focused on intense analysis of key passages of the Bible. Discussions moved between analysis of the texts and analysis of events that had occurred in individuals' lives, with the aim of drawing analogies, contrasts, and lessons from Scripture. Debates about rival interpretations of the Bible were frequent in these discussions. During the regular church service, members also volunteered extemporaneous meditations and prayers from the pews. A few moments were taken during worship for all members to write contributions to what was called "the burden box," a place to deposit worries, prayers, communions, and other private thoughts in written form. In keeping with the pastor's commitment to member participation in all aspects of church affairs, several of the interviewees held administrative positions, including stewardships, financial offices, and committee assignments, all of which required reading and sometimes writing. Two of the interviewees were teaching Sunday school to younger members, and both said they made written preparation for the classes. One of the men I interviewed served on a citywide, Quaker-sponsored commission that was planning and arranging financing for a low-income housing initiative. This man, a World War II veteran, was also preparing a poster and report about the Buffalo Soldiers as his contribution to a Black History Month event being sponsored at the church. His sister had recently mailed him some background materials on this topic from her local newspaper, which he added to a clipping file he kept about African Americans in the military.

Many aspects of the African American church's cultural and historical heritage wove throughout these church members' accounts of literacy and literacy learning. First, the bedrock connection between reading and personal redemption – which justified the acquisition of literacy among African Americans before emancipation – was still salient, especially among older church members. Some of this saliency was carried in memories of older relatives. Stanley James, born in 1920 in a midsize Kansas city, recalled the following about his grandparents:

> My grandfather was in slavery. And my grandmother was a full-blooded Cherokee Indian. She had a little education. But they could both read the Bible. It is one of the most peculiar things in my life. My grandfather could not read a newspaper but he could read a Bible and understand it. He was very religious. All of our family was.

Others named the basic responsibilities of their faith as the principal, even the sole source of their interest in reading. Reading demonstrated active faith. Bertha Nixon, born in 1915 in rural Georgia and schooled irregularly to the seventh grade, said the Bible was her main reading material. "If you want to be a Christian, you have to read it to know what God said," she explained. "And to know what he said, you have to read it for yourself, not just what somebody else said all the time." Lavinia Stokes, who was born in 1930 and raised by her grandparents, also in a farming area in rural Georgia, said: "I do a lot of reading. The Bible, different commentaries, any book concerning the Scriptures. I read because I want to know all I can about what Jesus wants me to do or what Jesus wants me to be or how he wants me to live."

The compensatory role of the church in providing against poverty and governmental neglect was most vivid in Nixon's memories of her earliest literacy learning. She was raised along with seven brothers and one sister during some of the harshest decades of Jim Crow.[13] There were telling contrasts in the ways she recalled reading and learning in school versus in church – differences that had significant effects on her literacy for the rest of her life. Although at 78 years old she was still proud of her identity as a good speller,[14] she described her segregated country grade school as a place where no one ever graduated. "[The students] went' til they got too old or quit," she said. At her school, it was typical for the white school board to economize in funding by hiring ill-prepared teachers. In fact, she said, it was not uncommon for the school board (over the objections of the principal) to appoint as teachers the black schools students who were only a grade or two ahead of the children in their charge.[15] The negative effects of such low investment in education were magnified by the economics of tenant farming that relied on children in the family to help with the work, a problem exacerbated in Nixon's case by her mother's frequent illness:

> I was a good scholar and could have been a good scholar, but, you see, in the South, most people, if you … well, my mother was sick a lot and the fathers kept the sons out of school a lot to work. I could have been a good scholar, but, you see there, if the mother was sick, you stayed home to cook for the father and brothers.

In contrast to these school conditions, Nixon recalled attendance at church as regular and mandatory. And in a home where there was no cash for books – not even a privately owned Bible – the reading materials at church were central for literacy learning. Further, for a person like Nixon, whose family moved around from tenancy to tenancy, the church's ownership of books was especially satisfying (the *we* in the following passage refers first to her immediate family and then moves seamlessly to the institution of the church itself):

> We lived in church. Yeah, we went to church, went to Sunday school, eleven o'clock service, walking, raining, muddy, dusty, and we walked back for dinner, and then round about five in the afternoon, we would walk back for night service, and then we walked back home. We had no Bible of our own. We had them in church. We also had books that we called Sunday school books that we bought every three months. The church ordered them and they passed them out in church and you studied them at church and then you left them at church. They were about this size [showing me a current church publication she had on hand]. And you'd read here and you'd read out of the Bible. You'd find the answer and things out of the Bible. We bought them from [the AME Book Concern] out of Nashville, Tennessee. Yeah, we own that place.

The status of the Bible as the sometimes inscrutable word of God gave Nixon a prerogative as a reader and interpreter of texts that kept her questioning and wondering even at 78 years old. Confirming that she read the Bible on a regular basis, she explained: "There are a lot of words in there I can't pronounce, but there's a lot in there I know people can't pronounce that got degrees." Around the time of our interview, Nixon was carefully working through an audiotape that her son had sent her of a sermon based on one of Jesus' parables. She was eager to engage in considering various interpretations of the words.[16]

Kansas native Stanley James (born 1920) also associated his early church training with explicit literacy learning and with a developing literate identity. He especially recalled Sunday school cards that children in his church were given that had the text of the weekly lessons printed out on them. "We used to save the cards and review them, go back over them," he said. "That was learning you to read. That was learning you how to pick up." Sunday school lessons and reading materials also helped children gauge their maturity and status. Sunday school books were associated with the grown-ups. "When you turned into a teenager, you moved into a book," he recalled about the reading sequence in his Sunday school.

"Then we went to young adult. We'd be reading the same thing as our parents were reading. And that was educational to us."

Several other members identified the Bible as their first primer and religion as a strong motivator for literacy. Frances Hawkins, born to Mississippi tenant farmers in 1956, said her earliest memory of reading was when her grandparents, who lived nearby and sometimes cared for her, encouraged her to open the Bible.

> They knew all about the Bible and still do. I was a little girl and didn't know a thing about life. My grandmother would let me do my prayers. She would say them to me and would tell me how I could recite them on my own. This was before I went to school. You know how nowadays we give our children book material? Sometimes it may not be the best material, but we kind of look through it and then we help our children understand it. That's the way [the Bible] was put to me. This is something good. You can read it now or you can read it in later years.

Hawkins said she wrote religious poetry as a child (an activity that got "misplaced" as she grew older) and recalled doing regular reading in connection with Sunday school at her childhood church.

For Stanley James, the family Bible, which had belonged to his grandfather, carried another vital function: It contained at the front a record of the family tree. This record was made more important by the fact that until 1929, James's county government refused to issue birth certificates to nonwhite citizens. "The doctor kept a record," he explained. "But if the doctor died, you had no record. So what you did, you went back to the Bible. That certified you. That's the way my grandfather and my mother's side, her people, did it."

The consolidating traditions of preaching and teaching, learning and worshiping, praying, certifying, and governing were all in place in the Metropolitan AME Church, particularly since the arrival of a much revered and dynamic pastor.[17] Several members discussed the kinds of learning and writing that went into preparing their special Sunday talks. They used not only the church library but also the pastor's private library to research their topics, and the pastor would photocopy relevant commentaries to help members with their planning. In addition, he would critique their presentations and offer advice along the way. Lavinia Stokes (born 1930) described her experience:

> When [the pastor] first came here, he started [the talks]. We have [a] third Sunday morning breakfast that the men prepare and they

have someone to talk after the breakfast. First Sunday night service, we have someone to talk. Second Sunday night service, we have someone to talk. Plus Good Fridays, we have talks on the seven words that Jesus said on the cross. When [the pastor] first came, I really didn't know how to do this or what to do. We have a library in church, plus [the pastor] invites us to his library at home. He has a very large library. And I do have some books myself. We usually ask [the pastor] for some guidance and help. He will go through his commentaries and he will photocopy from his commentaries and give that to us. We will just go through it and get what we want to talk about from that. I always write out my talk [beforehand]. When I write my talk out, I go over it many times so that I don't have to keep my eyes on my paper. Sometimes after a person gives a talk, [the pastor] will say, "I want you to put more emphasis on this," or "Do it this way" or "Do it that way."

Others discussed how preparing the talks created time for reflection and solitude. One woman, June Birch, born in 1939, recalled having an idea for a talk come to her as she looked at herself one day in a mirror. "I wrote on that, on looking at yourself in a mirror. I just got in a quiet spot and things just came to me, and I started writing it on the paper. After I wrote it, I kind of put it together. But when thoughts were coming to me, I'd just jot them down." She said she shared the essay with her husband before delivering it in church. Her husband, Marcus Birch, born in 1942, said he found topics for his talks during his general reading of church-related books. "I go to books and pick out a topic and just relate to the topic," he explained. "I'll write [the talk] out and then type it out. Once my writing gets cold, I can't read it. So I'll type it out."

As these accounts suggest, the Metropolitan AME Church served as a consolidating force in the literacy development of its members. It unified sponsorship for literacy that in other contexts is more often distributed across multiple institutions. It also preserved and highlighted original relationships between literacy and faith, which helped to make the past present in the practices of the church and in the consciousness of the members. Above all, it provided an unquestioned entitlement to literacy. Democratic access to the Bible and equal treatment under its laws held remarkable currency for a people who were not extended such equality in secular society. Democratic principles were upheld not only during exegesis that took place in public worship but also in decisions regarding church finances as well as in the many committee assignments and leadership positions. Through worship services, Sunday school, and administrative functions, the church provided material, spiritual, and social incentives for critical reading and writing. Within any given span of months, participation in the church could engage adult lay members in reading and writing a wide array of genres in both religious and secular forms. Additionally, the pastor was accepted, in Lavinia Stokes's words, as both "a preacher and a teacher" among his parishioners. He performed many of the conventional functions of an educator, creating opportunities for reading, writing, and learning; supplying relevant reading materials; inviting outside research; and affording feedback and correction – all in addition to his role as a spiritual guide. Lay members also played multiple and revolving roles – teachers and learners, speakers and audience, supplicants and grantors, leaders and followers – within their various duties at the church. For some members, especially the older ones, these consolidated forms of sponsorship provided compensations for blatant education and political injustices of their childhoods. They also provided for interpretive license among all members. Even for younger members who experienced relatively greater opportunities in education and economic spheres, the church provided holistic uses of reading and writing that helped to sustain, comfort, and instruct.

As one of the few life-affirming institutions for African Americans in American society, the church developed literacy as part of a larger spiritual effort to practice a form of Christianity that resisted and repaired the insults of racism. These orientations favored synthesis and consolidation over separation and diversification and collectivity over hierarchy. For instance, in the Metropolitan AME congregation, college-educated people were pointed out with pride, and extra collections were taken up during services for college students whose families belonged to the church. At the same time, however, entitlement to reading and freedom of interpretation were shared equally among all the members. Leadership positions also were held by people of all education levels. Practices were imbued with an explicit racial solidarity, with what Bertha Nixon called "the we."

Finally, and perhaps most significant, is a strong connection between the spiritual and the material, the then, now, and later. This orientation, which was favored in discussions and reflected in the structures and activities of the Metropolitan AME Church as a whole, works against the rather sharp divisions between secular and religious literacy that widened generally through the twentieth century. The effects of this orientation were subtly evident in the explicit way several church members talked about the moral implications of their secular writing and their responsibilities as writers and leaders. Kyle Barnes, born in the industrial midwest in 1958 and raised mostly in the West, faced a moral dilemma as a teenager after he began to sell original love poems to his less articulate male friends for their use in romantic endeavors. Nicknamed "Word" for his facility with poetry, song, and fantasy, Barnes said he initially enjoyed ghostwriting as a lucrative sideline. However, he discovered that some of his friends were using his poems to romance several girls at the same time. That violated his ethical sensibilities, and he eventually quit writing and selling the poetry. "I had to be accountable for my writing," he said. "I was building a vehicle for them and I didn't like what they were doing." Two older church members, June Birch and Rosa Parnell (born 1942), expressed concerns about honoring principles of fairness in connection with writing they undertook at their jobs. As a fraud investigator for a public utility, June Birch said she was well aware that the facts she documented could result in the withholding of an important public service. "You couldn't add anything and you couldn't subtract anything," she said. Rosa Parnell, a caseworker for a government entitlement program, discussed determination reports she composed in response to people's requests for benefits. "These things have to be correct according to the laws and regulations," she explained. "You just can't do it haphazardly. You're dealing with people's money and you're dealing with people's lives." Stanley James, a retired postal supervisor, talked about his commitment to honoring human values in what was sometimes a dehumanizing work environment:

> I had a hard time when I first became a supervisor to instruct other supervisors that you must respect the individual workforce. They didn't believe that. They believed they could treat you any kind of way and you had to take it. That wasn't my philosophy. I was always under the concept that I'll treat you the way I want to be treated.

Another intersection of the spiritual and the secular arose in the inspirational writing and reading that a few of the members said they undertook. Kyle Barnes served as a sports coach at a Catholic high school for several years and said he always wrote prayers that he recited with teams before games. He also sent to individual players cards and letters that served as inspirational devices. These messages captured in brief verse the personalities or particular skills of his players and referred to events in their lives as occasions for reflection and learning. "This writing brought people closer to me," he reflected. "Kids from ten years ago still have the cards I sent them or they still remember that speech I gave."[18]

Nowhere were the long-standing core values of the black church more wholly instantiated than in the daily practices of Mississippi native Frances Hawkins, who had been schooled in one of the poorest counties in the United States and was, when I interviewed her, raising three children in a high-tech university town in the Midwest. Born in 1956, she was the third of 11 children of tenant farmers. Fifteen years after *Brown v. Board of Education,* schools in her county remained segregated and services for the black majority were still baldly neglected by the white government.[19] Her account of her earliest literacy learning in school, which covered the years 1963 to 1970, expresses the details of economic and educational oppression:

> I started out in a little two-room school a long time ago. It was in the South. We had two teachers, husband and wife, and they taught school. We didn't have a school bus. The teachers transported us by their truck. They had a truck they put us on, maybe twenty children on a truck. And then we'd go into this little two-room school, one side for the smaller children and one side for the other children. We used to call them side schools. They had real good teachers, but it wasn't like we were in a big school.

In 1976, unlike her grandparents or parents, Frances Hawkins graduated from high school, attended college briefly in a medical technology program, then joined relatives working in manufacturing industries near Detroit. By the mid-1980s, she had moved to south central Wisconsin, one of thousands of African Americans who arrived to the region via the Rust Belt in search of a stronger economy and stronger schools. In the early 1990s, at 36 years of age, she was raising school-age children in a public housing project. A steward in the Metropolitan AME Church, she worked as a classroom aide in her children's school, supervising the playground, occasionally tutoring, and trying to observe closely to learn what she could to improve her children's chances for educational success. The school was participating in a controversial desegregation plan that paired children of the city's heavily white, affluent professional west side with the children of the city's heavily minority, working, and nonworking poor south side. Hawkins belonged to a district-sponsored organization for low-income parents that provided instructional guides on how to compose letters and place telephone calls to teachers and administrators. As earnings permitted, she was gradually buying children's books on African American history and culture, "unfolding" a library that she was dedicated to accumulating, and lending the books to other children in the housing complex. Pinned up on the wall of her living room, along with Christian images, were pro-reading posters she had rescued from surplus at the school library.

In the late 1990s in her northern home, Hawkins was calling on integrated values of faith, advancement, liberation, and survival that were remarkably similar to the earliest formulations of AME church doctrine. This heritage was tangible in the wall decor of the Hawkinses' living room, where images from the sanctuary and the schoolhouse hung in one unified inspirational message. Faith in God and faith in learning, once integrated incentives for the spread of literacy in mass American society in the late eighteenth and nineteenth centuries, increasingly grew apart as secular literacy and education eclipsed religious literacy in social and political value. In industrializing and postindustrializing America, the moral imperative to read *the* Good Book was overtaken by the message to read *a* good book and eventually by the intransitive imperative of late twentieth-century library posters and family literacy programs: *Read.* Yet in Frances Hawkins's home, the original connections between faith and learning were still alive. This connection was also apparent in some of her methods of communicating with her children. She explained:

> I kind of dictate notes to myself, notes to my children. I leave notes all around. I have what I call positive information up on my [bed-room] door upstairs. This is what I love to do. I love other people who live, who learn, and who help others learn. It all goes with life and how we enhance ourselves and kind of move on in this world we're living in today, because it's certainly not an easy one.

The association between the church and public schooling remained strong for many Southern African Americans in part because public school classes started out in church buildings and continued to be held there through much of the early twentieth century. George A. Davis and O. Fred Donaldson (1975) reported that in 1934, in some parts of Mississippi, only 51 of 226 schools for African Americans were actually school buildings. Transportation to school was rarely provided to African American students. These conditions, they said, "contrasted with the consolidated and well-constructed schools for whites in these counties" (p. 163). In *An African-American Exodus,* Katharine L. Dvorak (1991) suggested that the close relationship between education and religious sensibility for southern African American Christians arises from historical conditions in which religious leaders served as teachers and public school classes were held in church buildings. Anita Taylor, who was born in 1917 in rural Missisippi, not far from where Frances Hawkins grew up, recalled, "I didn't go to no school. I went to a church. It was a church house, but they had school there."

Just as the church served as a multiple sponsor for education and uplift, Hawkins's position as a classroom aide sponsored multiple initiatives within the family economy. It provided a (very modest) living, but it also allowed Hawkins to communicate to her children the importance of a collective effort toward learning. On a practical level, it enabled her to observe how things worked in her children's school and how teachers responded to students. She also monitored the curriculum and was sometimes displeased by what she called "outdated" material in use in the grade school.

As a high school student, Hawkins said she had written quite a number of book reports, but, she said, speaking of the early 1970s, "We didn't have all these good books available to us, like black history books. That wasn't available to us. We didn't know who the heroes were back then, who was the first black doctor and those kinds of things." She also said she did not have easy access to public libraries as a girl. Asked if she ever used the public library to write her school reports, Hawkins replied, "We were thinking about doing it. But at that time, people of color didn't have the same privileges as whites had, if I can say that." In recent years, Hawkins acquired a typewriter for herself, had paid for but did not complete a correspondence course on academic guidance, and was building a library that was of keen importance to her. Her description of this effort incorporated the values of self-determination, collective uplift, and religious and secular activism that have been part of the tradition of the black church:

> We're trying to start a library, a home library. We have stuff like three sets of religious books and we have all kinds of magazines, from children's magazines on. I'm ordering a set of black history books about how black Americans achieved their own life and where they have come from and where they are going. I think I owe every book company in America. I'm going to do some basic research some day. I'm going to start with basic research and move my way up and then kind of set up a home library and it's going to be important for myself, my children, and other people who would like access to it. Someday if I live long enough – I hope it will happen – I'd like to set up a scholarship for all children, no matter what age, what color, what ethnic group. It would just be for your education. I would like to be president of my own company. So I still have my materials, still have the typewriter, all this stuff. But I haven't really unfolded all the things that I've got in the back of my mind.

Meanwhile, Hawkins displayed for my visit her son's perfectly scored spelling test and a script for a school play in which her older daughter had a role. She kept her workbook from the parents' group next to her Christian Keepsake Organizer, a daybook bordered by short religious messages and filled mostly with family photographs.

To sum up, for many African Americans the black church functioned as a multiply performing sponsor of literacy and literacy learning that provided important opportunities and rewards for its members. The links among faith, moral uplift, educational improvement, and self-determination that launched the African American church at its onset carried on both in contemporary church practices and in the interpretive orientations of people raised in its influence. These traditions in some ways stand in contrast to a prevailing concepts of literacy that critics and historians identify as secular, technical, specialized, and fragmented. With a spiritual emphasis on recuperation, unification, collectivity, memory, and persistence, the religious literacy of the African American church invites members to affiliate with much older-seeming literacy traditions.

The literacy values and practices of the black church illuminate the relationships between literacy learning and agents associated with the deep structure of African American cultural survival. The church remains one of the important channels within African American society to provide what larger political systems withhold and to offer conscious alternatives to the hostility and negativity that those larger systems often deliver.

This chapter will continue to seek the presence of African American self-help institutions of long standing as they appear as enabling agents – directly and indirectly – in the literacy learning of ordinary African Americans. As we will see, the values of persistence and keeping whole – which function as both practical and spiritual necessities – favor some of the oldest aspects of literacy's historical development. They also favor a multiplicity of roles for literacy agents and their practices. These conditions bring a multiplicity and simultaneity to the meanings of literacy – a synergy that often combines practical and spiritual significance and that makes one meaning less compelling without the other.

Educators

Another component in this deep-rooted survival system are African American educators. V. P. Franklin (1990) explained the practical and symbolic value of education within African American culture. In a society in which land, jobs, and human rights were not secure, education became "valuable not merely as means of social or educational advancement but as an end in itself" (p. 40). Once obtained, education was an asset that could not be taken away.[20] Further, although in the general society education in the twentieth century often functioned as an edge in economic competitions with others, in black society it could more often function explicitly and deliberately as a resource to be shared and as an achievement for which all could take pride. So, for instance, just as church members might take up special collections for the college students in the congregation, support was expected to flow the other way. "Anyone who acquired literacy or advanced training often recognized the obligation to pass that knowledge on to others within their family, community, and cultural group," according to Franklin (1990, p. 40).

This practice was favored by the structure of collective self-help in segregated communities generally. Especially in years before official desegregation, secondhand sharing was an essential means by which to spread the few fruits of opportunity. Segregation affected the spread of education in yet another way. Because of professional constrictions placed on the black intelligentsia, teaching black students was one of the few careers comfortably open to those with advanced education. Although teacher shortages and inadequate teacher preparation were a feature of many black schools in the rural South, this same system of discrimination also concentrated highly talented and educated black people in the teaching profession. The principal of Stanley James's Kansas elementary school in the 1920s, for example, was a noted educator from a politically prominent family. And even in cases in which credentials came from regional normal schools, certain teachers were referred to in memories as "professor." Jordan Grant, born in 1948 and a member of the last generation to be reared under legal segregation, recalled "extraordinary" elementary- and secondary-school teachers who, thanks to "the ridiculousness of racism," taught in the public schools he attended in Mississippi, Arkansas, and Tennessee:

> At the time [i.e., 1950s and 1960s], black people were not permitted to go to the graduate schools in the South by law. But the states would pay for black people to go to the northern cities. Rather than to bother desegregating Ole Miss, for instance, the state of Mississippi would pay for a person to go to Harvard, Yale, Princeton, and get these degrees. And many of them came back to our little classrooms. And when they came back, we had very enriched experiences because in any other time, these people would not be teaching. They might be a physician or an attorney or a CPA or an engineer or an accountant. It does not encompass the entire experience because there were poor schools and poor teachers, but because the professions in the South were typically limited to preaching or to teaching one's own people, we had an enriched vein of knowledge back in our classrooms.

The constrictions of segregation also meant that teachers usually lived in the same neighborhoods as their students and were considered in many instances as surrogate guardians.[21] As one interviewee put it: "Your teacher was considered one of your many parents, so whatever they said went. It was reinforced at home. So it was like a real extended family in going to the school. You didn't do anything without it getting back." Another observed, "The principal of the high school was the superintendent of the Sunday school. So we were trapped, locked in. Besides, the peer pressure was very high because we went to school with the sons and daughters of the teachers and the ministers and maybe an attorney or a black dentist. But the most important thing was that teachers had confidence in us because they at one time were us." In some instances, children took lessons from the same teachers as had their parents. Stanley James, who attended elementary school in the late 1920s, said he picked up handwriting both from his mother, who worked as a domestic, and from his fifth-grade teacher, who had taught his mother how to write – a reinforcement of a style that pleased him (despite the corporal punishment that sometimes went with it!):

> My mother had beautiful handwriting. She's the one who taught me writing. She was the one who was very particular about us being able to punctuate at the proper time. But I had a schoolteacher. Her name was E_____ T_____. She had taught my mother and she had taught my father. And she was strict on penmanship. She whipped everybody in that class. And the reason she did it, she said, "When you leave here, I don't want them to think you were my pet." And she had beautiful penmanship. I picked up from her. I started writing like her. And now my sister and them tell me they can't wait for me to write to them.

For June Birch, born in 1939 in urban South Carolina, the schoolteacher most vivid in her memories was her seventh-grade teacher, a man who taught all subjects, played the piano, and typed like the wind:

> He had a typewriter right in his classroom and if we were working on assignments, he would type whatever. We'd be working, and this thing would be ringing. He could probably type like ninety words a minute. I said to myself, "One of these days, I'm going to be able to do that."

Jordan Grant, who eventually became an English teacher in northern integrated schools, was enthralled by grade-school teachers with exceptional ways with language: "I liked the way they expressed themselves," he said. "I liked their style. I liked their comfort with the written word. Their knowledge of literature. Their love for it."

Interestingly, several interviewees were related to schoolteachers and named them as early influences on their writing and reading.[22] Antonia Lawrence, born in 1939 in Chicago to factory workers, was befriended early in life by her grandmother, a former Southern schoolteacher. Asked about her earliest memory of writing, Lawrence responded:

> I guess my earliest recollection, a real pleasurable one, would be my grandmother, my maternal grandmother. She had an ink pen and she always had this bottle of ink. There was a cloisonné design on the pen, and she promised me that if I learned to write certain things, she would allow me to use this pen, and that encouraged me a lot. I guess it would have started when I was maybe three. The first time my grandmother let me use the pen was on my fifth birthday. It was great. And I've grown to love cloisonné.

Lawrence's grandmother also taught her to read:

> She read to me. A lot of times I remember her taking my hand, taking my finger and following the words. I remember her teaching me the alphabet. She taught me sounds and letters and she would encourage me to write short sentences. She would let me spell words the ways they sounded to me and then she'd write them the right way. When I got older, my grandmother would read things that I wrote and would correct my spelling. My grandmother subscribed to this magazine for me called *Wee Wisdom,* and I would get that every month, so I looked forward to that.[23]

At the time of our interview, Lawrence was serving as president of a neighborhood association at a low-income housing project in which she lived. In her spare time, she was working on a collection of short stories, begun in a college creative writing course she enrolled in on a returning-adult scholarship. No longer in possession of the cloisonné pen (lost in one of many moves), she used a typewriter that she was able to borrow from time to time from the office of the neighborhood association.

Government worker Rosa Parnell was born in rural Missouri in 1942. Much younger than her other siblings, she was instructed in reading and writing early in life by a sister-in-law living in the household who was a part-time teacher. Like Lawrence, Parnell began her literacy learning early under the tutelage of this teacher-relative:

> My sister-in-law taught me how to read and write before I started kindergarten. We had a book. I don't know how she came by it,

maybe through her teaching part time. And it was about monkeys and bananas and it had a lot of counting in it. I can remember sets of two and threes and fives. She kind of started out with that with me. And she would have me write like a page a night, just copy the page from the book. There might have been other books, but that one seems to stick out as the one I used the most... We didn't have a car, but during those first few years [before school], my sister-in-law would take me to the library on the bus. We would get a lot of books. She would let me pick out what I wanted.

June Birch, born in 1939 in South Carolina, was the daughter of laborers. Her great-aunt was on the faculty of Howard University. As a girl, she was helped in her schoolwork by her mother's sister, a high school teacher, who was part of an extended family sharing a 15-room house. The aunt would organize the six children of the household for evening homework sessions and served as a general resource for questions and assistance: "She was a schoolteacher, and she had things she wanted us to learn. Any questions we had, we would go to her and she would help us out," explained Birch, who would go on to enroll in an education course at a black religious college in the late 1950s.

These memories emphasize the school-like instruction that could take place in the presence of teacher-relatives. Other times, teaching provided by other household members was less formal but no less influential. Parnell, a civil service employee who also kept the books and filed the tax returns for her husband's small business, was introduced to the world of finance early in life by her father, a farmer in rural Missouri. He was not schooled past the third grade but had something to teach her:

When I was eight [i.e., 1950], my father taught me about money. They didn't have a checking account, so he paid all the bills in cash. When I was eight, he used to send me around to pay the bills, the light company or whatever, with cash money. And I'd have to come back with the right change or else I'd really get it. So maybe that's why I have such a good business sense. And I remember when I was nine, he had me selling perfume. Somebody cheated me or didn't pay or something and I remember getting a spanking about that. So, I guess I learned how to take care of money. I'm real good at that.

Anita Russell, working at the time of the interview as a home health aide, was born in 1946 in rural Mississippi. Because her mother had migrated north in search of work, she was raised to age 16 by her grandparents, who were rice farmers. It was an older brother, who also stayed behind, who "did most of the helping" when it came to literacy. She explained:

> My brother would carry me over. I was kind of a hard learner and
> he would take the time and carry me over the little primer. He
> would tell me, "Now you read it back to me." I would forget half
> the things he was reading to me. Then he just said, "You will learn."
> And then I started catching on to reading.

Claire Harvey, born into urban poverty in 1960 in Chicago, graduated from high school in 1977 but continued to have trouble reading and particularly writing as an adult. As a mother of three school-age children in the 1990s, she relied on the aptitude of an older sister, a medical secretary, when her children requested help with written projects assigned in school. She explained, "A lot of times my kids come to me and ask, like once my daughter had to write something on Martin Luther King and I asked my sister to rewrite it for her because I don't really know what I'm doing as far as writing." This sister, who lived two states away, also prepared résumés for Claire Harvey whenever she went on the job market.

Stanley James, born in 1920 in eastern Kansas, took an early and abiding interest in the law. For him, significant informal instruction came from educated people beyond the family. Although the financial hardships of the Depression would cut short his college career and send him into the army, he still relished, at age 73, the informal apprenticeship he developed as a teenager with two attorneys in his hometown:

> I wanted to be a lawyer so bad. I came out of a town that had two
> black lawyers. I have some of the law books of one of the lawyers
> upstairs in my attic. In his later years, he was the one that gave me
> the prep before I went to the University of_____. He had a style. A
> lawyer is a showman. He would have certain cases that he would
> want me to see him perform. And I used to go [to court] and get
> the biggest thrill because he would be against a white attorney and
> he would be so sharp. He was one of the first to ever use a writ of
> habeas corpus. He got people out of federal prison. He explained
> to me that to become a good lawyer, I had to remember. And he
> would test me in a week to see if I could remember what happened
> last month. I would go to his house and sit around with him. And
> he'd be training these young lawyers, too. There were young
> lawyers there and he would be training them. There was one young
> lawyer there who went on to become a senator of_____. He was
> really a brilliant fellow.

Several features of these recollections deserve notice. First, they put into context Franklin's observation about the sharing of the resources of literacy and education among family and community, what Gadsden (1993) called the "communal nature of learning." Throughout much of the twentieth century, formal education and sometimes even basic schooling circulated as rare assets in many places. In the cases of June Birch, Rosa Parnell, and Antonia Lawrence, the teacher-relative was the only professional figure in otherwise laboring households. In the 1930s in the town where James grew up, there were only two African American attorneys in a population at the time of nearly 20,000. After Anita Russell's literate mother moved north for better work, her older brother had to step into a critical teaching position that their grandparents could not perform. When Antonia Lawrence's grandmother and Rosa Parnell's sister-in-law endowed the young girls with lifelong interest in the written word, they did so not to replicate an inherited place in the professional middle class (as was the case for virtually all the teacher-relatives who appear in the memories of white people I interviewed), for no such place could be ensured. Indeed, at the time of the events recounted in these memories, African American teachers themselves were targets of discriminatory pay, limited appointments, and layoffs.[24] These memories underscore how closely education resources have coexisted with economic oppression in the history of African American life – often, quite literally, under the same roof – and how literacy instruction has had to be couched more in hope than in destiny.

Another notable feature in these memories is the role of apprenticeship. Whether in the cloisonné pen, the ringing typewriter, the literature lessons, the sermon, or the court performance, these teachers and their materials modeled ways of using language that encouraged emulation. Stanley James's experience is most significant in this regard, as he "picked up" legal language by watching and listening to his mentors. Owing in no small part to the resources of literacy, craft apprenticeship as a form of training virtually disappeared through the nineteenth and twentieth century. Specialized knowledge was increasingly embodied in print. Credentials – rather than performed skill – became the preferred qualifications.[25] Rather than what they could do, it was what teachers knew and could transmit that took prominence. Interestingly, however, before the rise of law schools, legal education had been conducted almost entirely through apprenticeship. And James's memory illustrates how this older tradition was retained informally in the small community of African American attorneys in his town. Apprenticeship was a powerful medium for transferring professional skills and, maybe more important, professional identity. Here again, we see a retention of and preference for an older, recessive tradition in the history of literacy, one that preserves itself by preserving knowledge, skill, performance, and human relationships in one embodied and holistic form. Interestingly, Lincoln and Mamiya, writing in 1990, observed the persistence of apprenticeship in the preparation of African American clergy. Most African American clergy, they wrote, "are still educated and socialized in the ministry in an apprenticeship mode, learning on the job from senior clergy."[26] There are many practical explanations for the apprenticeship relationships observed and experienced by James. They allowed black attorneys to transmit know-how and perspectives needed to function in a white-dominated legal system, skills perhaps so subtle and subversive that they were best left to performance than to explicit explanation. Further, the mentor relationships could compensate for exclusions from the white power structure, building an alternative network for advancement and social support. At the same time, apprenticeship loosened emphasis on credentials, so that even a teenage aspirant was admitted into a circle of learners. Above all, for James, performance, which is at the center of the apprenticeship model, made visible to him the embodied powers of African American language, literacy, and learnedness.

Finally, in some of these examples of education we can see how instruction at times could occur in the context of what interviewees described as strict punishment. In some of these reported memories, learning basic skills occurred simultaneously with learning how not to be cheated or how not to count on preferential treatment. These were harsh but realistic lessons in the context of African American life.

Taken together, these scenes of literacy transfer suggest how the strictures of African American economic and political life are quietly communicated (and resisted) within ordinary acts of literacy teaching and learning. They also provide at least partial evidence of how African American literacy achievement was bootstrapped in various times and places throughout the twentieth century. For many, the ways that such bootstrapping occurred remained relevant to literacy development and habits over a lifetime. Reading and writing skills that developed under segregated conditions could carry the lasting distortions of lost opportunity but also the residual and persistent resources associated with survival, self-help, and racial affirmation. Nowhere was that legacy more tangible than in the mature reading and writing habits of James, who was 73 years old at the time of the interview. Thwarted in his ambition to be a lawyer and curtailed in his early army career by official discrimination against blacks in the military, James nevertheless had managed to blend his flair for handwriting, his two years of college, and his infatuation with law and regulation to gain administrative positions in the armed forces, including some in the judicial system.[27] During some of his years in the army, he served as a court recorder, allowing him to continue to observe trials and to master manuals of army regulations and codes of conduct. In addition, throughout the war years and beyond, he used letters, news accounts, and storytelling to keep track of the careers and accomplishments of the African American men who were managing to work themselves into the officer ranks. The career of Jackie Robinson – both before his racially charged exit from the army and during his rise to baseball fame – also was carefully followed by James and his associates via newspaper accounts, personal letters, and eyewitnesses. Letters also were used to tell and retell accounts of racial insults in the service, sometimes turned into humorously triumphant stories and passed around for the release of tension and the protection of dignity. And throughout the war, James maintained a diary to record names of associates and their whereabouts so that he could stay in touch in the future. In his retirement, he maintained an extensive clipping file about African Americans in the military, with particular emphasis on news about the black cavalry unit in which he had served. At the same time, he was a frequent viewer of televised court trials and news shows. He could recount the family connections of several African American newsmakers and even some of the news reporters who appeared on national networks. Many of his anecdotes began with the genealogies of both the actors in the story and the chain of sources by which he had come by the story. He had recently written to a black music company in search of old recordings of a favorite gospel group from his childhood on a tip that had been provided by relatives of a hometown friend. Finally, he was an avid reader of a wide array of books about the law, including a recent biography of Supreme Court Justice Thurgood Marshall, and he said he often reread books as a way to test himself on how much he could remember.

This inventory of literate practices illustrates in fascinating ways how James kept faith with his earliest teachers and with the communication patterns of the local community in which he had been raised. But it also shows how he could adapt elements of increasingly depersonalized and decontextualized communication systems to maintain orientations learned in his boyhood even as he adapted to social, economic, and political changes in his life and work. Institutions like the modern military and mass media are usually credited with forcing interpretive habits and identities on citizens that favor the faceless, the nameless, what Berger, Berger, and Kellner (1974) might have called "homeless" ways of perceiving and communicating. Certainly as an army administrator and later government supervisor,

James made those adjustments recurrently over a 40-year career. But in addition, he was able to use resources like the army bureaucracy or the television set or the bookstore to stay connected to developments and accomplishments of black America in a remarkably personal way. If James didn't know the family line of a notable African American in a news account, he almost always knew of someone who knew of someone who did.

This practice of establishing elaborate networks of personal relationships went back to the influence of James's uncle, who, although educated only to ninth grade, became a high-echelon executive in a national insurance company. This uncle was a prodigious letter writer and often served as a conduit for family and race news that he passed in letters and through the circuit of visits that he frequently made to various branches of the family. He would bring books as well as news on his visits and was known to finance the educations of younger relatives. James also wrote frequent letters to immediate and far-flung members of his family and was staying in touch with (and even caring for) aging relatives of childhood friends who happened to live in the vicinity.

James used letters to represent personal experience and maintain personal relations, and he revisited and amplified personal experience through resources of mass media. Especially as the events of World War II and, more slowly, African American experiences in World War II, were rendered as history in newspapers, books, and television shows, James's perspective on his personal experiences during the war continued to expand.[28] He used instruments of mass bureaucratized and commercial culture as added resources for the ceaseless work of maintaining racial solidarity and connectedness. For James, not only did literacy achieve the practical ends of staying in touch and staying informed but it also served as a constituent act of community making itself.

Mass Movement and Mass Literacy

The civil rights movement was born with the institution of slavery. There was never a time when African Americans were not in secular struggle for the recognition of their human and civil rights. By the early twentieth century, several political organizations were competing for the allegiances of African Americans, including Marcus Garvey's nationalist campaign and the more integration-minded NAACP. Franklin (1984) regarded the exodus of African Americans from the South in the opening decades of the twentieth century as itself a mass civil rights movement in protest against the remnants of the agrarian-slavery regime, a social experience with enormous influence, he says, on the liberatory consciousness of African Americans.[29] The "Double V" campaign during World War II to end discrimination toward blacks in the military was a "seed time" for the modern civil rights movement and lay the groundwork for the orchestration of African American newspapers, politicians, and civil rights organizations that would characterize the later mass movement.[30] By the 1950s and 1960s, the modern civil rights campaign arose from a unique alliance of religious and secular organizations. The mass protest movement engaged African Americans in countless local settings in the push to end legal discrimination in employment, housing, commerce, and education. The movement continued to build in the late 1960s as a broader cultural expression of black pride and black power.[31]

Throughout this history, the African American press served as an ally if not a manifestation of the civil rights movement. Born in the nineteenth century in religious, abolitionist, and protest causes, the black press proliferated in the twentieth century. Local independent black newspapers as well as larger syndicated ones in major cities numbered 500 between the end of the Civil War and the turn of the twentieth century and grew to nearly 1,400 between 1910 and 1930.[32] Newspapers and journals brought visibility to black social life and political thought usually ignored by the mainstream press. The black media helped African Americans interpret the social conditions that modernity and migration were bringing, helped to maintain at least abstract versions of racial ties during diaspora, and provided a consistent editorial voice for justice and equality. In the years after World War II, mass-market magazines like *Ebony* and *Jet* emerged. Although geared, like other magazines of the period, to entertainment and consumerism, these publications nevertheless were pressured by the times and by the tradition of black journalism to report on racial and social issues of concern to African Americans (Wolseley, 1990, pp. 142*ff*).[33] These magazines provided coverage of the civil rights movement from a black perspective. In his autobiography, *Ebony* and *Jet* founder John H. Johnson (1989) boasted of the coincidence between the publishing successes of his magazines and the political and legal successes of the civil rights effort (pp. 237–238). By the 1960s and 1970s, African American publishing exploded, with many more books, including children's books, devoted to black history, culture, and literature.[34]

No histories that I have yet been able to find explicitly explore the mutual impact among the rising levels of African American literacy, the broadening of the civil rights movement, and the influence of the black press, although the relationships seem patently obvious. Civil rights consciousness and the black press traveled together on the broad back of mass literacy. By midcentury, for the first time in history, the individual reading skills of ordinary people could be recruited to the traditional missions of the African American self-help system. Reading could maintain the perspectives and critical knowledge needed for racial survival and advancement. Rising literacy levels were vital to the development of the mass consciousness on which the civil rights struggle depended for its many local manifestations and successes. At the same time, the need for political activism stimulated reading and writing in the lives of ordinary African Americans of various ages and classes throughout the second half of the twentieth century. In very practical ways, mass literacy and mass movement were realized together.

Evidence of this synergy was evident in both direct and indirect ways in the life-history accounts of the African Americans that I interviewed. Ethnically oriented books and magazines were widely in use in some working-class and most middle-class households I visited, serving as supplements and correctives to mainstream (white-oriented) media. *Ebony* and *Jet* were most commonly read, almost always in tandem. "I try to go through the whole thing for any interesting articles and try to keep up with what's going on," explained 50-year-old government worker Rosa Parnell about her subscription to *Ebony*. "It has a lot of information about our ethnic roots. I want to be informed. I like to be informed about what's happening with us and to us. I use it as a way to improve myself if I can, to try to keep up on health aspects and things like that." As a teenager in the 1970s, Kyle Barnes was reading *Ebony, Jet, Sports Illustrated,* and a local mainstream newspaper. He also was reading *Muhammad Speaks* and other publications by the Nation of Islam, provided by an older brother who had converted to the Muslim faith. "I didn't get into the Koran," Barnes explained. "But I liked the literature that talked about black people, the newsletters, the books. My brother also shared his world knowledge with me."

Book reading among other African Americans I interviewed also frequently functioned to build up ethnic knowledge and understanding. Marcus Birch, born in 1942, had grown up in rural Arkansas as one of 11 children of a lumber-worker father and a homemaking mother. The only two books in his childhood household had been a Bible and a "wish book," (i.e., a mail-order catalog). Birch's skin color barred him from using the public library in his town, and, as a student in an underfinanced segregated school, he had to share textbooks with other students because there weren't enough to go around:

> We had to share books. At that time, in that era, when you went to an all-black school you got the hand-me-downs from the white

school. That's how it was in the South. We all didn't have enough books. One person would take the book home this time and next time you had to make sure to bring it back so the other person could use it.

Although there was a library in Birch's school, preference for its use was given to older students. "We weren't allowed to go to the library until up about the ninth grade," he explained. "They didn't have enough books, so [high school students] were the ones that got to use the library." At the time of our interview, as a 50-year-old postal supervisor, Birch was living at a great distance from his birthplace. He was one of the most active, self-sponsored readers that I encountered in the project and one of the few who reported reading books on his own to improve his job-related writing. Bookstores and occasionally the public library were his source for reading materials. Describing himself as "a history person," he explained:

> I read religious type material and different books. I read books on black managers, what to expect in life as a black manager. A lot of time I feel a need to read up on some things related to my job. Sometimes I'll be looking and a book will catch my eye and I'll just buy it and keep it for my collection. I read black history. I try to read up on where my ancestry came from, how it related to me, what the struggle was. These are things I wanted to know. It makes me appreciate where I am and what my mother and father went through and why they went through these things. My father served in the army. He came out and couldn't get a house where he wanted to live, he couldn't get a job where he wanted, he couldn't go in restaurants. That always bothered me, you know. And that got me into reading about why all these things happened.

Just as Bible reading for members of the Metropolitan AME Church served as both a channel for developing religious consciousness and for enacting and demonstrating that consciousness, so did the reading of black-authored secular material serve as both a channel for developing civil rights consciousness and for enacting it. We have already seen these dual functions in the home library of Frances Hawkins, which served as a material residue of her self-sponsored education and as a contribution in itself to righting the wrongs around her. Kyle Barnes's mother was a civil rights activist who held elected local office while he was growing up in the 1960s. Together, mother and son carried this activism into his predominantly white elementary school. He explained:

When I was in sixth grade [i.e., 1968], I was questioning a lot of the teaching I was getting at that time. Because of my mother's training of us on all the contributions [by African Americans], I was able to go to the library to get books that they didn't have in the classroom. Even those books were outdated and not really factual on the contributions. So Mom came to the school and got them to purchase titles that she gave them that talked more about the contributions. It was in all of that that my teacher began to see that I liked to write.

The preponderance of memories recounted here involves generations that experienced directly the rise of modern civil rights activism. As individuals, most of them had made profound political, regional, and occupational shifts from the positions of their parents. In the 1990s, they resided in a multiethnic yet predominantly European American city where desegregation was the law of the land yet full equality was rarely experienced. Significantly better educated overall than the preceding generation, they participated as citizens, workers, and parents in many mainstream social and economic systems. Unlike most of their parents, they were no longer closely or uniformly tied to the local institutions that characterized segregated society in the rural South. In their lives, the black press and the civil rights movement functioned primarily as abstract and diffused resources that assisted principally at the level of consciousness.

This influence also registered in the many incidences of protest writing reported in these accounts. Nearly half of the African Americans I interviewed said they used writing at one time or another to speak out against racism and injustice affecting them, their children, or their community. For instance, Anita Russell, born in 1946 in rural Mississippi, a part-time bus driver and home health aide, discussed the often dispiriting process of searching for jobs in the late 1970s in the urban Midwest. To cope with discrimination, Anita Russell and her friends wrote down their reactions. She explained:

A group of us ladies would go out job hunting together and if we felt we were discriminated against, we would write letters. We'd all just come along with it. "What do you think about it?" "I don't think it was fair." We'd get together and just write what we thought. Then we might call [the employers] and tell them we didn't think it was fair. We would talk to different ones. Whatever one we got to talk to, we'd tell them we didn't think this was fair.

Antonia Lawrence, born in 1939 in Chicago, was, at the time of our interview, serving as president of a low-income neighborhood association.

She was elected, she said, "because I talk a lot." She had recently written a letter to the editor of the local newspaper to answer racially insensitive remarks made in an editorial by an elected county official. She said:

> He was making lots of derogatory remarks about minority people, about our mentality, about our habits, about how most of our daughters have babies before they are out of high school. Someone made a point of showing me his letter. I was offended and a little angry, so I wrote a response. Certain thoughts went through my head when I read it and I just wanted to respond to him.

Janine Williams, who was born in 1951 and raised in rural Tennessee, was working in the 1990s as a civil servant in southern Wisconsin. Her three children were attending predominantly white public schools. Distressed by racial insensitivity that her children were witnessing in their classrooms, she eventually appeared before the local school board to speak out. Writing both propelled and structured her response:

> The kids would come home and tell me stuff. I would kind of jot it down and then it got to a point that, as they say, the straw broke the camel's back. This is it. So I take all of my little notes and write out [the presentation to the school board]. The first try is real harsh and bitter, so you read through it and edit it 'til you get to the point where they are not going to escort you off the stage. I used the writing to keep focused on what I was going to talk about so I wouldn't ramble on and get off track. I just wanted to go there and present what my kids had said and ask for a solution to it.

These reports invite speculation about how mass movements sponsor literacy learning. We see how a sustained period of well-publicized civil rights protest could disseminate into public consciousness various formats and stances to structure the release of anger and the exercise of rights and self-determination. The civil rights era helped to make these forms of written protest recognizable for what they were to the authors and their audiences. We also see how literacy learning furthered the interests of traditional sponsors of African American survival because it made more people capable of caring individually for the ongoing interests of racial advancement, especially as those interests intersected with the political, bureaucratic, and legalistic forums of contemporary social life. Because Russell, Lawrence, and Williams could write, they could exert pressure single-handedly on local social and education systems. If African American religious literacy in the nineteenth century helped to internalize liberatory consciousness among people in slavery, African American secular literacy in the twentieth century helped to internalize text-based routines for liberatory actions within political and economic domains.

"How It Manifests Itself On Paper": The Writing Career of Jordan Grant

The discussion turns here to an extended examination of the literacy learning account of Jordan Grant, who, in the 1990s, was a member in good standing of the Information Age. Highly educated, affluent, entrepreneurial, mobile, he was an independent human resources consultant, a prolific writer and speechmaker working within the communications-driven, secular, postindustrial economy that dominated late-twentieth century life. Grant might readily be viewed as a beneficiary of the widening education and economic options open to African Americans in post–Civil Rights Act America. Yet he was more truly a beneficiary of the accumulating boost of the oldest agents of African American cultural survival: a man into whose life converged most of the major nourishing forces for African American literacy, old and new. For Grant, developing as a writer in the second half of the twentieth century entailed amalgamating and transforming these traditional resources to respond to – and contribute to – a period of tremendous political and cultural change. His case is of added interest here because the stages of his writing development synchronize so vividly with stages of African American political and cultural struggle.

Grant was born in 1948 to two parents who had attended religiously affiliated, historically black colleges in their native South. His father, a CME minister, also attended seminary. His parents made their education available to Grant and his brothers principally through church-related activity. At two years of age, Grant memorized an Easter pageant speech, coached throughout by a mother who was "steeped in the Southern tradition of memorization." His mother also read and recited often from her favorite poetry anthology. Grant had vivid memories of watching his father compose sermons in the parsonage. Amid a collection of theological texts, concordances, and various versions of the Bible, Pastor Grant would pace the floor, often with a baby son on his shoulder, rehearsing under his breath. "You could hear the tremor of his voice," Jordan Grant recalled. "His eyes would be fixed and he would just be walking around in circles with this sleeping child on his shoulder, preaching these sermons. And then at some point he would go to this old Underwood typewriter and start hunting and pecking about." The younger Grant named this technique "clouding up and raining," adding. "I use the same technique that he used when I do presentations." He had equally vivid memories of helping his mother, who served as church secretary, crank out church bulletins between the ironing and the cooking. She composed the church bulletin each week, including the full worship service and responsive readings, then printed it out on a mimeograph machine that was kept on the porch. Grant described in detail a process of cutting out and pasting stencils and, later, with an electric mimeograph, hanging up freshly printed sheets of paper to dry. "Then you would have to collate them and staple them," he said, "which was always a big job on Saturdays in our home."

Grant earned a reputation early in life for his essay writing. As an eighth grader [in 1961], he entered a writing contest entitled "On My Career," held among all the black schools citywide. He wrote an essay on why he wanted to be a minister like his father:

> And I won it. I think top prize was five or ten silver dollars, which in those days was big stuff. There was an article in the paper, and they had my picture and the other winners from the other grade levels. And my father kept the essay in the Bible, waiting for me to become a person of the cloth until the day he died.

In accounting for his success, Grant was "confident" that his father's sermons served as an important model for his writing. In the following memory, we can see how a style of sermon writing that Pastor Grant would have developed during his seminary training impressed its form in dramatic ways on his young son:

> [My father] did neat sermons. And *neat* means he would always begin with a text and he would actually have a theme for it. So he would say, "Our sermon for the day is entitled..." and he would have an actual title for it. And in the church – this was very profound – the ushers who served in the church would be lined along the walls, two down front, two in the middle, and two in the back. And I remember on [my father] giving the text, the ushers would all turn and all move to the back of the church to be seated. So very profound, dramatic moments. [My father] did not like it when people just got up and started preaching without having thought about both the Scripture, typically both an Old and New Testament scripture, [and] a theme for it, and there would be a beginning, a middle, and an end. He would start off with the written word; he'd have the sermon written out. In most of his sermons, you see dot, dot, dot, which meant that by that time, the Spirit had taken over –

he didn't need the text anymore. He'd just go off. And that's when he became the black preacher.

This scene of literacy transmission – from father to son – is layered with a legacy of literacy, race, and religion. By the midnineteenth century in America, the seeds of a liberatory literacy had been sown through a growing network of African American churches, mostly Baptist and Methodist, as well as church-sponsored schools and seminaries. For generations, the ministry was one of the few careers comfortably open to educated African American men. As a descendent of that tradition, Pastor Grant infused the worship service of his congregation with the resources of his formal education, impressing exegesis, thematic development, and – in the dramatic about-face of the church ushers – a topical structure on a young son watching and listening in a church pew. As a young writer, Jordan Grant appropriated a sermonic style learned from his father for use in secular channels of expression, including essay writing and school success.[35]

In an earlier section on African American educators, we saw the influence of Grant's teachers on his enthusiasm for English and language study. Lessons in poetry awakened his interest in imagery, alliteration, and metaphor. He also learned the debate process during the Kennedy–Nixon presidential campaign, researching and defending Kennedy's position before a schoolwide mock vote. In addition, he wrote an occasional speech as a student government leader. Identified early as a proficient writer, Grant confided that as a teenager he helped one of the members of the church congregation rewrite a thesis to fulfill master's degree requirements.

Also by the time that Grant was a teenager, African American churches throughout the South had joined up with other groups focused, as Grant said, "on clearing the brush of Jim Crow." His father's Tennessee church hosted training sessions organized by the Student Nonviolent Coordinating Committee and the Southern Christian Leadership Conference (SCLC) in preparation for picketing at downtown stores. Grant characterized this period as a time of intense writing. In public, with his older brother, he composed messages for picket signs. In private, he wrote "constantly" – "thoughts, ideas, essays," he said.

> Obviously in those times I was concerned with the apartheid
> racism we were experiencing. Everybody was angry about it. Frustrated about it. My father was a person who didn't tolerate it very easily. He would speak out against it. So I saw how he handled these things and he was not afraid of anybody. So in these very critical times, the early years of the King movement, the civil rights era and then the Black Power movement, all of that was happening

while I was down there. It was a very emotionally charged time and you had lots of things to say.

Writing, for Grant, often served as "a vent. It did not hurt later on to have had those experiences, but at the time, you're not thinking of practicing. You used whatever means you could to work off these frustrations."

With his father still waiting for him to become a minister, Grant entered a nearby church-affiliated college, where he soon found his truer calling in a college class in transformational grammar. "The system of language," he said, extolling his chosen field. "To find out that it was much more scientific than I had thought – it was just a wonderful, wonderful thing." Before graduating with a degree in English, he won another writing contest, this one on the theme of "My People and Power," sponsored jointly by the United Negro College Fund (UNCF) and the Reader's Digest Foundation.[36] Recruited out of college to teach in a multiethnic public school system in the upper Midwest, Grant taught English while pursuing a master's degree in school administration at a state research university. In the early 1970s, he became the first affirmative action officer in a large, predominantly white metropolitan school district in the region. It was then that the "flowery English major with the Ciceronian writing style" was put to work writing an affirmative action plan and training manuals in a field that never existed before. "There were no prototypes," Grant explained. A district consultant provided some advice; the rest was trial and error. As he described his new identity as a public-sector bureaucrat, it was clear that there was more than a little of the black preacher in Jordan Grant. "My memoranda were very long and pretty or piercing or whatever," he said, "but they were not typical." Some tension developed with the "hard-nosed administrators." He explained:

> I never wanted to write anything that was so dull and deadly that you couldn't flourish every now and then, but the manual was tough for me. The interplay between what I wanted to write and the way I wanted to write it and what they wanted me to write was pretty hard. I remember a couple of times having the writing reviewed and having been told they didn't particularly like it – which also frustrated me because I didn't particularly like the way they wrote.

Later, while completing a doctoral degree in educational administration, Grant encountered similar tensions with his dissertation committee of four white male professors. "I was tending to have all these Ciceronian flourishes and lots of words and lots of analogies and lots of imagery, and the thesis advisor kept saying, 'You're bleeding on the paper. Stop bleeding on the paper. This is a scientific piece of work.'"

By the 1990s, Grant had left public education and had founded his own freelance consulting firm that assisted in the development and management of multicultural work forces. He was active in a local civil rights organization and was working intermittently on a book on civil rights issues. Grant said that he worked on the book during odd moments in his frequent business trips, "clouding up and raining" in airplanes and hotel rooms on a laptop computer that he taught himself to use. He said his fascination with writing throughout his life resided "in the power of it. A lot of times, I was surprised and still am surprised about what I just had written, how it manifests itself on paper." A wide-ranging reader, Grant said he was continuing to develop a professional language that left room for the part of himself he called "the artist." Boxes of his informal writing piled up in his home, where he also was working through a collection of his late father's sermons. He often included copies of his father's sermons in holiday messages to friends and associates.

In Grant is the most complex example yet of how individual literacy development manifests developments among the sponsors with which one makes contact. His literacy learning rode along on the backward-reaching, forward momentum of the African American self-help system as it amalgamated at midtwentieth century into the modern civil rights movement. In this amalgamation were the accumulating traditions of black theology, education, and freedom struggle as they pushed with increasing power against the contradictions in American laws and mores. Especially significant were the efforts to transform historically church-based resources, ranging from ethical power to oratorical power to organizational power, into projects of secular activism. These efforts involved not only hybrid agents like the SCLC and SNCC but also the UNCF. When founded in 1944, it consolidated the resources of dozens of historically black colleges, many rooted in nineteenth- and early twentieth-century church sponsorship, to serve the needs of an increasingly literate and educated African American population.[37] All of these organizations touched the life of Grant and sponsored his writing. Just as emerging political organizations appropriated the assets of African American church tradition, so, too, did Grant during the same time period appropriate these assets for writing in secular contexts and for breaking old barriers of a segregationist regime.

As the radical successes of the civil rights movement of the 1950s and 1960s were pacified in the 1970s by federal legislation and government oversight of education and employment, new bureaucratic genres like "the affirmative action plan" emerged. Amid racial and regional tensions, the adult Grant found himself trying to integrate his Southern black sermonic style into a Northern white, bureaucratic, and scientific style. In his struggles as a writer were the quintessential elements of the larger political struggle going on as an aftermath of official integration. It was not only the rich cultural assets with which Grant was blessed but his ability to transform and adapt them to new conditions that marked his adult literacy development. In the 1990s, as Grant carried his father's composing technique of "clouding up and raining" along with a laptop computer into airplanes destined for presentations at human resource seminars for secular, multicultural workforces throughout the country, the complexity of his literacy – indeed, all literacy as it must be practiced at the turn of the twenty-first century – was amply manifest.

Sponsors of African American Literacy

This chapter has traced the presence of an African American survival network as it appeared in the literacy learning accounts of ordinary African Americans who learned to read and write in various regions and periods across the twentieth century. Core cultural institutions, including the church, educators, the press, and the civil rights movement, organized originally to help African Americans defeat slavery, continued to provide life-affirming support in response to ongoing economic and political oppression. This network operated as an economy in which cultural resources, including the resources of literacy, were produced and distributed. This system helps to account for the rising levels of mass literacy among African Americans in the absence of (or the merely begrudging presence of) wider economic and education sponsorship.

As other chapters have already demonstrated, sponsors of literacy leave their marks on the literacy of the sponsored. For many historical reasons, the ideological context of African American–sponsored literacy retains a strongly spiritual component. Religious and secular values and styles can coexist within the same practice or the same interpretive stance. The church has been a primary scene of literacy learning for African Americans throughout their history and continues, for many, to be a key sponsor of literacy use and development. The ideological context of African American–sponsored literacy also retains a strong association with political rights. Historically, literacy has been used as a weapon against the civil rights of black people, and the achievement of literacy and education often has been at the defiance of oppressive forces. At the same time, as the movement for full citizenship continued through the twentieth century, primarily in the arenas of government, law, and mass media, reading and writing were a practical mechanism for carrying out that work. Reading and writing were used often by the individuals studied here to make the African American world visible to themselves and others. And literacy and language learning took their value in serving the broader goals of critical consciousness and, often, social activism.

In many ways, the ideological potency of African American–sponsored literacy stays true to earlier traditions of mass literacy in America. In the nineteenth century, reading and writing were more regularly acquired in connection with explicit religious and political causes. These included religious salvation and citizenship duty. As schooling became mandatory and as economic values eclipsed religious and civic ones, school literacy began to neutralize, as Jenny Cook-Gumperz has described it, becoming a "decontextualized skill" with little intrinsic connotation.[38] However, African American-sponsored literacy has stayed more consciously connected to the original traditions of American literacy emphasizing collective faith, democracy, and citizenship.

Older formations of literacy also were favored by the economic conditions in which African American–sponsored literacy grew. Because of the economic and professional constrictions imposed by racial discrimination, African American sponsoring agents for literacy were fewer in number yet denser in power and, again, more likely to be connected more directly to founding forces of mass literacy. As an earlier chapter disclosed, in European American farm communities at the turn of the twentieth century, strong individual cultural agents with ties to long-standing religious and secular print traditions served as informal teachers of literacy in the absence of formal education opportunity. Similar cultural agents appear in the accounts of the African Americans interviewed for this study and, in fact, did not drop out as the century progressed but remain influential. Although apprenticeship has become a recessive teaching tradition in the history of American education overall, it is not an uncommon format in the literacy accounts of contemporary African Americans. Preachers, teachers, doctors, and lawyers – the basic components of African American professional networks from earliest times – touched the lives of a high proportion of the 16 African Americans I interviewed, appearing as sources of literacy teaching and educational encouragement throughout the century.[39]

Agents of African American self-help systems were not the only influences on the literacy development of the African Americans I interviewed. Nor do I wish to imply by my emphasis on older orders that African

Americans have not been involved in the great economic and social transformations of the past century. Indeed, much of the challenge has been in making the leaps required by these changes without the educational and economic assets that were accumulating in white America. However, legacies of literacy within systems of African American cultural survival potentially bring certain meanings, styles, postures, and inflections that reflect a unique racial history. They supply a set of interpretations and values that, as we have seen, can shape reading and writing in many direct, indirect, and long-lasting ways.

Traditional sponsors of African American literacy ask their sponsored to reach deeply into the original sources of American literacy – into human spirituality, solidarity, and citizenship rights. If these ideological contexts for literacy were to be embraced more regularly by schools, workplaces, and other sponsors of literacy, racial equity in access, achievement, and reward for literacy might become more possible.[40]

5

THE SACRED AND THE PROFANE

Reading versus Writing in Popular Memory

In a study of popular literacy in nineteenth-century England, Thomas Laqueur (1976) recounted how on July 6, 1834, in the industrial town of Bolton, England, nearly 1,000 Sunday school students and their teachers took to the streets against efforts to eliminate writing instruction from their Sabbath schools. Although public education was beginning to be well established, working-class children who labored through the week depended on the lay-administered Sunday school for instruction in reading and, increasingly, in writing and arithmetic. Writing was an especially desired skill, according to Laqueur, and admission to Sunday school writing classes was often a reward for good behavior.

By the 1830s, however, an antiwriting movement was afoot, led, Laqueur reported, by the Wesleyan Methodist Conference. Unlike reading, with its direct and traditional connection to piety and Bible study, writing was considered too secular, worldly, and vocational and too strongly associated with upward mobility (a process that conservative church leaders wanted no part in encouraging). Although the antiwriting effort appeared on the surface to be an attempt to purify the Sabbath for prayer and worship, Laqueur argued that the real motive was to suppress the growing power of the lay Sunday school and restore control to the ministry. "Writing instruction on the Sabbath," he wrote, "came to be considered the identifying mark of the independent, lay-dominated, and locally controlled Sunday school."[1]

A similar story emerges in Furet and Ozouf's (1982) detailed study of mass literacy development in France. Education sponsored by parish

146

churches was restricted at first to reading. Writing, on the other hand, "always belonged to the civil domain."[2] As peasant families articulated to themselves and others the connection between education and upward economic mobility, they brought pressure to bear for more schooling and, particularly, more instruction in writing, at least for males. Furet and Ozouf suggested that developmental differences between reading and writing as cultural activities had their roots in the conflicting interests between institutional authorities and the people. Through the eighteenth and nineteenth centuries in France, reading continued its association with conventional morality and religious duty, whereas writing was associated almost exclusively with trade, earning, and other utilitarian functions. In this relationship of cultural dissociation, as Furet and Ozouf treat it, writing also continued to be eyed suspiciously within early church schools. Not only was writing considered dirty in the literal sense (involving messy inks and fragile pens) but also some church leaders believed that exposure to writing actually ruined students' devotion to reading.[3]

Although these accounts suggest something about how the politics of literacy were waged in the decades before universal public education, state-sponsored schooling eventually did much toward making reading and writing into more equal and more simultaneously taught skills. Yet these long-standing divisions between reading and writing continued to play out in nineteenth- and twentieth-century education. E. Jennifer Monaghan and E. Wendy Saul (1987) have picked up the story of the cultural separation of writing and reading as they have been manifested in the American public school. Reading, in their view, has always enjoyed more "divine" status in education, in terms of budget expenditures, scholarly attention, and public concern. Reading, they said, has always been a more clearly defined curricular activity, whereas definitions of writing in school have continued to shift, from the mechanical art of copying to grammar to exposition to creative expression and personal growth. Reading, they observed, fits more easily than writing with traditional roles of student and teacher, one as receptor of knowledge and the other as conduit. Students engaged in reading and teachers engaged in reading instruction, they suggested, are more subject to the control of school administrators and textbook publishers than they are when engaged in writing and writing instruction. In addition, Monaghan and Saul pointed to the matter of measurability: Reading is more conducive to assessments by standard instruments.[4] They observed:

> Reading has been and continues to be clearly defined and therefore better able to define itself and its assumptions to the pedagogical community at large. Moreover, reading as a field has embraced

those who identify themselves as interested in the teaching of reading, whereas writing is the servant of many masters. (p. 91)[5]

Divisions in the sponsorship histories of reading and writing are salient
for understanding challenges posed by what many call the "new" literacy
or "higher" literacy being forced by economic and social conditions today.
This new literacy is often characterized as an ability to go beyond rote
skills of deciphering text into the more mentally challenging levels of
interpretation and critical reasoning.[6] As Resnick and Resnick (1977) put
it, the need now is for a mass of people to be able to do things with words
that until quite recently were done only by a small group of the highly
educated. Basic literacy is no longer adequate – advanced proficiency is
required. Another way to understand this transformation in literacy is to
see that writing is beginning to overtake reading as the more fundamental
literate skill. Writing is the productive member of the pair, and with literacy now a key productive force in the information economy, writing not
only documents work but also increasingly comprises the work that many
people do. The economy demands more people in more spheres able to
render what they do in writing and other symbols. More people also are
entering institutions of higher education, where writing remains a major
medium of engagement. Writing now more regularly activates reading. In
front of computer screens and keyboards, people typically read from prior
positions as composers and messagers. The quickening spread of interactive media and genres is another indication that writing is the skill that is
riding this second wave of mass literacy – a transformation coming 100
years or so after the nation established a basic reading literacy.[7]

Yet the role of the writer has never really been mass-distributed in society before. And if the history of the struggle over writing is any indication,
potential tensions are rife between the sponsors of writing and the sponsored, between institutions that teach and exploit the powers of writing
and the individuals that seek them. The productive skills of interpretation,
critical reasoning, and creativity so coveted now by American capitalism
are also skills that historically have been used for resistance, rebellion, the
claiming of voice, and the development of critical consciousness. If the
question by ruling interests in the nineteenth century was how to instill a
dutiful reading while constricting writing altogether, perhaps the question
today is how to instill a dutiful writing while constricting the other, latent
powers of writing. How will the "profane" skill of writing be sanctified
and controlled? It should be an interesting era.

This chapter cannot foretell what may happen as the skill of writing
and the expansion of audiences via the Internet continue to grow.[8] How-

ever, it does look back into the cultural connotations that have accompanied the learning of writing and reading in the recent past. As we will see, cultural dissociations between reading and writing still exist in popular memory along the same lines that historians have charted in the past. Appreciating these differences may provide clues to the shape of future struggles between the sponsors and the sponsored in this second wave of literacy – clues to how ideological residues inherited from literacy's past may be appropriated in competitions over the meanings and means of literacy campaigns, instructional imperatives, and individual and collective experiences with writing. For teachers of literacy, these memories also can shed light on how general cultural attitudes toward reading and writing affect encounters with reading and writing in school. Above all, as this chapter visits some of the earliest memories of literacy learning in people's lives – those that occurred in contexts of childhood family life and early schooling – we will see from yet another angle how conservative traditions of literacy continue to function even in periods of great change. Whatever new relationships are yet to emerge between writing and reading (and other forms of communication), this history will be present in latent and influential ways.

The following discussion, then, treats all 80 life-history accounts in which people born between 1895 and 1985 recalled with me everything they could about how they learned to read and write. As I analyzed their accounts, I saw pronounced differences in the ways that they remembered early learning in reading and writing. They discussed them differently and seemed to value them differently. Differences especially pertained to the settings in which early reading and writing were remembered to have occurred, as well as the personal and cultural significance assigned to each. What we will see is how the histories of literacy sponsorship become abstracted into the practices of family and school life, no longer attached, perhaps, to the original ideological or economic campaigns that gave rise to them but still sending powerful messages not only about literacy but also about family, self, and world.

Cultural Dissociations: Reading versus Writing

Although there were some exceptions, people typically remembered their first reading experiences as pleasurable occasions, endorsed if not organized by adults. On the other hand, many early writing experiences, particularly those set outside of school, were remembered as occurring out of the eye of adult supervision and, often, involving feelings of loneliness, secrecy, and resistance. Further, whereas reading with children and encouraging them to read was regarded as part of normal parental responsibilities in many working-class and middle-class families, teaching or encouraging writing (beyond showing very young children how to form letters or checking the spelling on homework assignments) was nearly unheard of and sometimes actively avoided by many of these same families.

"Part of the Good Stuff": The Prestige of Reading

Three quarters of the people I spoke with said that reading and books were actively endorsed in their households. Mostly this endorsement took the form of being read to by parents (usually mothers), grandparents, or older siblings, usually at bedtime or nap time and often in the presence of other family members. The vividness of early reading memories suggests their importance and their association with pleasure and family intimacy. For instance, Betty MacDuff, a retired journalist born in 1924, whose father's education had ended in third grade, recalled her mother reading to both her and her father, whether it was from *Hans Brinker* or *Five Little Peppers and How They Grew* or the *A* volume of the 1936 *Compton's Encyclopedia*. Carol White, who was born in 1940 and led an otherwise stressful childhood, had pleasurable memories of her widowed mother reading to her and her older brother. She recalled:

> She used to have a big old storybook. I kind of wish I had it today, but I don't. My brother and I would jump into bed and that would be our entertainment. She'd read stories from the book. And it was just like they were alive. I can still see some of the pictures even now.

In several households, reading religious materials was part of a family routine or holiday ritual. There was only one book in the house of former Missouri sharecropper Johnny Ames, who was born in 1950. The book was the Bible, from which his grandmother would read parables to her children and grandchildren. Another Missouri man of similar age, this one from a St. Louis suburb, remembered having to remain at the supper table after the meal was over to listen to his father read from a book of Bible stories. A 20-year-old rural Wisconsin man recalled that his mother cut out Christmas stories that appeared in serial form in the local newspaper, pasted them into book form, and read the stories to the family each Christmas Eve thereafter.

In other homes, secular reading predominated, and reading storybooks or comic books was regarded as a form of entertainment or relaxation.

Reading to preschool children cut across class, race, generation, and sometimes language. A 25-year-old woman remembered her parents, Holocaust refugees, sharing with her their own childhood storybooks, translating into English the German words beneath the pictures. Miguel Sanchez, born in 1959 and raised in San Antonio, Texas, recalled:

> We would read with my mom at home. At night, we would have a reading time and we would sit down and do some reading. My dad would not because my dad didn't read very much because he only had an eighth-grade education. But he used to sit there with us while we were reading. And my mom would correct us. When my mom read to us, she would read in Spanish. We didn't speak Spanish, but we understood what she was talking about. That's how I came to learn Spanish.

In a few cases, parents did not read to children but did give them books. A 23-year-old Hmong man, a college student at the time of the interview, recalled his father instructing him to read an English picture dictionary that had been purchased by the family's American sponsors.

All parents were perhaps not as conscientious as the mother of Rebecca Howard, who, when she went to the hospital to give birth to her firstborn in 1974, packed children's books to read to the baby. Nevertheless, reading and the teaching of reading were widely considered as a normal part of responsible care of young children in many households. The heavy hand of mothers in organizing book-based activities especially indicates the close association between reading and child rearing. A few of the people I interviewed served as surrogate parents for younger siblings. Anthony Stassi, who was born in 1956 and grew up in a tough neighborhood in Chicago, said he was responsible for the well-being of his siblings while his parents were at work. "I read a lot to my younger brother and sister," he explained. "It was something I did not as a distraction for them, to keep them in line or anything. I just did it because it was good for me, good for them."

Beyond the home, public libraries also signaled the cultural value of reading. Among those I interviewed, public libraries were used more by urban dwellers, especially if they could be reached by public transportation or on foot. Small children would be accompanied by parents, older siblings, or in-laws, sometimes to a library-sponsored story hour. Harry Carlton, born in 1949 in South Dakota, recalled his hometown library sponsoring a summer reading contest. Traveling libraries and bookmobiles reached into rural schools and neighborhoods. Itinerant farmworker Jack Wills, who was born in 1930 and left school at the age of 10 to begin a life on the road, pursued his education by using public libraries and, later, a library on an army base in Germany where he served in the 1950s. Wills wept recalling his encounter with a public librarian who befriended him. "She saw me roaming around the library and she said, 'You're trying to further your education, aren't you?' I said, 'Yes, that's what I'm doing.' So she picked out about fifteen books there and said if I read them, I'd be able to read just about anything in the library." Computer programmer John Roe, blinded at birth in 1969, depended on a public library for early reading material. "Books in Braille are pretty expensive," he explained, "so if I got things to read, it was usually out of the library." Two people I interviewed worked in their school libraries during junior high school or high school.[9] A Chicago woman, 33 years old at the time of the interview, remembered her single mother, who worked as a cook, would drop her off, along with younger siblings, in front of a downtown library and urge the youngsters to go inside.

Buying books, particularly children's books, was another indication of the value of reading that was communicated to children. Buying books and magazines was, in fact, more common in families than using the public library. Books were frequently kept in prominent locations around a home. Several people reported that their working- or middle-class parents purchased sets of encyclopedias. Where bookstore prices could not be afforded, used books were purchased at garage sales, secondhand shops, or library discard sales. Housekeeper Linda Hagger, born in the Midwest in 1960 as one of eight children in a low-income family, said her mother would come up with books "anywhere she could find them. Garage sales. She bought a set of *World Book*s for us. Anywhere she could come up with books. She made sure she got the *Child Craft* for us." Privately owned books tended to be preserved across generations. Jasper Tannen, who was born in 1927 and raised in a wealthy family in Wisconsin's state capital, recalled, in addition to contemporary books purchased through book clubs, older books that had been part of his mother's inheritance. Sidney Vopat, born in 1913, remembered several handed-down books in his rural Wisconsin household, some of which he believed were written in Polish, one of the languages of his ancestors. Jack May, born in 1958 in south central Wisconsin, recalled that his parents kept their college manuals and books in a room in the house called "the library." "And they are still there," he said. "I don't think they ever threw a book out or gave one away." Registered nurse Beth Barrett, born into a dairy farming family in 1951, also recalled a "full set of *Child Craft* books" that her parents purchased. "And, oh," she said:

I remember there was a drawer upstairs that was sort of like a built-in linen closet, and there was one drawer that was full of books. And we would pull it out. It was filled with books from when my mom and dad went to school. It was their schoolbooks. And I remember looking at those books and, in fact, reading most of those books.

Books also were given as gifts. Several rural people recounted especially how urban relatives – usually of a higher economic station – would send them fine books on birthdays or at holidays. Rosa Parnell, born in the South in 1942, remembered that one Christmas as a young girl she was given two identical copies of a desk dictionary, one from her father and one from her adult brother. Former school teacher Olga Nelson, born in rural Wisconsin in 1896, told me how, each Christmas, she and her sisters would find an orange and a book in their stockings:

> That great big, long stocking. I can see it up there now. And in the toe was an orange. And in those days oranges were scarce, don't you know. And [my mother] would always give us an orange and a book. It was always that. And maybe something else, but not a lot of stuff. We didn't have a lot. But we had good stuff.

For Nelson, books and reading were clearly part of the good stuff, part of the way their finishing-school mother taught Olga and her sisters to distinguish themselves as a little more refined. "We were," she explained, "a reading family."

In general, reading was remembered as an activity, indeed a ritual, that was knitted into holiday celebrations as well as into the ordinary routines of daily life. There was a reverence expressed for books and their value and sometimes a connection between reading and refinement or good breeding. Reading was not without its troubles. Minister's son Jordan Grant, born in 1948, was subject to a minor inquisition when his father noticed a mystery book with the word *murder* in the title among the books that Jordan, as a young teen, had brought home from the library. Art historian Ellen Blum, a precocious reader and regular library user in a large eastern city where she was born in 1947, recalled a librarian chasing her out of the adult section of the library when she was 11 years old. Jasper Tannen reported the anxiety he experienced as someone for whom reading always came hard. "One of the ways I tried to improve my reading was to read at church – read the Bible, or the lesson for the day at church. And it would absolutely petrify me to do this. I would mix up my words. I would bring a noun before [an adjective]; I'd mix them all up." However, despite occasional tensions, reading was most typically remembered and described as a deeply sanctioned activity in the culture at large. Jack Wills, who was on the road alone as an itinerant farm worker between the ages of 10 and 23, said he always carried a book or two with him to read at night in the makeshift camps where he would sleep. "If you were reading," he said, "people generally left you alone."

"It Was Nothing Encouraged": The Ambiguity of Writing

Although the ability to write was widely – almost unanimously – regarded as precious, memories of writing and learning to write diverged significantly from those of reading. Writing appeared to develop in situations and out of psychological motivations that were saliently, jarringly different from those surrounding reading. These differences surfaced in the memories that people had of their own early writing, their memories of how writing was used and modeled by adults in their households, as well as the uses they made of writing at various times in their lives. Writing was more often recalled in the context of humiliation and anxiety. Compared to reading, writing seemed to have a less coherent status in collective family life, and much early writing was remembered as occurring in lonely, secret, or rebellious circumstances.

The difference is most dramatically captured in this early memory of South Dakotan Harry Carlton: "I wrote all the bad words that I knew," he said, "on a blackboard that was on an easel while my mother was having card club. I was at one end of the room and all the women were there in the room for cards." Asked to explain his motivation, he continued, "I think it was a just a wild juxtaposition, that I could be writing all these nasty thoughts with all these people in the room and they didn't know."

Although there was a certain thrill retained in Mr. Carlton's memory, more typically, the feelings surrounding early self-initiated writing were described as lonely. In stark contrast to cozy bedtime reading, a 50-year-old disabled woman remembered her first writing occurring alone in a hospital bed when she was 4 years old. Eleven-year-old Michael May wrote his first story at 5 when his family moved to a new neighborhood. The story was about a pig who was having trouble making friends. Carla Krauss, a Midwestern woman born in 1926, remembered her first poem was inspired by sitting alone on the front steps of her house waiting for her older sister to arrive home from school.

It is, of course, likely that these young authors of stories and poems used technical knowledge derived from their reading to make their compositions, but it is noteworthy that the motivations for the writing in these cases were not books and the motivators were not adults. Rather, the occasions and impulses to write emerged from the children's immediate circumstances and feelings. Whereas people tended to remember reading for the sensual and emotional pleasure that it gave, they tended to remember writing for the pain or isolation it was meant to assuage. People's descriptions of the settings of childhood and adolescent writing – a hospital bed, the front steps of a house, and, in other cases, a garage, a treehouse, and a highway overpass – were scenes of exile, hiding, or at least degraded versions of domesticity, in marked contrast to the memories of pillowed, well-lit family reading circles described in so many of the interviews.

In another twist on writing–reading relationships, several earliest writing memories involved defacement, including, ironically, defacement of books. "I remember writing in little kids' books," recalled college student Barbara Hunt, born in 1971. "We had those hard covered books and I just remember writing 'Barbaras' all over the covers." Jack May, who remembered many of the details of his family's library, also remembered getting caught by his displeased mother while he was writing on the library wall. Susan Parsons, a farmer born in 1973, remembered that at three years of age, she wrote the word *apple* (learned, she believed, by watching *Sesame Street*) on the wall of her grandparents' house on the afternoon of her brother's birth. Relatedly, a woman born in a Wisconsin mill town in 1968 said her earliest memory of writing was making marks and scratches on the door of a bedroom she shared with four sisters. She did it, she said, "Because I wanted my mom's attention. She was constantly reading and I think I wanted her to see my writing."

If early urges to write were frequently associated with ambiguous and complex motives and feelings, including self-assertion, violation, jealousy, and guilt, adult relationships to youngsters' early writing efforts could also be ambiguous and unpredictable. After Susan Parson's grandparents reprimanded her for writing on the wall, they took a picture of her scribbles, a record that became part of the legend of Susan's precociousness. As a postscript to the card-party story, Harry Carlton's mother later discovered his work and calmly pointed out to him that the word *butt* should be spelled with two *t*'s. College student Aileen Markero, born in 1970 and raised in the suburbs of Chicago, remembered during a visit to an aunt's house secretly taking from her mother's purse an envelope on which her mother's signature was written. Alone, she began to copy the signature, "trying desperately not to get caught." She was, in fact, discovered by family members. But, she said, "Instead of being punished for practicing my art of forgery, my beautiful and skillful penmanship was celebrated." These accounts further demonstrate the mixed messages that can encase literacy memories. In these examples, lessons about the proprieties of language correctness or adult delight in literary precociousness are remembered in connection with misbehavior or rebellion.

The ambiguity that surrounded memories of writing actually began at a more fundamental level: with the definition of writing itself. In confirmation of Monaghan and Saul's (1987) analysis, reading was usually recalled as a clearly demarcated activity: the names of first books, even, in some cases, the first lines of first primers, surfaced in people's descriptions. Memories of writing were decidedly more vague. "It's difficult to remember writing as a separate activity," remarked Sam May, born in 1925, about his growing-up years. "I don't have memories of people actually sitting down and writing," said his son Jack May about his childhood household. More often than not, writing went under the rubrics of "work," "doing the bills," "doodling," or "homework." Vague definitions of writing posed an interesting problem in the conduct of the interviews. In asking people to describe in general how they learned to write, I deliberately left the term *writing* undefined at the start of each interview. Many people assumed the topic was handwriting, whereas others equated writing exclusively with literary or creative composition. Many of the latter group initially reported that they did no writing, when, in fact, with more probing, they reported using writing for an array of purposes. This mundane writing was practically invisible to them because it did not rise to the level of belle lettres.

A dual association of writing with the invisibly mundane and the creatively elite probably helped to account for the lack of memories of parental endorsement or specific parental teaching of writing to offspring. Johnny Ames, mentioned earlier in connection with Bible reading by his grandmother, said he had no recollection of writing anything as a boy, even though his grandmother, who he said taught him everything he knew, wrote in connection with her work. Probing, I asked:

Would you have seen your grandmother writing?

Yeah, I seen her write.

What would she have been doing?

Well, see, my grandmother's job was to hire people to pick cotton, fill out, do all the figures. She had to put the name of the people, how much they worked, how much they picked a day. Every time they picked, she had to weigh the cotton and tally it up at the end of the day, take it to the gin, get it weighed, get the money, pay the people off, and take the money and turn it in. She had to keep books for the person she worked for.

Would these books be in your house? Would she do this at home?

Right.

Did you help her? Would you be hanging around?

I'd always hang around. Where she went, I went.

Okay, but you don't remember…

It was nothing encouraged. There was no encouragement of writing in my household when I was coming up. It was just a necessity for her to do that. I saw her do it – I understood why she was doing it – but there was no encouragement for me to do that.

For Ames's grandmother, writing was just a necessity for her job and not thought of as a separate activity or skill to be passed along for its own sake. Judging from the interviews as a whole, Ames's experience was not all that unique. Although adults in many households considered reading with children to be part of their parental responsibility, they didn't seem to extend that responsibility quite so articulately to writing. This included many middle-class, school-oriented households in which parental writing was frequent. Hope Moore, born in 1909, was a college graduate who married a college professor. She wrote extensively herself, especially when she was involved in the League of Women Voters. She described her only child, a daughter, as being "kind of a writer":

Oh, she was really a writer all the way through. She had a long saga about some imaginary girl she wrote.

So these were things she would do on her own?

Oh, yes, and she did sort of a novel. She called it a novel.

But you didn't teach that explicitly to her?

No.

You didn't encourage her to do it?

Well, I encouraged her because it kept her busy and it was something to do sometimes. And I thought it was nice that she had that interest. But I never would have said, 'Go write something on your novel.' I would never have thought of it.

Carla Krauss, born in Michigan, wrote creatively as a child and went on to attend college. She read regularly to her two sons. But she rejected the idea that writing could or should be actively encouraged by parents. She explained:

I think the idea that you must be creative is sort of wrenching it out of the natural. It always seemed to me that it was a natural thing if it was going to come. And the idea of psychologizing it and thinking, now, if a person can express themselves, well, they'll have a bigger sense of themselves and this is good for them is nonsense to me, frankly.

Betty MacDuff, another mother of three, herself a journalist, echoed the reluctance to intervene in what she believed to be a natural and mysterious process. "The ones that had the creative spark did it," she said of her children's writing. Martha Day, who at 89 was organizing a lifetime of journal entries, said she always kept the writing that her children did at school or home. "But," she said, "I didn't push it."

It is interesting to note how a cultural ideal that could have derived from literary reading – the romantic writer as natural genius – plays out in parents' hands-off attitudes toward children's writing development. Even further, negative stereotypes of the creative writer sometimes translated into active or at least passive discouragement of an offspring's literary pursuits. Hedy Lucas, who was born in 1907 and immigrated to New York City from Poland, told me that she read to her only son Benjamin every night before he went to sleep. In an interview later with Benjamin Lucas, born in 1936, I learned that he not only read voraciously as a child and young man but also wrote poetry and eventually drama. When asked what kind of encouragement there was in his household for writing, he explained:

> Not only did I not get encouragement at home but I got a lot of discouragement because this was something that was so totally an anathema to [my family]. First, they didn't understand it, but what they thought they understood about it was something they identified with poverty and wastefulness.

Similarly, Yi Vang, born in 1969, whose father encouraged him to read an English dictionary, recalled becoming enthused about writing after a semester of journal keeping and creative writing taken in the class of a particularly supportive high school teacher. He tried to keep up the momentum on his own during the summer. "I thought maybe I wanted to be a writer," he recalled, "so I would write my stories and it went pretty long. But after a while, you ran out of ideas and there was nobody there to help you. There was nobody there to acknowledge you were doing a good job."

It is not surprising, given the ambivalence and vagueness that surround writing as an activity, that developing an identity as a writer is rather difficult. Many people took pride in calling themselves an "avid reader" or "quite a reader" or "always reading." Yet there was reticence among the people I spoke with – including a well-established, published poet – to regard themselves as writers, despite avid energy in their pursuit of writing. Some of this reticence had to do with not seeing writing as an end in itself. Carla Krauss, who was a retired government worker, wrote poetry and plays as a schoolgirl and, at the time of our interview, was composing philosophical essays that she shared with distant friends. Of her childhood writing, she said, "I enjoyed it. I really had no sense of it as writing at all. It was almost for another purpose." Benjamin Lucas, a writer and critic, remarked, "I think I never had a sense of myself as a writer. I think I had a sense of myself as wanting to do something that my peers and my family just weren't doing." Antonia Lawrence, a former medical technician and telephone operator who has written fiction and poetry intermittently all of her life, was working on a series of short stories at the time of the interview. Asked when and how she began to develop an identity as a writer, she said, "I don't think I ever thought about it."

Although ambiguity surrounded writing and parental involvement in promoting writing, writing as an activity and a skill were regarded highly, especially if preservation is an indicator. Even more than schoolbooks, children's writing was a tangible medium that linked home and school. Many people recalled bringing home written projects from school for parents to read and, if the project received a high grade, displaying it on a refrigerator or bulletin board, sometimes along with blue ribbons from contests. When Michael May wrote his story about the friendless pig, he showed it to his mother, who, in turn, showed it to a teacher for whom she was doing baby-sitting. Many adults still had in their possession research papers, family genealogies, and other papers they had composed in grade school and high school. Twenty-five years after graduating from high school, Janine Williams, born in 1951, tried to retrieve from her former high school teacher an essay she had written on the death of her mother. Nor were all early memories of writing charged with ambiguous or difficult feelings. A few individuals indeed described scenes of intimacy and adult sponsorship of writing that resembled accounts of early reading. College student Luann Wallitsch, born in 1968, would read her school-assigned writing aloud to her approving mother. Ted Anderson, Wisconsin farmer, born in 1973, recalled that he would sit next to his mother as she wrote letters to relatives and pretend to write himself in a small notebook that she had given him for just such occasions. Fifty-year-old Chicago native Antonia Lawrence, who was writing fiction at the time of the interview, remembered her early interest in a cloisonné pen owned by her schoolteacher grandmother. Her grandmother promised her that she could use the pen if she learned to write certain things. "The first time my grandmother let me use the pen was on my fifth birthday," she recalled. "It was great. And I've grown to love cloisonné."

Writing (at least as it translated into school success or economic gain) also appeared to be encouraged through the giving of gifts. Typewriters were widely purchased by parents and given to offspring (most commonly, the firstborn) before they went off to college or when they enrolled in secretarial courses. Two women I interviewed remembered as teens being given diaries for their birthdays, one by her mother and another by her aunt. Another recent high school graduate was given a journal as a graduation present from her German teacher in anticipation of the student's planned trip to Germany. But all in all, diaries and journals were more frequently self-purchased than received as gifts, and writing-related gifts seemed much less prevalent and much less strongly associated with holidays than did book giving.[10]

On the whole, it must be said that the status of writing in everyday literacy practices appeared decidedly more ambiguous and conflicted in comparison to reading. Except for the dutiful thank-you notes or letters home from camp that some people recalled being required to write as children, writing did not appear to play a standard role in the activities or rituals of families, especially not in the communal way that reading was. Nor was writing so readily identified as a separate activity. Rather, writing seemed to be experienced more as an embedded means than a demarcated end in itself. Writing did not seem to be as broadly sponsored or endorsed by parents, nor did the identity of "writer" seem as easily available as the identity of "reader."

Reading and Writing across Generations

A closer look at the functions of writing and reading in households revealed how much more stratified writing was than reading, by which I mean there seemed to be more natural opportunities to share reading and knowledge about reading across generations than is the case for writing. Parental reading was associated primarily with learning, relaxing, and worshiping – all activities that are equally available to children and adults and that often take place in communal settings. On the other hand, parents' writing was mostly associated with earning money, paying bills, and maintaining communication with distant family relations – activities more strictly in the purview of adults. People were aware, as children, of the functions of their parents' work-related writing, but that kind of writing usually remained out of the realm of most children.

Eighty-three-year-old Hope Moore did recall helping her grocer father sort and record checks at their kitchen table. Twenty-year-old William

Bussler had close-up memories of his father's dairy delivery records because he used to ride along on the delivery route. Several of the younger people I interviewed mentioned that their first exposure to computers occurred when parents bought computers or brought them home for work; these included a young boy whose mother worked part time for an insurance company; the daughter of a school superintendent, who routinely checked out computer equipment from the school for home use; and the daughter of a self-employed accountant, who taught her how to use a computer and to "ten key" on equipment that he kept in the home. In addition, accompanying a parent to work increased the chance of at least seeing that parent writing, if not always joining in. On the whole, however, children were not really invited to participate in their parents' writing nor were they ready or natural audiences for it. It was not unusual for children of professional fathers to say that their fathers' work-related writing went on behind closed doors in studies or offices that were off-limits to children.

Although it was rare for children to read their parents' writing, it was quite common for children to read their parents' magazines. *Saturday Evening Post, Look, Reader's Digest,* and *Ladies' Home Journal,* as well as farming and hunting magazines, were standard reading fare for many children and adolescents. But there was nothing really comparable on the writing side. Parents might have read to children, but parents seldom wrote to children (although parental divorce, incarceration, military service, or other family breakups increased those chances). One woman reported that when the oldest of her seven siblings was drafted into the army during the Vietnam War, her mother organized a collective letter-writing effort by which each family member took a turn writing a weekly letter. Overall, though, writing appeared to be more segregated and stratified between adults and children than was reading. It was more likely to be associated with work or with family crisis or separation.

The link between writing and adult work was not the only cause for segregation. Rather, the privacy, even secrecy, that surrounded many forms of writing diminished occasions for teaching and learning. Two people reported that their parents wrote poetry (one a dray-operating father and the other a day-laboring mother), but interestingly, neither of these people were aware of their parents' creative writing until they themselves became adults. Thirty-six-year-old Anthony Stassi reported during our interview that his father had just been sent a journal that had been being kept by Anthony's grandfather in Italy and that he and his father were arranging to have it translated. An 84-year-old woman who rarely wrote throughout her life confided in our interview that she was writing a long, autobiographical letter to her grandchildren but that she did not wish the existence of the letter to be revealed until after her death.

The writing mentioned above all might have been kept secret as a kind of legacy meant for eventual disclosure, but many of the people I interviewed had at some time in their lives written things explicitly meant to be kept from others. Sam May remembered a retreat he made as a teenager in the 1930s out of an old car seat set up in a barn, where he wrote thoughts and plans in a notebook. Carla Krauss said that at 9 or 10 years old, she became "intrigued by the idea of having secret diaries." Carol White, the woman with warm memories of storybook reading with her mother and brother, recalled: "There was an old, dilapidated garage in the back of one of the houses we lived in and the ceiling was coming down. I used to keep my diary up there. I'd write in there and keep it up there so nobody would see it." The girl who copied her mother's signature in secret went on, as a grade schooler, to write stories in secret. "I rarely told anyone about my private writings," she said, "and kept them hidden in a special folder under my mattress." Several people mentioned that diary keeping or private writing ended bitterly when a sibling or someone else discovered and violated the secrecy of their writing.

Many people I interviewed reported using private writing to purge feelings, primarily anger or grief. Much of this writing was never shown to anyone and was, in fact, destroyed (certainly another obstacle for passing along knowledge about writing). Using writing as "a purge" or "vent" (frequently used expressions) was especially common among white and black women and among black men that I interviewed. This writing tended to occur at times of crisis: death, divorce, romantic loss, incarceration, war. Betty MacDuff remembered writing a lot during her divorce and still was resorting to writing "to get through a lot of feelings of family situations. I just write it out, and when I'm done, I throw it away because it's down." Eighteen-year-old Susan Parsons, remembering her parents' divorce when she was nine, said, "I would write down as to how I felt, and it seemed to help." Forty-six-year-old Anita Russell, sometimes in the company of friends, would write down her experiences with job discrimination in the form of protest letters than she never sent. Jordan Grant, recalling the civil rights protests in the 1950s and 1960s, some of which were organized at his father's church, said, "It was an emotionally charged time and you had a lot of things to say." Writing was, for him "a vent," "an alternative to hitting people." Johnny Ames started writing regularly after he moved from a maximum- to a minimum-security prison. "I saw things that didn't set right with what I felt," he explained. "I'd write my feelings about that and throw them away."

The focus on connections between writing and secrecy does not imply that reading goes on in the absence of privacy and secrecy. The history of censorship and punishment around reading is at least as long and as volatile as it is around writing. Nevertheless, a salient difference arose in these accounts having to do with the way that children and adults relate to each other through reading and writing. It appeared that what gives writing its particular value for people – its usefulness in maintaining material life, withholding experience for private reflection, venting feeling, and resisting conformity and control – are the very qualities that make writing a problematic practice for adults to pass on to children or for children to share easily with adults. Paradoxically, writing remained more invisible than reading in the young lives of these Americans, both because of how it was embedded in mundane, workaday concerns and because of how it was shrouded in secrecy and suspicion. Consequently, parents and children had fewer ways of seeing, naming, and talking about writing than appeared to be the case for reading. Not only do people spend considerably more time reading in their lives than writing but also opportunities for learning about the acts and activities of writing are usually fainter than those for reading.

Writing and Reading Relationships in School

When memories turned to literacy practices in school, prestige around reading and ambivalence around writing played out in yet more various and paradoxical configurations. As was mentioned above, in the history of literacy instruction in school, writing almost always has played second fiddle to reading in terms of the time and resources spent on each. This subordination was reflected in people's memories of writing assignments that were primarily in the service of reading and books. Writing served to induce, support, or verify reading.[11] Harry Carlton, schooled in South Dakota in the 1950s and 1960s, remembered doing no writing through junior high school save for making elaborate outlines of assigned readings. Book reports were, by far, the assignment most frequently recalled among those I interviewed. A 50-year-old rural man spoke for many when he described how, in third or fourth grade, students "used to get a certificate if we read so many books. But we did have to write a report on those books to get our star." Expository reports, usually on animals or states, were also commonly remembered across the generations. Students began by going to the school library, reading on their subject, and then producing an essay that usually resembled the texts they had read. A man born in

1945 and schooled in a university community in Missouri recalled reading Dick and Jane stories in kindergarten and then receiving a lined sheet of paper with printed prompts inviting him to invent simple stories making himself, his family, and his pet the protagonists. Jordan Grant, educated in segregated schools in Arkansas and Tennessee during the 1950s and early 1960s, remembered a major poetry unit in high school that began with extensive lessons on the conventional forms and technical vocabulary of poetry. Next, students designed and produced book covers. After that, they filled their books with five or six poems by white poets, five or six poems by black poets, and then, in the back of the book, a number of their own poems in the different forms they had studied. Younger people whom I interviewed, those born from the late 1960s onward, tended to remember more creative writing assigned, especially in the early grades. In an episode similar to one involving Dick and Jane, Rebecca Howard, born in a university town in 1974, recalled being introduced to writing in kindergarten via a storybook in which the protagonist, this time, was a child story writer. She explained:

> *Harold and the Purple Crayon* was a book. It had this kid named Harold and this crayon, and he'd make up stories and he'd draw them. In kindergarten, they'd give us a big, long piece of paper and they'd have us make up Harold and the Purple Crayon stories. We'd draw them out and then dictate them out and the teacher would write them above our stories. They were little, short two-sentence things.

Younger people also tended to describe school-based writing that was based on television or movies rather than merely books – among them, research reports on Walt Disney and Marilyn Monroe. But even these projects required trips to the library for book-based research.

At the same time, across the generations, school-based writing was widely associated with pain, belittlement, and perplexity. Handwriting was recalled as a heavily monitored activity, and those who struggled with it remember it as a source of humiliation or defeat. A 68-year-old former Spanish teacher said that poor handwriting in her early education discouraged her from writing. Benjamin Lucas's memory stood for many people across the generations, male and female and often left-handed, when he explained: "My handwriting is terrible. Very unclear. I remember teachers complaining to my mother about my handwriting, asking her to try to correct it. I remember my handwriting being a topic of conversation, particularly during early school years." Jack May was pulled out of his regular classroom for extra work on his handwriting. Anthony Stassi said, "My teacher made handwriting a big problem for me and my parents. That was a bad experience and it turned me off to school."

At other times, the suffering associated with school-based writing was more private, brought on by assignments that could produce roiling conflict. "We were to write something about our mother," recalled college student Patricia Nyland, who was born in 1942 and attended Catholic schools in Chicago. Her mother was suffering from depression at the time:

> I broke out in a cold sweat. I couldn't write about my mother. I had no words within myself for the big glob of bad scariness that I felt. I managed to dredge up eight or nine sentences of bland and phony clichés. When the paper came back, it bore a huge C-minus.

One girl remembered ending her first grade-school composition with the phrase "And they lived happily ever after," a flourish that received a negative comment from the teacher. "And I was like, come on, I'm in third grade," she shrugged.

Poor grades were not the only potential source of pain or embarrassment. A young farm woman recalled the utter humiliation she felt after a peer found one of her school papers, inadvertently dropped on the floor of their school bus, and read it aloud to the merciless howls of the other children.

Secrecy and rebellion that we saw associated with out-of-school writing also pertained to in-school writing – that is, the unofficial kind that many people recalled participating in. In these contexts, school reading assignments became the objects of spoof and satire. One man remembered writing satiric newspaper accounts, including unflattering items about his teacher, and passing them furtively around his fourth-grade classroom. Several people, like highway maintenance worker Charlie Smith, born in 1942, associated note-passing in school with "big secrets," some remembering that they resorted to pseudonyms or secret codes in case notes were apprehended by teachers or otherwise fell into the wrong hands. An 18-year-old farmer remembered a social ritual in his middle school in which girls stored their diaries in their lockers and boys stole the diaries and read them. Compared to reading, writing in school was more often discussed in the context of censorship. Student Rebecca Howard, born in 1974, who served as an editor of her high school newspaper, recalled her principal closing down the paper in the late 1980s because of a controversial article that she and the other students had insisted on publishing. Another student of similar age, Michelle Friedman, said she would never forget that "horrible moment" in sixth grade when her teacher caught her passing a note about one of her classmates, a note, she said, "that was not very nice."

"Mrs. C _____ seized the note from my hand," she explained, "and after class warned me gravely, 'Never write things down, Michelle. *Never!*'" Like out-of-school writing, writing in school could be accompanied by mixed messages from adult sponsors, who could teach and require it yet also express wariness and disapproval of its powers.

If writing in school was more associated than reading with emotional conflict, surveillance, and punishment, it also could be associated with sharper pride and individual accomplishment. Many people remembered receiving certificates for excellent penmanship or accurate typing. Others recalled with pride instances when their compositions were selected to be read aloud or published in school publications. Student writing was often on display during parental visits to schools. Several people I interviewed recalled participating in and sometimes winning writing contests, sponsored by, among others, the American Legion, the Ayn Rand Foundation, a Detroit automobile manufacturing company, *Reader's Digest,* and the United Negro College Fund (UNCF).

To sum up, as remembered, official school-based writing often functioned in subordination to reading, as assignments principally engaged students in displaying the results of their reading or imitating or adulating published texts. Assignments typically highlighted text structures or literary qualities, and students were invited to occupy positions of authorship. Shirley Brice Heath has conjectured that the emphasis in the schools on literary and expository writing, with a stress on individual authorship and professional models, was actually a way of imposing elitist values and domesticating amateur popular forms of writing that had flourished in earlier times.[12] Linking writing to reading was a way to curtail or control writing, not necessarily to develop it on its own terms. However, although official assignments may have asked students to pay homage to authors or validate their reading, unofficial writing in school often rose in resistance to those practices, taking the form of satires, spoofs, code, or other forms of challenge. Sub rosa writing was used to comment on school authority. In comparison with reading, writing in school was recalled in much more heavily evaluative and even competitive contexts. Judgments about one's writing, generally rendered by teachers, stayed in the memory as sore points or keen accomplishment. Like writing at home, writing in school could bring punishment and censorship more readily than reading. Although reading was treated as a resource, as an experience from which one could draw lessons or on which one could reflect, writing was treated more wholly as a performance and as a responsibility, more revealing, riskier, and fraught with consequences.

Compelling Literacy

Messages about the prestige of reading are sent to children early and often. Reading is incorporated into shared family rituals and is supported independently of school through such avenues as religion, hobbies, and the values of parent–child involvement. School-based campaigns such as D.E.A.R. (Drop Everything and Read), in which all members of a school community, from principal to custodian, are supposed to devote 15 minutes a day to reading, is matched by television commercials and library posters featuring sports figures and other cultural icons extolling the virtues of reading. Writing enjoys no such broad sponsorship.[13] Though far from absent in households, writing is less explicitly taught and publicly valued than reading, largely because writing practices are embedded in mundane work and are more stratified generationally. Though parents do not hesitate to endorse and promote reading, their involvement with children's writing seems more restricted and circumspect. Many parents intervene only to provide technical information or assistance with school projects, and many are outwardly wary of what they sense are the creative and mysterious origins of writing. Conventions of gift giving favor books over materials associated with writing. And perhaps because of the private subject matter of much self-initiated writing at home, there are barriers to adult–child sharing. Writing overall seems more associated with troubles. There were more accounts of getting into trouble with writing than with reading and about using writing as a response to trouble. Even in school, where reading and writing are most explicitly connected in official tasks, unofficial literacy lessons occur and, as in the home, may send mixed messages about the consequences of reading and writing.

School and home practices together participate in the broader cultural diffusions of literacy across time. Other chapters have demonstrated the impact on these practices of convulsive changes in economic and communication systems, especially in the way they multiply the contexts in which the young encounter and acquire reading and writing. Here we see pointedly how installations of earlier, powerful systems remain in the life of literacy – sometimes long after their practical and ideological powers remain relevant. The sacred status of reading – established through the once commanding influence of religion – still winds its way into family relationships, gift buying, and secular literacy campaigns. The profane status of writing, with its origins in the same hierarchical structures, survives even as writing has been absorbed steadily into the interests of the economy, sanctioned more regularly in school, and, with the mass acquisition of computers that was just beginning at the end of the twentieth century, practiced as a form of information gathering and entertainment. Always associated with commercialism, writing now is sponsored most heavily by keyboard-driven technologies and takes place on the commercialized surfaces of the Internet. However it may turn out that new relationships emerge between writing and reading (and other communication systems), the histories of their differential sponsorship will continue to inhabit encounters in big and small ways. Student Fran Kaplan, born in 1965 near Washington, D.C., recalled how, at age seven or eight, she read for the first time the heavily censored FBI file of her father, an attorney disbarred during the McCarthy investigations. The only thing she could remember about the conversation afterward was her father telling her that she should always put a date on anything she wrote, "a compulsion," she said, "that has stayed with me." To understand better what literacy instruction represents to people in the future, it will be important to remember the settings in which knowledge about reading and writing have come to people. We must understand better the histories that are compelling literacy as it is lived.

6

THE MEANS OF PRODUCTION

Literacy and Stratification at the Twenty-First Century

Despite expanding democracy in educational chances, access and reward for literacy still travel along dividing lines by region, wealth, and prerogative. National tests of reading and writing performance routinely turn up correlations between higher literacy achievement and higher socioeconomic status. And although literacy among America's racial minorities rose steadily across the twentieth century, gaps by race endure.[1] At least in the aggregate, literacy clusters with material and political privilege. It favors the richer over the poorer, the freer over the jailed, the well connected over the newly arrived or the left out. These disparities have always existed in the history of literacy, but they took on new connotations at the start of the twenty-first century as the status of literacy itself grew so high, so central to economic and political viability. Where once literate skill would merely have confirmed social advantage, it is, under current economic conditions, a growing resource in social advantage itself.[2] On the one hand, this intensifying worth of literacy brings renewed possibility to the democratic hope in public education that more equal distribution of literate skill can moderate the effects of inequality in wealth and civil rights. But, as a matter of fact, the advantage of literate skill is helping to aggravate social inequity. Just, as it seems, the rich get richer, the literate get more literate.

Analysis of this problem frequently focuses on the school or on relationships between schools and families. According to some critics, disparities in literacy achievement are proof of the school's complicity in

169

maintaining inequality. Schools, they suggest, devise curriculum and assessment tools that protect society's pecking order and justify its reward system. Other observers use this clustering of literacy with social advantage not to question what is happening in school but to explain it. Students' family backgrounds – namely, the education and income of their parents – are treated on their face as sources of advantage or disadvantage for a student, and differences in socioeconomic status are used to make sense of differences in academic performance. Middle-class families are perceived on the whole as more school-oriented, and that explains why their children enjoy better success in school. Children from families with poor earnings or poor understanding of school culture are more poorly prepared, and that explains their relative underachievement.[3] For school apologists, differences in literacy achievement by race and class serve to rationalize the status quo. If apples don't fall far from trees or cream rises to the top, then schools can only do so much, or so that thinking goes. School activists, on the other hand, often regard these disparities as a call to intervene in the families of the underperformers to help them negotiate the institution of the school in their children's interests. Hence the popularity of family literacy programs that draw lower-income and lower-skilled parents into school-sanctioned literacy practices. Despite this range of interpretations around the same set of facts, however, debates and deliberations generally give primary attention to relationships between schools and individual students or schools and individual homes.[4]

This chapter, like earlier ones, seeks a broader angle of investigation from which to explore issues of access, proficiency, and reward in literacy learning. Correlations of literacy performance with individual socioeconomic status capture yet, in their shorthand way, obscure larger conditions that lie behind differential outcomes in literacy achievement. Literacy learning, in school and out, takes place within systems of unequal subsidy and unequal reward – systems that range beyond the influence of any individual family's assets, beyond any one pile of cultural capital that a student or a home might accumulate.[5] Gaining a clearer vision of how these larger historical and economic conditions bear on acts of literacy learning can clarify why literacy remains so susceptible to the complex effects of economic inequity and political discrimination. It also may suggest alternative positions that schools can take up in relationship to their society to strengthen their democratizing influence in literacy and learning.

My argument begins again, as it has in earlier chapters, with a focus on the economic changes that occurred in the last half of the twentieth century, the move into what is often called the Information Age or the Knowledge Economy. In this transformation, economic production came to center less on making things and more on generating new knowledge and exchanging, manipulating, or exploiting information. As we know, much educational discussion gestures toward this change as an incentive, indeed an imperative, for raising achievement in reading, writing, and other symbol-wielding skills. However, we have paid less attention to the effects of these economic changes on the status of literacy more broadly as it becomes integral to economic relations, and as it is pulled deeply into the engines of productivity and profit. What happens when literacy itself is capitalized as a productive force? And what impact does such investment have on the course of individual literacy learning?

Literacy takes on unusual status in an information economy. It is a form of labor power, to be sure, a human skill, an input. Yet it also is an output, a product of varying value in use and exchange. The transformation of the American labor force from principally manufacturing in the 1940s to principally knowledge production and control by the 1980s gauges the ascending role of literacy as both labor input and product output, its increasing centrality in both production and consumption.[6] Further, however, literacy is also a means of production – that is, a tool, an instrument, a technology. We can feel the capitalization of this dimension of literacy in the unprecedented pace of development and change in communication technologies, particularly computers, over the last several decades. As profits have come to depend on making or moving information more quickly, more cheaply, more powerfully, or more meaningfully, investment in literacy-based instruments has surged.[7] Finally, it is not too farfetched to regard literacy as a kind of raw material, an element or constituent in production. If this economy buys and sells written and spoken words, graphs, charts, images, software, and many other symbolic products, these products themselves are often formulated out of rawer but still symbolic materials: Budgets are made of numbers; forecasts, out of trends; insurance policies, out of actuarial tables; texts, in general, out of other texts. Indeed, one of the key features of an advancing information economy is that its raw materials are more and more highly processed to begin with. Many people now work at making representations out of other representations. So, to reiterate, in an information economy, literacy shows up in all aspects of production: as raw material, as labor power, as an instrument of production, and as product.[8]

This ubiquitous presence of literacy in all modes of production certainly can account for the intensifying pressure for literacy achievement at the start of the twenty-first century. Literacy is the energy supply of the Information Age. This unusual status also illuminates why highly developed literacy skills – or, I should say, skills of a certain sort – can be a source of economic and social advantage (because their worth can be cashed in, as it were, at so many points in the production process), just as it also confirms why illiteracy has become such a thorough liability from the standpoint of economic productivity (because it cuts a person off as supplier, producer, and consumer). It also may help to pinpoint current gaps in literacy achievement as occurring not so much between human skills and an absolute standard but between literacy as a human achievement and literacy as a technological achievement. But my real interest in reflecting on the role of literacy as a productive force is to deepen the gaze into the processes of individual literacy learning and to consider how possibilities for individual literacy achievement are augmented or not by economic forces. How are the means of production by which individuals become literate related to the means of production in a nation's economic system, and particularly to structural changes and developments within that system? As reliance on literacy as a productive force intensifies, investment, exploitation, and innovation around literacy also intensify. How individual literacy learning dovetails (or not) with these larger systems of investment, exploitation, and innovation can give us access into the deeper relationships between literacy achievement and class stratification – that is, the processes by which the richer can have their literacy enriched and the poorer not.

The inquiry into this dynamic begins with two individuals, Raymond Branch and Dora Lopez, whose differences in family background and literacy achievement embody the familiar breakdown along categories of gender, race, and class. Both Raymond Branch and Dora Lopez were born in 1969, he in Silicon Valley in Southern California and she in the Rio Grande Valley in southern Texas. Raymond Branch's grandparents had been farm owners and ranchers. Dora Lopez's grandparents had been migrant farm workers. When they were young children, both Raymond Branch and Dora Lopez moved with their parents to the same city in the upper Midwest, where both their fathers took work at a state university. Raymond Branch's father, who had a doctoral degree from an Ivy League university, was a member of the science faculty. Dora Lopez's father, who had a two-year community college degree in accounting, worked as a shipping and receiving clerk. In 1995, Raymond Branch, at 26, had recently graduated from the university where his father taught. He was a freelance writer of computer software and software documentation. Dora Lopez was, in 1995, at 26 years old, a part-time liberal arts student at the same community college that her parents had attended. She was earning a living by cleaning office buildings in the city's downtown.

During their early teen years, that is, during the early 1980s, both Branch and Lopez undertook projects of self-initiated learning – learning propelled mostly by their own motivations and occurring largely outside of school. They both undertook the learning of a second language. Branch taught himself programming language to write computer software, a skill that neither of his parents had to any great degree. Lopez taught herself to read and write in Spanish, a recovered skill known to her Mexican American parents but not carried forward into her generation. Attending closely to their accounts of this self-initiated learning can expose the wider systems of resources, subsidies, and barriers that influence literacy learning yet often lie outside attention in debates about literacy achievement in school. As in other chapters, the analysis proceeds through an examination of sponsoring agents and primarily attends to how these two individuals described particular processes of self-initiated learning during adolescence.

Branch, a European American, was born, as mentioned above, in 1969 in southern California, the son of a professor father and a real-estate executive mother. He recalled that his first-grade classroom in 1975 was hooked up to a mainframe computer at one of California's elite private universities and that as a youngster, he enjoyed fooling around with computer programming in the company of "real users" in his father's science lab. This access continued uninterrupted when, in the late 1970s, Branch moved with his parents and sister to south central Wisconsin. Branch received his first personal computer as a Christmas present from his parents in 1981, when he was 12 years old, and a modem the year after that. By the mid-1980s, computer hardware and software stores were popping up within a bicycle-ride's distance from where he lived. The stores served the university community and, increasingly, the high-tech companies that were getting established, partly with university help, in that vicinity. As an adolescent, Branch spent his summers roaming these stores, sampling new computer games, joining user groups, swapping pirating information, making contact with founders of some of the first electronic bulletin boards in the nation, and continuing, through reading, writing, and other informal means, to develop his programming techniques. As was mentioned, at the time of our interview in 1995, he held a bachelor's degree and was a self-employed writer of software and software documentation, with clients in both the private sector and the university community.

Lopez, a Mexican American, was born, as was mentioned, in the same year as Branch, 1969, in a Texas border town, where her grandparents, who worked as migrant laborers, lived much of the year. When Lopez was still a baby, she moved with her parents and brother to the same Midwest university town as would Branch's family. They were eventually joined by her grandparents. Her father pursued an accounting degree at a local technical college and worked as a shipping and receiving clerk at the university. Her mother, who also attended technical college briefly, worked part time in a bookstore. In the early 1970s, when the Lopez family made its move to the Midwest, the Mexican American population in the university town was less than 1%. Lopez recalled that the family had to drive 70 miles to a big city to find not only suitable groceries but also Spanish-language newspapers and magazines that carried information of concern and interest to them. (Sometimes, but only when reception was good, they could catch Spanish-language radio programs coming from Chicago, 150 miles away.) When she was 12 years old and before she had access to foreign-language courses in high school, Lopez undertook to teach herself how to read and write in Spanish, something, she said, that neither her brother nor her U.S.-born cousins knew how to do. Although her parents were both literate in Spanish, they did not use written Spanish very much in their household, in their schooling, or in their work.

Lopez began to learn written Spanish on her own, first by reading. She had been exposed to some Spanish-language children's books earlier in her life, books that her mother had purchased while working at a campus bookstore. Later, Lopez started teaching herself how to write, composing letters and sometimes writing poetry. She sought out novels by South American and Mexican writers, and she practiced her written Spanish by corresponding with distant relatives and friends. She said she would try reading and writing on the basis of her phonemic sense of spoken Spanish, and then later would check her accuracy with her mother. She recalled the process this way:

> I learned by reading first. I read phonetically. The way I spoke is the way I figured it was said, and later on, I asked either my mother or somebody who knew Spanish if that was right. Then, writing, I tried to write phonetically, the way you hear it, then eventually you catch on to the little tricks you got in there. I practiced for a long time, and then I would write letters to my cousins in Mexico. I also write to Colombia, to a friend of mine. The poetry, I just liked to write. No particular reason. It was my own.

As in the case of Branch, Lopez's general literacy was influenced and supported through her father's education and employment. Her father owned a typewriter, as a result of his college training, which she would use on occasion. And Lopez especially remembered seeing her father writing by hand when she visited him in his mailroom office at the university.

Lopez first encountered computers at the age of 14 when she worked as a teacher's aide in a federally funded summer school program for the elementary-age children of migrant farm workers. The computers were used to help the children come up to grade level in their English reading skills, and Lopez learned to use the computer to run preprogrammed study drills aimed at third- and fourth-grade vocabulary building. After high school graduation, Lopez entered college with the goal of becoming a bilingual social worker. Her father bought her a used word processor that had been advertised for sale by a university student. While in school, Lopez worked as an attendant in a nursing home and, by 19, had become a mother.

At the time of our interview in 1995, Lopez was still pursuing a two-year degree part time. She was finding some outlet for her biliterate skills in her janitorial job, where she performed extra duties as a translator, communicating on her supervisor's behalf with the largely Latina cleaning staff. "I write in Spanish for him," she explained, "what he needs to be translated, like job duties, what he expects them to do, and I write lists for him in English and Spanish."

In Branch's account, we can see behind the scenes of his family's socioeconomic profile. There lies a thick and, to him, relatively accessible economy of institutional and commercial supports that cultivated and subsidized his acquisition of a powerful form of literacy. One might be tempted to say that Branch was born at the right time and lived in the right place – except that Lopez's experience troubles that thought. For Branch, a university town in the 1970s and 1980s provided an information-rich, resource-rich learning environment in which to pursue his version of second-language learning. But for Lopez, a female member of a culturally unsubsidized ethnic minority, the same town at the same time was information- and resource-poor. Although both young people were pursuing projects of self-initiated learning, Branch in computer programming and Lopez in written Spanish, she had to reach much farther afield for the material and communicative systems needed to support her learning. Also, although Branch, as the son of an academic, was subsidized in his learning by some of the most powerful agents of a research university (its laboratories, newest technologies, and most educated personnel), Lopez was subsidized in her learning by what her parents could pull from the peripheral service systems of the university (the mailroom, the bookstore, the secondhand technology market). In these accounts we also can see how the development and eventual economic worth of Branch's literacy skills were underwritten by late twentieth-century transformations in communication technology that created a boomtown need for software and software documentation. Lopez's biliterate abilities developed and paid off much farther down the economic-reward ladder, in government-sponsored summer programs and commercial enterprises that, in the 1990s, were absorbing surplus migrant workers into a low-wage, urban service economy.

To get a better picture of how economic forces work their influence at the scenes of literacy learning, let's consider Branch's detailed account of his initiation into early computer culture during his adolescent years. This account is interesting not only as a window into the literacy practices associated with the early phases of the computer age (to be more exact, the consumer dimensions of the computer age). It also shows how the amplification of Branch's programming skills stemmed from larger contexts of investment, augmentation, and innovation that went on around this form of literacy as a productive force in the economy. We will see in this account lots of evidence of individual motivation on the part of Branch and lots of strategically supportive action on the part of his family. We also will see evidence of an emerging community of programmers and pirates, who, through a variety of communal efforts (some of them illegal), taught themselves how to compose in new forms. However, as the description unfolds, it also will become clear that the impact of these initiatives – personal, familial, social – derives from much larger levels of economic structure and activity. As subsidies flow to computer literacy as a consumer commodity and a productive force of increasing prominence, so flow subsidies to Branch's brand of literacy development. In the following excerpt, Branch recalls returning from a summer enrichment camp in 1980, at the end of his sixth year of elementary school. The program had been held at a distant college campus where, in addition to traditional academic enrichment, he took a course in the computer language Basic. It was at this camp that he wrote his first computer program, an adventure game modeled after a popular commercial version. He recalled this period of development:

> I came back from that class, and, at the time, Atari game machines were the rage. So from October through December, all I did was hound my parents for an Atari for Christmas. I remember distinctly memorizing the size of the Atari box, so I could look under the Christmas tree and see immediately. Christmas morning came and there was no Atari box, so I was all depressed. But I started opening other boxes, and it turned out to be an Apple II computer system. […] At the time, there was a computer store in town called [New Wave] Computing. That's where my computer came from, and they had a selection of games and peripherals. It soon became a habit after school – my friends and I would always stop by [New Wave] and spend a few hours there checking out the computers, talking to the salesmen. We got to be really good friends with them. They'd loan you hardware and so forth, trying to get you addicted to things. […] One of the first little projects I did was to try to rewrite my submarine exploration game on the Apple. Apple had some graphics. I tried to add graphics to it. At the time the only people who had Apples were people who were programmers, too. At the time, [personal] computers weren't made to be used for much. You had to

learn a little about the language to get anything done, so the books that came with [the computer] were fairly good about teaching you Basic and so forth. The way you really learned, though, was probably the same way you really learn to write. And that's by picking apart other people's published work. If there's a game that you like, you look at it. Find out how the person did what they did, and then you duplicate that. [...] There was a company called Beagle Brothers, which developed this excellent software for the Apple II, and they had a number of published charts with computer information about the Apple II, just little topics and tricks. So there was a pretty good community there. So there were quite a few publications. Beagle Brothers had what's called utility software – software to help you write programs. The games generally were copy-protected to prevent you from looking at them. So the first thing you had to learn is how to pirate software, so that not only could you look at the code but you could also copy the program for your friends. That was what everybody did back then. Usually, when you had a program that had been cracked by someone else, they usually included a little note about how they cracked it. I got pirated materials from trading with friends that had Apple IIs, and there were a fair number of people. You'd meet them through user groups. They advertised in the computer stores. The first people to buy computers were generally either parents trying to get their kids involved, and then the kids immediately took to the computers, or else they were older, usually older men that just liked the hobby, liked to tinker. It was kind of a narrow bunch but a colorful bunch. [...] When I got the modem, it was very liberating at the time, when I was fourteen or whatever. At the time, there were only about three or four places [in town] that you could call and log into them. But it sped things up considerably. I could transfer software to people in Minnesota or Washington or whatever. There were new ways to transmit data and communicate with people that you may not know and communicate ideas back and forth, completely unrestricted, unrestrained.

This is a fascinating account of the maverick days of early computer aficionados, the gamers and pirates, principally male, many young, who claimed early control over programming languages largely as a form of entertainment and developed early versions of networked communication practices that would eventually engulf the nation. Adventure games were made more adventurous by the challenge of cracking the programming code and gaining bragging rights as well as solidarity by sharing illicit results with fellow pirates. Branch's access to this world owed in no small part to surplus wealth within his family that permitted the purchase of relatively expensive equipment that wasn't "made to be used for much." At the same time, however, the growth and reach of Branch's skills owed more profoundly to the commercial growth in computer hardware and software products orchestrated by the mutually sustaining activity of hardware manufacturers, software manufacturers, and retail outlets – not to mention the university–government relationships through which the Internet was made and maintained. New Wave Computing was a site where consumer desires were not only stimulated but organized into product-loyal communities and ratified by a steady stream of written aids. In this recollection, we see how, at least in this period of development, the expansion of the computer market depended on the expansion of technological skills among users and their growing "addiction" to the functions of the computer. This early group of retrofitted ham operators and young, middle-class gamers helped to consolidate capital and push out the tendrils of networked communication that would, over the succeeding 10 years, entrench the Internet as a key mechanism in workplaces, homes, and schools. In on the ground floor, Branch was literally helping to build the economic expansion that would subsidize and reward him as an adult.

By the time Branch enrolled in the university in the late 1980s, computer technology was widely distributed throughout the campus community. In addition to putting personal computers at the desk of every faculty member and many support staff, the university was investing quickly and heavily in developing a central computing center where users could get advice and technical help. The university also produced its own Internet software, including e-mail services, distributed free to students, faculty, and permanent white-collar staff. It sold computer hardware and software at deep academic discount to qualified buyers. Branch took a part-time job at the computing center while a student and worked there briefly full time following graduation. He wrote software documentation, experimented with the latest equipment that the university received as complimentary sales promotions, and started picking up freelance work from which he would eventually launch his own business. He also coauthored with his father some original software applications that his father used in teaching and research. Although, ironically, too underprepared in mathematics to major in computer science, Branch took as many electives as he could in the computer science department.

Before continuing to probe the means by which Branch's literacy development was subsidized as part of economic production, it is necessary to explore the very different experience of Lopez as she set about her project of self-initiated literacy learning. One of the most pronounced differences pertains to the social and economic status of the second language to which Lopez dedicated her learning. In Branch's world, the language of computer programming enjoyed stable, in fact, escalating value and status across many of the contexts through which he traveled, including his home, the science laboratories in California, the summer enrichment camp, the retail outlets, the user groups, and the university where he studied and worked. For Lopez, the value and status of Spanish–English biliteracy fluctuated dramatically as she moved between the private and the public spheres. Spanish had high status in her family context, where it served as the vital medium of communication between older and young generations. Lopez also earned respect and distinction within the extended family because of her highly developed skills in Spanish and her interest in teaching it. Lopez explained the role of Spanish in her household:

> My grandfather was living with us, so my mom said we had to speak Spanish in the house because, one, she didn't want us to forget our language, and, two, because my grandfather didn't understand English. My grandmother on my father's side lived outside the house, but everybody had to speak Spanish to her. Other members of the family primarily speak Spanish at home. Some English, but primarily Spanish. But most of their kids speak more English than Spanish, and they don't comprehend the Spanish language very well. I'm the only who can really comprehend both. I carry it on with my children. My children speak Spanish and English. I take care of my niece, usually five days a week, and her mother is Caucasian. She prefers me to speak to [the child] in Spanish so that she can have her second language, too. In my family, I am the most fluent of the nieces and nephews. There are about twenty of us. I am the most fluent.

At the same time, as was mentioned above, Spanish was nearly inaudible and invisible in the larger community to which the Lopez family had moved. It was not a significant productive force in the economy. There was little advantage at first for local shops to carry materials – including literacy materials – that catered to Spanish-speaking cultures, although incentive increased as the city's Latino population increased sharply in the 1990s. The industry of Spanish–English biliteracy was primarily confined to nonprofit social service agencies and government programs that dealt with the social effects of poverty and dislocation. Translators were sought by the police department, courts, government entitlement programs, and some community organizations. Bilingual teachers were hired in small migrant education programs and in some ESL (English as a Second Language) programs in area schools. Almost all of these positions required post-secondary certification (and it was to a position as a bilingual social worker that Lopez aspired). However, this industry – decentralized, not for profit, and usually minimally funded – generated few spin-off activities or products from which opportunity for literacy learning could be sponsored.

As Lopez entered public high school in the late 1980s, she gained access to formal course work in Spanish, enrolling in it in each of her four years of high school.[9] But here, too, status of language and speaker was not consistent with other contexts. For one thing, Spanish was taught as a "foreign" language. For another, foreign-language courses were taken mostly by Anglo college-prep students, some of whom eyed with suspicion the presence of Spanish-heritage students in the classes. More than a little defensiveness lingered as Lopez talked about her Spanish classes in high school: "I took the courses for my own personal use," she said, "just to advance my reading and writing skills and comprehension skills." She went on to add, "It wasn't because of an easy A. It's hard work to speak and write properly."[10]

Across Lopez's life, Spanish–English bilingualism fluctuated as an unstable currency as the family migrated from Texas to Wisconsin and as she moved between private and public spheres. Unlike for Branch, the legitimacy of her project of self-initiated literacy learning was unsubstantiated in the broader economic life of the community in which she lived. These conditions were reflected in the relative isolation and low-tech support in which Lopez pursued her biliterate learning. No "user group" was present to serve as a catalyst for learning or a conduit for materials – no technological infrastructure beyond primarily solitary reading and writing with pens, papers, and an occasional book from the bookstore. We might note that it is not the lack of family support for her literacy learning – but the fact that family was the only source of support – that distinguishes the experience of Lopez so sharply from that of Branch. Her network for Spanish literacy learning was sustained not by a modem connection to anywhere but only by her connections, via mail, with willing relatives and friends. This lack of substantiation and wider subsidy reverberated in her economic prospects, as she translated cleaning chores from English-speaking boss to Spanish-speaking laborers. That is, the outlets for her biliteracy were shaped by the low status given to Spanish and its native speakers, part of a general economic devaluation that put Latinas as a group on one of the lowest rungs of the economic reward ladder.[11]

A comparison of the informal literacy learning efforts of Raymond Branch and Dora Lopez suggests not merely how one social group's literacy practices may differ from another but how everybody's literate practices are operating in an economic structure that affects opportunity and reward. Through the economic structure come different access routes, different degrees of sponsoring power, and different scales of monetary worth to the practices in use. This is not to say that the value of reading and writing is confined to potential monetary rewards. (Neither Branch nor Lopez pursued learning for those reasons.) But it is to say that people who labor equally to acquire literacy do so under systems of unequal subsidy and unequal compensation. Economic values circulate along with systems of literacy sponsorship, affecting, among other things, the relative rarity and power of literacy opportunities. Rarity, as these two case studies suggest, pertains in both senses of that word. For Branch, an unusually early inclusion in the adventures of computer programming gave him a rarified advantage in developing his "second language" skills. For Dora Lopez, on the other hand, transplanted from the Texas border to an overwhelmingly Anglo culture in the upper Midwest, supports for developing her second-language skills were as rare a commodity to find as tortillas at that time in the local grocery store. And as for power of opportunity, we see that the critical differences between Branch and Lopez are not in what the individuals did for themselves or in what their families did for their children. In these two cases, those efforts are uncannily similar. Rather, the difference is that in Branch's case, those efforts were able to pull on so many other powerful agents – so many other "peripherals," to borrow a term. Not only could Branch's parents afford to buy him expensive computer equipment but also the technology itself was becoming worth so much more in his society and was being so heavily subsidized by academic and commercial agents in his sphere. As a learner, he reaped rewards of those subsidies secondhand. He was positioned to have his own literacy augmented when literacy as a productive force was augmented as part of economic growth. No such level of endowment supported the Spanish language where Lopez was growing up, and opportunity structures for her preferred versions of learning were more limited, fragile, and fraught with contradiction. If Branch reaped secondhand benefits from the economic structure, Lopez reaped secondhand liabilities as that same economic structure suppressed opportunities for augmentation.

Probing relationships between the means of individual literacy production and the means of economic production can bring deeper insight into configurations of inequity and class stratification that are affecting the new grounds of literacy development: particularly access to computer technology. And it is to the different ways in which Branch and Lopez came in contact with computers that the discussion now turns. Knowing programming languages, like knowing Spanish, may not – at least not yet – be a universally required component of American literacy. But knowing how to use computers as a communication tool is. Young Americans need to learn how to mediate their writing and reading through computer technology to gain access to information, audiences, voices, and genres of increasing social and economic importance. Yet, it is no surprise that access to computers and control over them is unequally distributed in the same ways that traditional literacy has been unequally distributed: by income, race, region, and occupation.[12] Understanding the deep structural sources of that inequity is important for finding solutions to it.

In the case of Branch and Lopez, the differences in their encounters with computers are keen and telling. Whereas Branch experienced computers first in the context of play, Lopez experienced them first in the context of work, as a teacher's aide in a summer school program. Whereas Branch learned to program in Basic in his academic enrichment program, the children in the migrant summer program practiced recognizing English antonyms and synonyms. When Branch visited his father at work at a university, he had access to the latest hardware and software at the disposal of elite universities and their science labs. When Dora Lopez visited her father at work at same university, there was no computer in his basement office. As an entry-level shipping clerk, Mr. Lopez was not issued a computer, had no e-mail address, and no Internet access. Nor could Mr. Lopez benefit from the free computer instruction sessions regularly offered to faculty and white-collar staff. Family finances did not allow him to take advantage of university discounts offered in the purchase of new computers. When he bought his daughter a word processor, it was purchased privately rather than through the university's technical support center, and the secondhand equipment came to Dora Lopez without a user manual. Whereas Branch described his experience with computers as "very liberating," Dora Lopez was still trying to figure out how her word processor worked. "I've been trying to get ahold of a manual so that I can use the whole system," she explained, "but I still don't know how to use it yet. I'm just messing with it, just figuring it out."

In these small details of ordinary existence are writ large histories of class discrepancy and racial discrimination that continue to condition literacy achievement. As landowners in an earlier point in the twentieth century, Branch's grandparents had some control over the means by which agricultural-based wealth was produced. By their grandchild's time, productive power for this social class had shifted from land to professional status, knowledge, and skills. We could see in Branch's account how his parents orchestrated resources to assist where they could in helping the family keep step with the society's dominant productive forces.[13] However, this effort was not merely – and not even mostly – a family accomplishment. The effort drew copiously from public assets, especially material and intellectual assets of a state university, that put Branch near the core of the production of computer knowledge and skills. As an entrepreneurial programmer at age 26, he had won some degree of ownership over the productive forces of the new economy and enjoyed some ownership over his own labor. Unlike Branch, Dora Lopez was a descendent of people historically dispossessed of land and capital and unentitled to first-class political and education rights. Although recent generations of Mexican Americans in Wisconsin have shifted from migrant farm labor to light manufacturing and, lately, to small business and social service, they remain overrepresented in low-wage labor and underrepresented in property ownership. Although education levels are rising in increments, class disadvantage and dispossession around the means of production persist. As with the word processor without the manual, Lopez cannot yet use the "whole system" of her literacy in a way that is available to Branch.

This analysis has brought attention to the status of literacy as not merely an individual skill or a cultural practice but as an economic resource, as an object of development, investment, and exploitation around which both value and competition intensify. Recognizing the integral role of literacy in both economic production and consumption, its strange and unique status as a technology, a process, a product, a form of work and play, a currency, an energy source, all in one, expands the range in which individual literacy learning and achievement can be analyzed. Branch and Lopez both took advantage of public education, both exerted individual initiative and worked hard, and both enjoyed some parental support of their literacy learning – the core concerns of most education policy. However, taking a step back into the larger economic and social contexts of their lives reveals influences from other spheres that have palpable effects on their literacy development.

For one thing, in these times, consumer status matters a great deal in literacy experience. It was as a target of computer retailers that Branch saw his programming abilities augmented. Although his parents underwrote the cost of the technology, his demographic status in the consumer market as a young, white, affluent male provided essential stimulation. For Lopez, on the other hand, as with many members of ethnic and cultural minorities, there was no equivalent market to amplify her learning, as the surrounding economy found little incentive to cater to her desires. Even when she wanted to buy, the products often were not available. On a wider scale, Branch lived in a part of town where commercial supports for computer users abounded along with, as a matter of fact, bookstores and public libraries. Lopez, her parents, and her children lived in low-cost housing districts, where computers, bookstores, and libraries were in shorter supply and at a greater distance from them. The commodification of literacy can inflame the effects of discrimination by race and class that are embedded in the social and economic marrow of most communities.

This broader perspective also brings attention to the role of parental work in children's literacy learning, a dimension that is often overlooked in analyses that emphasize parents' roles as readers to children or as surrogate teachers. Neither Lopez nor Branch remembered their mothers or fathers reading to them as young children.[14] However, for these two individuals, as well as for many other people whom I interviewed, parental schooling and work brought books, paper, typewriters, computers, and other literacy materials into the home; made adult reading and writing visible; and provided contact with workplaces where literacy was in use. In fact, it may be parents' work more than their level of education that accounts for socioeconomic differences in children's literacy achievement. As parents with higher education win the access, autonomy, and closer proximity to the means of production that often accompany professional status, they can divert institutional resources and knowledge more readily into opportunities for their children. Many people I interviewed whose parents held high-skill or supervisory positions were sustained beneficiaries of capitalization around literacy that was occurring in their parents' workplaces. This is how stratified work reinforces stratified literacy, as we see so dramatically in the cases of Branch and Lopez. Although universities have been incubators for the technologies, skills, and knowledge at the base of today's economy, the benefits of those developments are stratified among the university workforce. As labor practices stratify adult access to communication technologies, they perpetuate inequities that reverberate in the lives of children. This stratification has been exacerbated by the infusion of capital into developing computer skills and stimulating computer purchases among the professional class – an advantage so profound it will contribute to inequities for generations to come.

Further, this analysis illuminates what may be the key difference in the literacy learning experiences of Lopez and Branch: that is, the relative stability or instability in value to which their literacy learning is subject, especially as the two moved between the private sphere of the home and the public sphere of institutions and commercial life. For Branch much more than for Lopez, the value of the skills he was learning stayed intact as he moved across multiple contexts. As we have seen, for Lopez, there were wide discrepancies in the valuing systems through which she moved on her path to learning. The value of the Spanish language fluctuated as she traveled in and out of family contexts. Spanish enjoyed high value and her biliteracy enjoyed high status in the family sphere. But finding nourishment for the Spanish language and for biliteracy was difficult for family members in the wider spheres in which they traveled. Although her parents spoke Spanish at home, they could not use Spanish, spoken or written, as part of their work. Its use was unrewarded. Likewise, Lopez's biliterate skills had limited outlets in her play, in her work, in her school, and in relations with the local economy. On a macrolevel, her chances for applying her biliteracy (and being rewarded for it) were suppressed generally by the economic devaluation that bore down on Latina workers in her city. Relatively lower investment in Spanish–English biliteracy followed her into her higher education, where investments in Spanish departments (and for that matter, departments of social work) did not match investments in computer science and other technical fields.[15] As a result, the legitimacy of her project was not reflected in the broader community in which she lived, and material reward was still elusive.

By looking at the day-to-day efforts of literacy learners and their day-to-day contacts with public institutions and other social infrastructures, we can see more explicitly how economic inequality connects to outcomes in literacy and literacy achievement. There was, for Branch, a greater consistency and congruity in the valuing systems through which he moved on his path to learning. The computer languages he sought, the locations at which he learned, and his status as a white man all had high-end value. He acquired his computer skills at a time when those skills were escalating in exploitability. He could use his second language at play, at work, in school, in relations with his parents, and in relations with the local economy. As a result, his form of literacy was actualized to a full capacity; it enjoyed a broad legitimacy.

Recent literacy studies have drawn attention to how middle-class students enjoy a higher congruity between the literacy practices of their home and the literacy practices of their school, an advantage that is less often in place for poor and working-class students.[16] If these case studies are a guide, such congruity and, more troubling, such incongruity, can extend far beyond the school–home relationship. We must look to broader histories of economic relations to understand the contexts in which efforts at literacy learning are conducted. As children raised in the last quarter of the twentieth century, both Branch and Lopez belonged to families that were adjusting to economic transformation. Lopez's family especially made a significant change as her parents broke with the life of the field, migrated north, pursued post-secondary education, and performed forms of primarily mental rather than physical service. However, we can see how both a legacy of dispossession and the rapid pace of economic transformation translate into new rounds of disadvantage. The traditional forms of print literacy with which the Lopez family finally was entitled to work – and could put at a daughter's disposal – were deflating in both educational and economic power as investments moved into computer literacy.

In undertaking this analysis, I do not wish to imply that Branch enjoyed perfect stability and ease or that Lopez endured perfect instability and hardship in self-initiated literacy learning. Nor do I wish to suggest that their life outcomes are inevitable or, for that matter, at all set. Given all the turbulence that accompanies intensified competition in the computer industry, technology workers face a steady demand to upgrade knowledge and skills, and the threat of obsolescence looms. And as the Latino population in the United States burgeons, Spanish–English biliteracy may become more of a coin of the realm such that Lopez's skills will escalate in value and find more opportunities for development and reward.

However, in the meantime, I do want to suggest that this extended case analysis offers lessons for schools and educators concerned with democratizing literacy and learning. The more schools find themselves replicating market interests within their institutional practices, the more they may disadvantage the already economically disadvantaged. As democratic institutions, schools must serve to stabilize and attempt to augment the value and development of all forms of literacy learning. Although there is understandable pressure for schools to march in step with productive forces, equity asks that we march in step with the needs of all students, to be responsive to their past histories and current aspirations.[17] It also requires ongoing management of resources, including curriculum, staff, equipment, materials, time, space, and other forms of subsidy, to compensate within the school for economic inequality beyond the school. Schools must make special efforts to provide for minority constituents the kinds of reading materials and other cultural products that consumer markets overlook and must devise language curriculums that better acknowledge the multilingual conditions in which English literacy finds its meaning for many Americans. Finally, these two case studies ask that we all look hard at the institutions where we teach, study, or work to think about access for literacy in its broadest terms. Equal opportunity extends beyond the mere potential for admission or employment and involves all of the systems of value that circulate in institutions. In its investment decisions, course offerings, and labor practices, the public university that employed the fathers of Raymond Branch and Dora Lopez reflected – rather than rebalanced – the disparities that the two experienced on the outside.[18] A comprehensive literacy policy must include efforts to democratize access to the formidable wealth of technological and symbolic resources that cluster in schools, government buildings, and workplaces – in fact, in all of the nation's great foundries of literacy production.

CONCLUSION

Literacy in American Lives

In 1923, in the center of Wisconsin's dairy region, Sidney Vopat's father turned his blacksmith shop into a car dealership. A few years later, he convinced his son, then in high school, to enroll in a business course offered by a correspondence school out of Chicago so that Sidney could learn how to keep records and communicate on his father's behalf with Ford Motor Company. "The old man could outsell anybody," Vopat recalled, "but he wasn't too good at penmanship."

This recollection carries many of the major formations of literacy and literacy learning of the twentieth century. First and foremost is the sheer acceleration of economic and technological change that courses through American lives. In the opening decades of the twentieth century, Vopat's father, a man with a fourth-grade education, hammered out horseshoes and made his own tools on an anvil in a shop that he owned in a small crossroads town in the rural Midwest. By the 1920s, his shop was a franchise for Model T's, then Whippets, then Chryslers, and, by the 1950s, Vopat's father would be dealing television antennas. Turbulent economic and technological changes force changes in the nature of work, rearrangements in systems of communication and social relations, and fluctuation in the value of human skills. With the unique kinds of economic and technological changes of the twentieth century, those fluctuations came especially to affect the value of literacy. Demands on reading and writing rose sharply. Rapid-process production, technological innovation, modern weaponry, corporate consolidation, the growth of consumerism, the rise in knowledge industries, and the spread of computer technology all made

controlling and communicating words and other symbols vital to the production of profit. To an unprecedented extent, literacy became integral to
economic competition and, as a consequence, became one of the human
skills most vulnerable to its effects.

This changing status of literacy reverberated in Vopat's adolescent
encounters with it. For one thing, he became the first man in his family
whose literacy and schooling would be needed for family well-being. But
beyond that, competition around the resources of literacy was bringing a
proliferation of sponsors – agents with vested interest in promoting, shaping, buying, selling, or suppressing literate skill. Sponsors were spilling
beyond the local school, church, and newspaper, those institutions out of
which had come an earlier, serviceable literacy. Sponsors of literacy
became more diversified, distant, sometimes abstract, eventually ubiquitous, yet often unstable. Change in the status of literacy and the sponsors
that it attracted captured a learner like Vopat in odd ideological contradictions and contexts of mixed meanings and values. His father recruited
him into the role of scribe through the fading principles of an agrarian
family economy, a communal economy that divided its labor and pooled
its assets. Yet through that role, Vopat fell into literacy practices linked to
economic forces that were destroying that way of agrarian life and its view
of literate skill. In such odd amalgamations of literacy sponsorship, a for-
profit business school in Chicago could reach by mail order a teenager living in a hamlet too small to have its own post office. And Vopat could
become one of many customers willing to pay to transform penmanship
learned in a one-room country school into marks that would be accountable to America's great corporate bureaucracies.

Literacy became a key resource, a raw material, for the American economy of the twentieth century, and that in turn has had untold impact on
the ways that literacy is accessed, learned, and rewarded – it affects the
materials we use for literacy, the routes we have or don't have to learning
it, the public meanings that are ascribed to it, the social inequities that
cling to it. This is not to imply that people pursue literacy only as a job
skill or that being literate ensures rewarding work. Neither was true for
many, if not most, of the people whose lives are represented here. It is to
say that the powers of a basic mass literacy, which developed out of
Protestant evangelizing and common schools of the nineteenth century,
became an irresistible energy source – a public utility – that was harnessed
for American capitalism in the twentieth century. Although literacy levels
at the start of the twentieth century generally surpassed the reading and
writing requirements of most jobs of that day,[1] such a surplus of human
potential enabled economic transformations that would quickly alter

ratios of literacy's supply and demand. First as consumers and then as producers, American literates became fuel for the information economy. And out of the drives of that economy, its need for always better, faster, stronger flows of information, came the invention of technologies whose demands now threaten to swamp the human capacity to keep pace.

Economic development became integral to literacy development, and that is because literacy development became integral to economic gain. The entwining of literacy with profit and exploitation reminds us that literacy problems in these times stem mostly from the successes – maybe we could say the excesses – of literacy, rather than failures. Only a population fairly highly skilled to begin with could make the current economy viable. At the same time, however, the direct entanglement of literacy with money making also makes it more vulnerable than ever before to the restless logics of capitalist competition. If the banner of Christian salvation or American democracy under which literacy was earlier taught provided – in all of its hypocrisy – at least some moral imperative to include everyone, no such imperative exists – not even in hypocritical form – under the rules of efficiency and productivity. Once the economy secures enough of a certain kind of literacy to move on, it does, leaving people (and places) behind.[2]

In his important book, *The Great Transformation,* Karl Polanyi (1944) argued that until the end of the nineteenth century, economic relations within and between countries were used to enhance the social and political domains. Material assets had value only in terms of what they could do to strengthen social ties or consolidate political interests and had no real worth separate from these spheres. However, he suggested, this relationship reversed with the rise of market economies, which imposed cash value on everything and made production incidental to buying and selling. Everything took on money value. Everything became exchangeable. So powerfully did this new economic system define its own rules and develop its own institutions that it separated from the social and political systems and often made them answerable to it. In this transformation, he suggested, the labor of free human beings became, for the first time in history, a sheer commodity to be bought and sold along with everything else.

The history of literacy runs in parallel to these developments. For much of its career, literacy in the United States found its value principally in social and political contexts rather than economic ones – in what several historians have called the moral economy. Not an end in itself, literacy was a useful mechanism for religious initiation and nation building, a means to assimilate people into dominant modes of conduct and beliefs.[3] The emblematic value of literacy was at least as important as its practical value, as its presence was a signal that a certain kind of socialization – a certain kind of capitulation – had occurred. As Graff (1979) and others have shown, literacy did begin to be coopted more aggressively into the needs of an industrializing economy toward the end of the nineteenth century. However, its value at that time continued to reside mostly in its socializing power, including its capacity to assist in the assimilation of immigrants and to sort and gatekeep in such a way that access and reward for literacy continued to favor the entrenched. Throughout this economic transition, literacy retained its connections to tradition and to social conformity and stability. As it linked citizens to an official cultural past, traditional knowledge, and centralized authority, literacy served as a counterbalance to the social disruptions and instabilities that industrialism was introducing. Although reading and writing were emerging as forms of skilled labor, literacy remained peripheral to most work. In short, for most of the history of literacy, its value remained only indirectly instrumental – going through the rigors of becoming literate mattered more than being able to trade on it (in fact, the more literate you were, the less you were likely to have to trade on it). Like the economic sphere in premarket economies, literacy was deeply embedded in the forms and functions of cultural cohesion. Its practices, meanings, materials, and effects derived mainly from its conservative and conserving role.

However, as the rise of the market economy rearranged relationships among economic, social, and political spheres, it brought radical pressures to bear on literacy. Literacy became directly and deeply implicated in economic life for many mutually reinforcing reasons. Buying and selling involved many more people in recording, moving, and promoting information; readers became targets both as audiences for advertising and as purchasers of literacy-based commodities. Although always an aspect of literacy in American society, its economic meanings surged prominently as the twentieth century unfolded.[4] At the same time, a market mentality was helping to separate out forms of human resources, including literacy skills, as commodities in themselves. Labor came to be treated as a cost in production rather than a value added during production. In increasing numbers, people found their mental and scribal skills rated and tagged for market to employers. Just as the economic sphere unmoored from the laws and logic of social control, literacy, too, gained more recognizable status as a productive force within the new system.

These developments tied literacy less to tradition and social stability and more to competition and change. Instead of serving as a counterbalance during periods of excessive or rapid economic transformation, literacy came to play an integral role in transformation; it became a major catalyst for changes in communicative and economic relations. As the original "information processors," human beings in technological societies saw the basic abilities to read and write drawn deeply into the assumptions of work. And, like other technologies vital to an information economy, forms of reading and writing were subject to rounds of obsolescence, upgrades, overhauls, augmentations, rearrangements, and replacements.

Of course, it might rightly be observed that literacy has always stimulated cultural disruption, especially to those on whom it has been imposed. And wherever and whenever new uses and technologies of writing have occurred, they have created new social circuits, affected the status of old ones, and set off other, far-reaching reverberations in intellectual and material life (Martin, 1994). However, in the twentieth century, the alliance of literacy with economic change intensified, the pace of change quickened, and the impact of the association broadened to affect more people than ever before. It would be overreaching to make literacy the cause of all the economic and social changes of the twentieth century – just as it is overreaching to make literacy the solution for all of the United States' economic and social problems. On the other hand, it would be equally wrong to underestimate the role of literacy as an enabling mechanism for much of what has happened – especially as literacy came to be capitalized as a profit-bearing resource. It especially would be wrong to underestimate the pressures that these developments have brought to bear on contemporary literacy learning.

I have tried in this book to trace the impact of these pressures on the lives of ordinary Americans, particularly as the changing status of literacy forced adaptations in the means and methods of literacy learning. Throughout the past century, with nearly every new generation, learning to read and write has meant learning to read and write for new reasons and often under new auspices. Literacy learning became part of a wider response to changes affecting individuals, their families, and their communities. Martha Day, the turn-of-the-century farmer's daughter introduced in Chapter 1, was raised in a household in which local newspapers, farm journals, and craft and canning magazines integrated the family into consumer society, fed the family's progressive identity, and stimulated Day to join other better-schooled young people in migrating to the city. There, as an agricultural journalist, Day abstracted her family farm background into written products that were, at least for a while, of commercial value to her employers. Across four generations of the May family, who remained in one geographical location through the entire twentieth century, we could see the meanings of reading and writing changing as the region was transformed by the impact of knowledge industries. A great-grandmother who, as a child, wrote on chalk slates for "no real reason" experienced literacy principally as a backward-glancing practice, tied to maintaining local and well-repeated ways of life. A great-grandson, as a child, experienced literacy principally as a multipurpose, multigenre practice taking place in a propelling stream of instruments, surfaces, audiences, and demands.

The changing status of literacy within economic production and competition did not necessarily dislodge literacy's older orders. The goodness of reading, the shame of poor spelling or handwriting, and the pride of cultivated taste, all remnant features of an earlier "moral economy" of literacy, continued to circulate in resilient and convoluted ways, mixing with newer incentives and values. The intrinsic tenacity of literacy to preserve – best of all, to preserve itself – kept older traditions around, piling up at the scenes of literacy learning, circulating latently, sometimes even carried in on the force of new practices or the appearance of new sponsors. These legacies of literacy, as Graff (1986) has called them, could make encounters with reading or writing especially opaque, resistant at times to the very contexts in which the encounters occurred. At other times, these legacies of literacy's older orders could serve as welcome stabilizers for those surviving disorienting change or chronic exclusion.

Excavating memories of how people learned to read and write excavates the transformations of literacy within the lived life. Competitions over the powers of literacy – old and new – animate the contexts of literacy learning and enter deeply into the processes of literate interpretation. These effects can reach way down into the ways that we see ourselves and others. One woman I interviewed, Ellen Blum, was born in 1947 in a large Eastern city, where her family lived for a time with her maternal grandparents, Jews who had fled persecution in Poland around the time of World War I. English and Yiddish were spoken together in the household. Blum's grandmother, not untypical of Jewish women of her time and station, could neither read nor write in either language. In this household, Blum recalled receiving a persistent message: "It was always important to read the newspaper and keep up with things." She went on to observe:

> At least for my grandparents, the newspaper symbolized literacy. If you could read the newspaper, you could know. Thinking back to Poland, you know, when you read the newspaper, you'd find out, my God, there is a pogrom or some terrible thing happening. So it was a way of staying informed and a sign that you had some kind of intellectual skill. You were really smart if you could read the newspaper. And later on, I was shocked to find out that a newspaper is written at a sixth-grade level.

This is not merely another story about the rising standards for literacy across the twentieth century. It also shows how the cultural heritage of Polish shtetls, including memories of racial persecution and wariness toward bad news, was telescoped into the shared literacy practices of a midcentury American household. Although many of Blum's contemporaries whom I interviewed said they learned to read principally as an act of social conformity, Blum could still, in the 1950s, because of her grandparents' experiences, view reading as a source of social distinction. Yet this status was subject to harsh reinterpretation against scientific measurements of reading that emerged in America by midcentury: readability formulas and precise categories of skills developed by psychologists first to sort American soldiers and then later, to sort Cold War era students.[5] These new bureaucratic definitions of literacy and learnedness eventually infiltrated the popular consciousness, causing Blum to reevaluate – indeed to devalue – her family's literacy.

The commandeering of literacy by economic interests in the twentieth century registers most profoundly in the changing networks through which literacy has been sponsored. Sponsors are embodied in the materials of reading and writing, the institutional aegises and rationales under which learning is carried out, the histories by which practices arrive at the scenes of learning, the causes to which teachers and learners put their efforts, and the advantages, both direct and indirect, that stand to be won by the sponsors themselves. As we have seen, sponsors organize and administer stratified systems of opportunity and access. They raise the stakes for literacy in rivalries for advantage. They certify and often decertify literacy. Sponsors can be benefactors but also extortionists – and sometimes both in the same form. Often (as we saw, for instance, in the case of prison-inmate-turned-legal-technician Johnny Ames), opportunities for literacy learning – including the chance to divert resources for projects of self-development or resistance – open up in the clash among sponsors. These clashes typically are between long-standing residual forms of sponsorship and the new: between the lingering influence of literacy's conservative history and its pressure for change. The to-and-fro of this competition can make openings for literacy learning multiple, various, yet also unstable and frustrating to learners.

The ideological and material complexity that builds up around literacy because of this history cannot be underestimated. As earlier chapters have tried to make clear, individual histories of literacy learning are rife with the confluences of these processes. Marsha Litvin, an affluent homemaker born in 1926, sat on boards of directors of several charities despite lifelong and anguishing difficulties with reading and writing. Recently, after federal civil rights legislation affecting special education was enacted, her youngest son, also a struggling reader, was formally tested by his school to qualify for special tutoring. It was in her dealings with her son's testers and counselors that Marsha Litvin quietly realized that, like her son, she suffered from dyslexia, a condition that had been unnamed and undiagnosed during her own schooling in the 1930s and 1940s. Yi Vang, at seven years old one of the first Hmong immigrants to make his way in the 1980s from a Thai refugee camp to central Wisconsin, learned to read and write English at a school for the deaf and blind, where his rural school district, absent an ESL (English as a Second Language) program, assigned him for his first year of public school. In the 1990s, Carol White, a municipal revenue clerk, took an on-the-job seminar called "Persuasive Communication" so that she could spruce up the door-to-door evangelizing techniques she used as a Jehovah's Witness. This is literacy in American lives.

This book has used the analytical lens of sponsorship as an approach to some of the basic questions affecting education and social policy at the start of the twenty-first century. The first chapter explored the impact of regional economic change on opportunities for literacy learning. We are inundated with warnings about the new economy, the evaporation of low-skill labor, and the need for all workers to become proficient readers, writers, and problem solvers, even as we experience high rates of failure and attrition in public education. This is especially the case in adult basic education and two-year community colleges, where those taking the full brunt of economic restructuring are typically enrolled. Yet literacy curricula rarely begin with the acknowledgment that economic shuffles, merges, and downturns alter the routes to literacy that have been laid down by earlier economies. The chapter treated literacy sponsors within the lives of two women born two generations apart in similar rural communities. Their literacy accounts showed how economic good times can subsidize and develop literate potential whereas economic bad times can dissipate (and disappoint) it. The chapter proposed ways for educators to search for the parts of literacy learning that undergo duress in periods of economic transformation as a way to build more realistic, socially responsive pedagogies.

Chapter 2 explored the impact of rising standards for literacy as they are experienced within the lived life. That chapter followed two working-class men caught up in different elements of a second phenomenon of twentieth-century economic change – the formation of "advanced contractarian society." For a variety of reasons, documents came more and more to regulate a whole host of twentieth-century political, economic, and social relations, including those between management and labor and individuals and the state. Where relations were by nature antagonistic, struggles for power played out over the authoring, interpreting, and controlling of documents. These developments raised the stakes for literacy. Reading and writing became more tightly associated with the exercise of economic and political rights. We saw the consequences of these developments as they played out over a 20-year period in the lives of a union organizer and a prison inmate, both in terms of how the two acquired forms of adult literacy and in terms of how the power of those forms of literacy fluctuated across time. The chapter linked rising standards of literacy directly to competitions that go on among sponsoring agents as they exploit and blunt literate skills as part of struggles for advantage. Through the relationship between individual histories of literacy development and collective histories of literacy sponsorship can be glimpsed the profound distance that many learners must travel today in their pursuit of literacy.

Chapter 3 treated the issue of intergenerational literacy learning. It explored the effect of rapid social and economic change on a family's ability to pass on the practices and skills of reading and writing to younger members. The chapter followed the literacy learning of four generations of one middle-class family. Members of the May family participated in many of the signature movements of the twentieth century – immigrant assimilation, moves from rural to urban to suburban communities, rising education achievement, and transformations in work from agriculture to manufacturing to technical services. Their lives were touched by bilingualism, divorce, the Depression, World War II, the GI Bill, big business and knowledge production, urban sprawl, mass media, and computers. As the family members made adaptations to the changing economic realities of their region, they learned to read and write by drawing in part on material and ideological resources created in the previous generations. However, as change accelerated, the duration of the practical value of these skills shortened. A rare achievement in one generation became a basic requirement in the next. Skills developed to appease dominant economies in one generation sank in tradable value in the next. More time, effort, and expense had to be given to literacy development as the twentieth century proceeded.

Chapter 4 addressed the strategies for literacy learning that were sustained in African American culture in the absence of economic opportunity and equal rights to education. By law for most of the twentieth century and in practice still, the nation has given little consideration to the human development, including literacy development, of African Americans. Consequently, African Americans have taught and learned literacy within collective self-help systems of long, traditional standing, systems that emphasize spiritual wholeness, reciprocity, resistance, and political activism. Sponsoring agents for many African Americans have been few

in number, dense in function, multiple in purpose, and collective in outlook. Resources circulate more durably and, in values and methods for literacy learning, adaptation rather than abandonment, consolidation rather
than proliferation have been common. The influence of this history of literacy
Americans in this century took place in double-action contexts: coping
with the changes induced by rising educational expectations and economic and technological forces while fighting for basic access to the systems inducing those changes. The influence of this history of literacy
sponsorship was manifest in direct and indirect ways in the literacy learning accounts of 16 adult African Americans treated in Chapter 4. For
many of these individuals, the worth of literacy lay close to the spiritual
and citizenship meanings of the first wave of American mass literacy –
meanings that are often eclipsed by the market values of literacy's second
wave. The legacies of this history including its differences from – indeed
its challenges to – prevailing literacy values, must be made much more
central to any genuinely democratic system of public education. Catering
only to the literacy histories of the economically dominant promises only
to reinforce within education the deep structures of racial inequality
inherited from the past.

Chapter 5 drew on all 80 life history accounts to explore distinct differences in cultural meanings between reading and writing. If the mass literacy
that was achieved by the start of the twentieth century in the United States
was principally a reading literacy, the mass literacy called for at the start of
the twenty-first century is a reading and writing literacy. As that chapter
suggested, the cultural traditions of writing literacy have descended more
warily in American society, never enjoying the same sacred status of reading
in the public imagination. Across age, gender, race, and class, the people I
interviewed associated writing with secrecy, censorship, pain, and opprobrium. Although highly valued and often sought, writing was a skill that was
not passed so explicitly from parent to child and did not have broad and
accepted roles in family routines. These experiences of contemporary individuals resonate within the broader history of literacy. Historically, writing
was less readily embraced by traditional sponsors of literacy and more
highly feared by suppressors of literacy. Even as it gained status as one of
the three R's, writing has always played second fiddle to reading in terms of
instructional time and resources.

This legacy is important to remember at this juncture in literacy history when the status of writing stands to change as quickly as the technologies with which it is now functioning. Writing is gaining value as a
productive skill within the information economy. More critically, it is
sometimes the only way to represent one's interests in a system in which

so many social and political relationships are conducted through print. Although still not getting the attention it deserves in government literacy initiatives and in other public discourse about literacy, the status of writing will continue to up the ante on literacy standards and demands on workers. As a productive skill, writing is also keenly linked to political voice and to the protection and exercise of free speech rights. In the society we are becoming, uneven access and achievement in writing will harm the integrity of civil rights. What the cultural traditions of reading and writing have to tell us at this juncture is an urgent question for literacy teachers and policy makers.

Chapter 6 probed issues of literacy and stratification as they played out around language and technology in the closing decades of the twentieth century. Stratification in access, achievement, and reward in literacy – by gender, race, and class – is related to the role of literacy in economic consumption and production. As the assets of literacy (human and otherwise) grew more integral to certain kinds of production (including the production of profit), resources flowed to literacy development in all forms. At the end of the twentieth century, individual literacy learning was intersecting with those processes of subsidy and production in ways that aggravated a heritage of racial and class discrimination. Thus, despite ostensible democracy in public education, access to literacy and its rewards continue to flow disproportionately to the children of the already educated and the already affluent. Rarely do schools redress imbalance through management of school resources or cultural subsidy in literacy education – and in fact often adopt practices that abet and aggravate the imbalance.

By the new millennium, economic competition had taken more and more control of the access and reward systems for literacy, including the standards against which everyone's literacy is measured and valued. The full implications of these developments must be made more relevant in thinking about literacy today. Here are several implications that are especially striking and far reaching:

First, literacy is being sponsored in much different ways than it was in the past. Through most of its history, literacy was affiliated with a few strong cultural agents – education, religion, local commerce. It tended to be learned in the same contexts in which it was intended to be practiced.[6] Now, sponsors of literacy are more prolific, diffused, and heterogenous. Commercial sponsors abound and reach all geographical locations, often through the channels of television, radio, and computer – as do other big arms of literacy, the national government and international conglomerates. Whereas people used to move to literacy, literacy now moves to people. As we saw in the case of Barbara Hunt in Chapter 1, literacy does not move to people in equal amounts nor does its arrival necessarily signal opportunity. In fact, print often arrives in underserved communities as part of economic downturn or political oppression. Nevertheless, like contemporary literates of all ages and places, the young Barbara Hunt wrote and read using complex blends of media, rhetoric, and formally organized knowledge – much of it tied to distant sponsors and interests. As a matter of course, she had to control multiple perspectives and sources of information. A proliferation of sponsors also means that people who move – sometimes from culture to culture – transport their literacy from one context to another or must adapt and amalgamate practices learned in one sphere to meet the new demands of another sphere. Global communications and increased migrations can only intensify this process in the future.[7] Schools are no longer the major disseminators of literacy. Literacy instruction needs to develop from a sense of a new role for schools, as a place where the ideological complexities (including the inequities) of literacy sponsorship are sorted through and negotiated. Basic literate ability requires the ability to position and reposition oneself among literacy's sponsoring agents as well as among competing forms of communication.

Second, the diversification of work, especially parental work, brings various kinds of materials, instruments, and other resources into homes where they can be appropriated into teaching and learning. Current adult and family literacy campaigns emphasize the connection between children's school success and parental literacy and encourage parents to spend more time reading to their young children. In some communities, new mothers receive complimentary children's books when they are discharged from the maternity ward. And much effort is expended in early childhood education programs to engage low-income and undereducated mothers in child-centered literacy practices. These campaigns broadcast images of parents, usually mothers, relaxing in chairs or perching at bedsides, reading storybooks to young children.[8] Although *Literacy in American Lives* has turned up plenty of evidence of recreational reading by parents with children, home literacy overall also was strongly associated in memory with parental work. When children saw adults in their households reading and writing, it was often work related. It also was through adult work or work-related education that literacy materials, extensive or spare, entered households. Though not always the focus of explicit instruction and not often school oriented, work-related reading and writing provided children real-world information about how literacy functions. More important, as we saw in previous chapters, these encounters often brought at least some children into contact with the material assets and social power of major literacy sponsors – corporations, industries, merchants, governments, and universities.

Farming magazines were some of the very few print items that rural people at the turn of the century recalled in their childhood homes. Dairy inspector Henry Schmidt, born in 1908, said his father would read aloud from *Hoard's Dairyman* as he instructed Henry's older brothers on changes he wanted them to make around their 180-acre farm. In urban areas, commercial life brought documentary practices into visible view. Town dweller Jasper Tannen, born in 1927, saw his father, a wealthy business owner, working sporadically on accounts at home, as did Carla Krauss, born in 1926 near Detroit. Her father sold real estate after the motor company that employed him went out of business. The Dale Carnegie books he bought to help in the transition became part of the family's shared library. Homemaker Marsha Litvan, born in 1926, remembered that her father brought home an old typewriter from the office of his liquor store for her older brother to use when he was in high school. Another woman, born much later, in the 1970s, learned 10-key operations and computer processing from her father, a self-employed accountant.

Children of teachers across generations remembered seeing their mothers or fathers grading papers or preparing lesson plans at night and sometimes served as guinea pigs for new lessons or techniques. One daughter remembered her father, a school district superintendent, bringing home several computers over one summer in the late 1970s to test them prior to entering a contract for the system. Nursing manuals, small business machines, scrap paper and pens, ledgers, and especially typewriters and, eventually, computers, all made their ways into homes through adult jobs or job training. Many people also reported childhood visits to parents or other adult family members in newspaper plants, laboratories, stores, and other offices, or traveling along on dairy or sales routes, where printed materials, writing instruments, maps, and other literacy materials were out and in use. Literacy experiences also moved in opposite generational directions through work activities. A middle-aged social worker was reading up on gerontology with materials given to her by an academic in-law. A woman nearing 80 had just received a second-hand computer from a businessman son and was using it to write her memoirs. And a high school student in the mid-1990s, working part time as a telemarketer, was showing her single mother how to use computer software of value to her in her work.

The relationship between parental work and literacy must play a more prominent role in approaches to family literacy. For one thing, this relationship can illuminate the role of men in literacy learning, a dimension that is often overlooked when family literacy is linked solely to the nurture of preschool children. The historically privileged position that men have enjoyed in education and employment made fathers in many households the conduits of specialized skills and materials that could be of interest and use to other family members. This especially became true as more and more men worked in information and knowledge production. Women who worked in subordinate positions, typing, filing, and dispatching documents and other forms of print, could borrow skills and concepts from more highly educated men for whom they worked, turning this knowledge into assets for their families. Sarah Steele, born in 1920, for instance, a bookkeeper for a law firm, learned accounting procedures from one of the attorneys for whom she worked and applied them to a strained family budget. Single mother Antonia Lawrence was encouraged to enroll in a medical technician course by her children's pediatrician, who later employed her. As late-twentieth-century women gained more regular access to higher education and professional work, they could bring associated materials and skills directly into the context of child rearing. Certainly, the growing use of home computers for earning a living will further contribute literacy resources to private dwellings. The circulation of work-related literacy in households has contributed significantly to the diffusion of formal knowledge and literacy practices in this society. When we appreciate the connection between parental work and household literacy, we might better see why it is so urgent to make expanding education and employment opportunities (and not just bedtime story reading) a cornerstone of family literacy programs. As was suggested in an earlier chapter, the resources of workplaces could be better recruited into the literacy development of adults and their children. Beyond donating often obsolete computer equipment to community organizations, workplaces could more genuinely increase access to literacy resources and human development opportunities for all workers and their families. This seems especially important in public institutions like schools, universities, and government and health agencies.

Third, the patterns of literacy sponsorship in a parent's lifetime may bear little resemblance to the patterns in his or her child's lifetime, and the same with teacher and student. In a society inured to change, the significance of this phenomenon should not be overlooked. Mass literacy arose from the premise that print would function, in the words of Soltow and Stevens, as "social cement."[9] The stable, fixed nature of print, its authority in religion and statehood, and its effectiveness for rote learning all made literacy salient in maintaining traditions and passing down official versions of experience. For many generations, reading took place principally as what Gilmore (1989) identified as an intensive practice, as most people read the same small set of texts (mostly religious) repeatedly over a lifetime. But as commercial culture grew in the late eighteenth and nineteenth centuries, more extensive and serial reading became more prominent, a trend that intensified significantly in the United States over the twentieth century as paperbacks and magazines became big business. The more people could read and the more specific tastes could be addressed by print advertisers, the more periodicals proliferated and the more readership fragmented. The development of the children's literature industry, including special children's sections in public libraries, helped to stratify reading experiences by generation. Specialized knowledge and political and ethnic activism also broke reading publics into smaller audiences.[10] But more than the fracturing of reading audiences, it has been revolutions in communication technologies as well as the competition for new uses of the resources of reading and writing that drive the biggest generational wedges in literacy learning. We looked at these phenomena in depth in Chapter 3, through the experiences of the May family, who saw the powers of literacy that surged in one generation finding shorter duration and reach in subsequent generations. But these general patterns could be found in many different ways across the cohorts that I studied.

Technological change around literacy has had the fastest and most disruptive impact from a generational standpoint. As if in a kaleidoscope, reading and writing shift with each new communication option introduced, including telephone, radio, film, television, home video, and computer. The ages at which people make contact with influential new technologies heavily influence literacy learning. Radio, when it was first introduced, brought news and narrative to millions of listeners, and people I interviewed who were born in the 1920s and 1930s credited radio with stimulating their interest in reading and writing. On the other hand, many members of this same cohort dismissed television, which arrived later in their lives, as irrelevant or even deleterious to their literacy. By the 1950s and 1960s, narrative and news shifted to the new technology of television, as commercial radio turned mostly to music. People raised in the 1960s and 1970s were most apt to name television and not radio as a strong and largely positive influence on their reading and writing. As the first genuinely digital youth generation comes to consciousness, early literacy experiences embedded in computer and Internet use undoubtedly will give that generation's literacy a different quality from that of members of older generations. Mass media and new communication technologies touch members of all generations, of course, but the meaning of that contact and its capacity to affect literacy learning seems strongly linked to age. This is partly because of the ways that new communication technologies jockey against or sometimes appropriate the social functions of earlier technologies, but it also has to do with what part of the individual life span is making contact with the new technology and how. Here is another arena in which competition – in this case, the competition posed to reading and writing by other communication options – affects the basic processes of literacy learning. Young people today encounter a learning climate in which reading and writing coexist with a greater number of alternative communication systems, and this climate inevitably affects the meanings and mechanisms of literacy in young lives in distinctive ways.[11]

Changes in the ways that literacy is sponsored force changes in the methods, materials, motivations, and very meanings through which writing and reading take shape. If literacy once served social stability, it now also regularly serves specialization, fragmentation, competition, and disruption. More and more people are now doing more and more of their reading and writing in the roles of buyers and sellers, broadly construed. Parents and teachers must prepare young people to be writers and readers in forums and genres that they themselves have not necessarily learned in. And this teaching takes place in technological and communication contexts that are themselves fast-moving and unsteady underfoot. These social conditions seem to defy the basic terms of contract in which intergenerational transmissions of knowledge have traditionally taken place. Both knowledge and the mechanisms for sharing knowledge have been undergoing unprecedented waves of change. More people now carry around in their life experiences accumulating strata of contact with multiple writing technologies and genres. Indeed, the twentieth century is a virtual junkyard of recessive and abandoned communication materials; the twenty-first century will be the same. The difficulties inherent in literacy learning and teaching under these unprecedented conditions should not be simplified.

Fourth, the insinuation of market forces into the meaning and methods by which literacy is learned pose crucial ethical and policy questions for public education. Especially dangerous are the ways that education is now being cast as a privatized and individualized commodity – something that families obtain singly for their children. This new approach to education obliterates the memory of how much opportunity for literacy and schooling have depended on generous public subsidy – how much that history rides in the background of families now enjoying the greatest private rewards in the Information Age. We especially must scrutinize the ways that market forces can cause racial injustices to snowball. Two generations ago, high school became widely available to the mass of white citizens. Thus began the accumulation of education that powered the economic transformations that in turn created more education opportunities for those poised to seize them. Advanced literacy and education, especially for men, began to pay off in many segments of white society. Yet two generations ago, African Americans and other people of color were, by law and custom, typically excluded from the opportunities of high school education or routed into vocational and industrial training. Literacy and education continued to spread anyway among African Americans, especially in the middle class, but because of segregation could not pay off in the expected ways. A lot of things were changing in the American economy of the twentieth century, but not its outlook on race. Governments at all levels underinvested in the education of nonwhite citizens and used schools to enforce low expectations. People of color, black, brown, and red, were expected to stay in their place: mostly landless and performing lower-skilled, lower-wage manual and domestic service. This treatment pertained in both private and public enterprises, including the military, through most of the twentieth century. People of color who attained advanced education were expected to keep it among their own; their literacy, as a national resource, was appropriated and exploited only in extreme emergencies (like war) and was not systematically amplified or rewarded by the mainstream economy. The capacity to parlay the resources of literacy into economic assets and intergenerational security was seriously curtailed. Under the moral and political pressure of the civil rights movement, this system of second-class citizenship was officially repudiated, yet the turbulence of official integration in some cases further suppressed or destabilized the literacy assets that had developed in segregated economic and education systems. The imbalances of this history, reaching back into the days of slavery, have never been redressed by the American body politic. We allow these imbalances to continue to organize systems of access and reward for literacy, a neglect that in fact feeds a climate for further economic and political discrimination. Although apprehended as differences in literacy rates, we really have different histories of literacy sponsorship operating in the United States – differential systems by which literacy has been subsidized, developed, and compensated.

The more that economics play a hand in sponsoring literacy development, the more that racial discrimination in that system hurts literacy development. And in the most vicious of vicious circles, injured literacy development in turn hurts chances for economic improvement. Under practices of segregation, people of color were on the whole bypassed when subsidies started flowing in the early and midtwentieth century into the foundations of what would become the information economy – public and private subsidies to schools, corporations, the military, libraries, technology. As these investments helped to raise the economic value of literacy skills, further injury befell those without these skills as well as those who had the skills but could not fully cash in on their real worth. Important remedies were put in place by the major civil rights legislation of the 1960s and 1970s, uncorking the human skills and potential of African Americans and others by opening access to education and employment. However, the pace of political change around race, begrudging and backsliding, has never kept pace with economic change. Expanding civil rights and an expanding information economy have been two mighty engines going down the tracks, but they seem to be going at different speeds. Minority citizens who made later transitions into expanded schooling, intellectual labor, and political rights did not have much time to stabilize this base before the value of new opportunities was overtaken by a high-tech economy in overdrive – one that was exploiting the earlier investments in education and human capital that had gone more regularly into the white population. The economy no longer was waiting around for education to accumulate over two or three generations, as it had for typical white families in slower-moving eras of the recent past. Neither was it investing evenly in the productive potential of all citizens. Many people of color were left in cities where "work disappeared"[12] and ailing tax bases meant smaller investments in human development, especially schooling. Other people of color, as in communities like mine, belong to school districts blithely organized around the interests of a white mainstream, whose children sit atop two, three, sometimes four generations of college education. As we have seen in earlier chapters, schools (along with other institutions) embed into their literacy standards and practices histories of economic transformation that not all of the students who must depend on the school have been a part of. Out of this discrepancy arise conditions of unequal access to literacy in the ostensibly democratic school. Many learners in America, some new to the society, now must achieve high standards in reading and writing without the economic and political entitlements – past and present – that are tacit to those standards. Yet still the race goes on.[13]

American public schools and universities have not adequately confronted the tensions inherent in the recent transformation in literacy, especially the insatiable appetite of capitalism for more, better, faster, cheaper literates. Although always accommodating to the dominant economy, schools were designed as the quintessential bearers of an earlier literacy – traditional, integrative, local, and, in some regards, democratic.

Now, schools strain to assimilate into their traditional practices elements of a new ideology of literacy that attacks them at their foundation. At one level, this registers as a problem of being out of date, of promulgating old ways and old reasons for reading and writing that grow further out of step with communication experiences in the surrounding society. At another level, it registers as a problem of institutional confusion and vulnerability as new demands are stacked on top of old ones and as ideologies of older literacy campaigns are appropriated by new interests. As some politicians and business leaders call for a market takeover of American education, we see how, perhaps for the first time in history, the institution of the school has gotten out of step with the dominant economy's ideology of literacy.

In closing, I would like to address those readers who are committed to democracy in public education and are trying to think through this juncture in the history of literacy and schooling. By charter, democratic institutions exist to rebalance injustice – to make sure that differences in health, inheritance, origin of birth, and other inequalities do not overdetermine liberty and quality of life. Democratic institutions serve this function by actively expanding the control that individuals have over the decisions that affect their lives and by making sure that collective resources and individual rights are equally accessible by all members. Many forces interfere with the mission of democratic institutions, of course. In this society, government and schools too often are just another site where struggles over resources (in this case, public ones) are waged and won by those with more political and economic advantage. But as market pressures on the school intensify, it is important to remember that things are not supposed to be that way. As democratic institutions, schools are supposed to exist to offset imbalances that market philosophy helps to create – including, especially, imbalances in the worth of people's literacy. The more that the school organizes literacy teaching and learning to serve the needs of the economic system, the more it betrays its democratic possibilities. The more that private interests take over the educational development of our young citizens, the less of a democracy we will have.

Literacy's link to democracy appears prominently in the rhetoric of the founding of the nation. Thomas Jefferson's famous preference for newspapers over government as the basis of a republic shows that he saw literacy as a basis for citizenship. Free public education came into being because of the interdependency of an informed citizenry, a free press, and the right to vote. Citizens needed free access to information and, presumably, comparable access to the same information. This link between literacy and democracy has grown more complicated yet also more vital than it was in Jefferson's day. As big business encouraged big government, documentary relations sprawled into all aspects of society. More and more interaction was conducted through or alongside print. These developments brought new advantages to literacy skills as they enabled people with them to be more effective in systems that ran on them. In a documentary society, literacy – especially of a certain sort – allowed some people to amplify their right over the rights of others. Those who could write (or could hire writers) potentially had more ways to activate and exercise free speech. Just as economic change introduced instability into the potential worth and reach of literacy, literacy introduced instability into the potential worth and reach of basic rights. We see this most dramatically in the post-print technologies of radio, television, and global computer networks – all organs that have greatly amplified the voices of some entities over others. Although rising literacy standards and new communication technologies potentially can expand the civil rights of all citizens, they just as easily can (and do) damage them.

What I try to suggest here is that the new economic order presents American literacy educators with a much bigger agenda than increasing the productivity of future workers. From all angles – policy to pedagogy – literacy needs to be addressed in a civil rights context. Understanding – not just accommodating – economic and technological change is a vital responsibility of a democratic school. What is the meaning of an informed citizenry in these times? What problems are posed to first amendment rights by inequitable access to communication technologies? How do schools validate, preserve, amplify, and equalize all routes to literacy, especially when those routes are undergoing devaluation or destruction by economic change? How might "literacy standards" be expanded to address not just individual performers but all the forces and agents that sponsor (and profit from) literacy? That is, how might we begin to talk about the responsibility that this economy has to teachers and students instead of only the responsibility that teachers and students have to this economy?

How would the democratic mission be strengthened if students learned to read and write as forms of civil rights? My hunch is that literacy achievement would rise. Literacy's link to democracy ran as a recessive thread throughout many of the lives represented here. Barbara Hunt, the young farm woman introduced in Chapter 1, reached back intuitively to the remnants of agrarian populism as a support for her literacy growth in tough economic times. Johnny Ames, introduced in Chapter 2, came out of prison literate and educated, his reading and writing skills expanding in concert with expanding access to civil rights. The connection between literacy and civil rights runs deep in African American history and, as we saw in Chapter 4, brought practical and spiritual significance to many of the everyday African American readers and writers studied in this project. Teaching literacy in a civil rights context could bring the relevance of the school into the lives of students most often alienated from the present system – students of color, of poverty, of political asylum. Starting with the twentieth century, literacy has increasingly been captured for the cause of private wealth. It is time for the public school to reclaim in a serious way the role of literacy in strengthening democracy. Maybe the school can put to good use its slowness to change, its long memory, its entitlement to local control. As the society's major repository of the history of literacy, the school can serve to stabilize literacy learning and use its formidable resources to augment – beyond the needs of the market – the value of all the pluralistic forms of literacy that enter there.

It is easy to acknowledge the escalating standards for literacy achievement that the new economic order demands: the relatively high level of symbol skill and education experience presumed in many of the good-paying jobs that are being created. It is harder to be mindful that the conditions giving rise to our current literacy problems also are the conditions in which these problems are experienced and the conditions in which they must be addressed. We should see not only that people must adapt to changes in expectations for literacy but also wonder how they manage it while the social systems that sustain literacy themselves undergo dramatic assault. We should not only appreciate that standards for literacy achievement keep rising but also examine what is behind that escalation: how games of economic competition – the wins, losses, and draws – destabilize the value of existing literacy skills such that "the literacy crisis" becomes chronic. We should not only appreciate the benefits of parents reading to their children but also acknowledge the complex demands on teaching and learning when knowledge, skills, and the communication systems they ride along all change even faster than children do. We should not only recognize how stigmatized groups go about accumulating literacy despite discrimination but also dedicate the resources of the democratic school more wholly to their cause. Above all, in matters of literacy, we should consider the problems not only of deficit but of surplus. This includes acknowledging the ideological congestion that hangs at the scenes of literacy learning and forms much of the mystery in learning to read and write. It also includes acknowledging how often the literacy skills that exist in American lives languish for lack of adequate sponsorship.

Appendix

INTERVIEW SCRIPT

Demographic Questions

Date of birth
Place of birth
Place of rearing
Gender/race
Type of household (childhood)
Type of household (current)
Great-grandparents' schooling and occupations, if known
Grandparents' schooling and occupations, if known
Parents'/guardians' schooling and occupations, if known
Names and locations of all schools attended
Other training
Degrees, dates of graduation, size of graduating class
Past/current/future occupations

Early Childhood Memories

Earliest memories of seeing other people writing/reading
Earliest memories of self writing/reading
Earliest memories of direct or indirect instruction
Memories of places writing/reading occurred
Occasions associated with writing/reading
People associated with writing reading
Organizations associated with writing/reading

Materials available for writing/reading
Ways materials entered households
Kinds of materials used
Role of technologies

Writing and Reading in School

Earliest memories of writing/reading in school
Memories of kinds of writing/reading done in school
Memories of direct instruction
Memories of self-instruction
Memories of peer instruction
Memories of evaluation
Uses of assignments/other school writing and reading
Audiences of school-based writing
Knowledge drawn on to complete assignments
Resources drawn on to complete assignments
Kinds of materials available for school-based writing/reading
Kinds of materials used
Role of technologies

Writing and Reading with Peers

Memories of sharing writing and reading
Memories of writing and reading to/with friends
Memories of writing and reading in play
Memories of seeing friends reading and writing
Memories of reading friends' writing

Extracurricular Writing and Reading

Organizations or activities that may have involved writing or reading
Writing contests, pen pals, and so forth

Self-Initiated Writing or Reading

Purposes for writing and reading at different stages
Genres
Audiences/uses
Teaching/learning involved

Writing on the Job

Same questions as above

Civic or Political Writing

Influencial People

Memories of people who had a hand in one's learning to write or read

Influential Events

Significant events in the process of learning to write

Purposes for Writing and Reading Overall

Values

Relative importance of writing and reading
Motivations
Consequences

Current Uses of Reading and Writing

All reading and writing done in the six months prior to the interview

Sense of Literacy Learning

Interviewee's own sense of how he or she learned to read and write
Sense of how people in general learn to read and write

NOTES

Introduction: The Pursuit of Literacy

[1] Scribner and Cole (1981) set out one of the most influential formulations of literacy as a contextualized social practice. Through a series of painstaking empirical studies conducted among the Vai of Liberia, Scribner and Cole showed how through a variety of uses and contextual conditions, literacy yields a variety of cognitive preferences and skills. Their study stood in critique of widely held beliefs (developed largely out of anthropological and classical treatments of oral–literate contrasts) that characterized literacy as a monolithic technology bringing predictable cognitive consequences for people who took it up. Scribner and Cole showed that what literacy does to people depends on what people do with literacy. Another important advocate of contextualized approaches to literacy is Brian Street (1984), who emphasized the ideological aspects that context brings to literacy. For an expert application of this approach in ethnographic research, see Besnier (1995), and for broad, useful summaries, Collins (1995) and Barton (1994). Heath (1983) is a classic study of the implications of literacy in context for educational justice. For a more historically oriented treatment of literacy as practice, see Gere (1997).

[2] It would be fair to say that most ethnography-oriented studies of the social contexts of literacy treat context largely as a present-tense "scenic" setting. Many provide inventories of literacy practices in use by families, schools, groups, or communities, often with a focus on adult–child interactions. See, for instance, work by Heath (1983); Purcell-Gates (1995); Taylor (1985); Taylor and Dorsey-Gaines (1988); and Schieffelin and Gilmore (1984). For intergenerational and life span perspectives, see Gadsden (1992, 1997) and Donehower (1997).

[3] See, for instance, the famous study *A Nation at Risk* (1983), which is frequently credited with setting off the most recent alarms about student achievement in

basic skill. Along related lines is Johnston and Packer (1987). Calls in the late 1990s by the Clinton administration to have all children reading by third grade is a clear manifestation of concern about future American workers and their productivity in the new economy, as is the growing national standards movement, sometimes called the accountability movement. For more on the implications of these pressures, see the Conclusion. For a somewhat dated but still useful historical perspectives on these matters, see Resnick and Resnick (1977).

[4] In contemplating literacy as a resource, I find literal, material definitions quite useful because they tend to match the way that I found people treat their own literacy, often in a very practical and instrumental way. In the field of accounting, for instance, *assets* have been defined by Smith and Parr (1989) as "probable economic benefits" (42). Literacy as a potential benefit, or what Smith and Parr would call an "intangible asset," can behave in a similar way. Smith and Parr noted that the value of assets can be affected both by use and by changes and developments occurring in other places. They wrote: "Assets of an entity are changed both by its transactions and activities and by events that happen to it... An entity's assets or their value may be increased or decreased by other events ... that may be ... beyond the control of the entity" (p. 43). This fluctuation in the value of literacy affected many of the lives I studied and was often an instigation for further literacy learning.

[5] Graff's definitive *The Literacy Myth* (1979) decimates the assumptions that literacy leads to upward mobility and that illiteracy is the cause of downward mobility. Looking at census data from Canadian cities in the last quarter of the nineteenth century, Graff demonstrated that discrimination by race, gender, ethnicity, religion, and class was far more determining of chances for upward mobility than was literacy, an analysis that would still pertain in North American societies. Yet the literacy myth persists, most potently around social issues like crime and welfare. There is a widespread belief, for instance, that illiteracy causes poverty or criminality, for instance, or that literate women are better mothers than illiterate ones.

[6] For more on the concept of cultural capital and its role in stratifying access to and benefits from education, see Bourdieu and Passeron (1977). Interestingly, in later writings Bourdieu suggested that a more accurate term would be *informational capital* (Bourdieu and Wacquant, 1992, p. 119). Although literate resources would clearly fall under Bourdieu's broad notion of capital, he also saw that the technology of print could rearrange the powers of cultural capital by moving them from memory to text (Bourdieu, 1980, p. 125). Nobel Prize winner Gary Becker (1986) developed the notion of human capital into a general theory of economic activity based on investments in and rewards for human competence.

[7] Castells (1989) observed: "The main source of productivity [in the information society] is the capacity to generate and process new information, itself dependent upon the symbolic manipulating ability of labor" (p. 351).

[8] See especially the work of Brian Street (1984, 1993, 1995) for useful conceptions of what is often called critical literacy studies. Also see Street and Besnier (1994).

[9] Also see Bertaux and Thompson (1997). Social structure and social change are at the heart of the investigations of these three researchers. Individual cases are

valued for what they can reveal about economic and social relationships. For weaknesses in this approach, see the Popular Memory Group's (1982) critique of Thompson's *The Voice of the Past* (1988), which they fault for not attending to the cultural constructions involved in life-story interviewing and life stories themselves, for disguising premises of researcher and researched in "the empirical fact." My study, in fact, is limited in the same way.

[10] Lummis, 1987, page 108.

[11] Ryder, 1965, page 844. Ryder captured the value of this perspective for the study of literacy learning when he wrote that "the principal motor of contemporary social change is technological innovation. It pervades the other substructures of society and forces them into accommodation" (p. 851).

[12] Bertaux, 1981, page 130.

[13] Brigg's (1986) book is a useful reminder that oral history interviews are as systematically related to the present (especially the ongoing demands of the interview itself) as to the past. He also called for more attention to the what he called the "metacommunicative repertoires" of the social groups from which interviewees come, especially so that the interviewer can learn the lessons offered in a particular exchange.

[14] For additional psychological treatments of autobiographical memory, see the collection by Thompson, Skowronski, Larsen, and Betz (1996).

[15] Halloran, 1990, page 155.

[16] More attention needs to be paid to the fact that many reading assessments require students to write out their responses to reading as proof of comprehension. The intermingling of writing ability with reading ability in these settings is not usually addressed. The National Assessment of Educational Progress in Reading, for instance, judges reading comprehension on the basis of students' written answers.

[17] As this book was going to press, this area of Wisconsin was, like many parts of the country, experiencing unprecedented levels of employment. Unemployment had fallen to under 2% by the late 1990s.

[18] Bertaux, 1981, page 134.

[19] Kett, 1994, pages 67–70.

[20] Nicholas and Nicholas (1992).

[21] Three of the keenest and most eloquent observers of economic impacts on writing and teaching and learning have been Faigley (1999), Miller (1991), and Spellmeyer (1996).

[22] For a more positive treatment of sponsors, see Goldblatt (1994), who explored the power of institutions to authorize writers.

[23] Laqueur (1976, p. 124) provided a vivid account of a street demonstration in Bolton, England, in 1834 by a "pro-writing" faction of Sunday school students and their teachers. This faction demanded that writing instruction continue to be provided on Sundays, something that opponents of secular instruction on the Sabbath were trying to reverse. The legacies of this period on contemporary reading and writing are explored in Chapter 5.

[24] See Cornelius's (1991) absorbing study, which provides ample evidence of how competing interests – economic, political, and religious – set the conditions for literacy and illiteracy among African Americans in slavery.

[25] Thanks to Ann Egan-Robertson for suggesting patronage as a useful model for thinking about literacy and sponsorship. See Bourne (1986), Hortsman and Kurtz (1978), and Lynch (1986).

[26] Hortsman and Kurtz, 1978, pages 13–14.

[27] Stevens (1988) drew on Rawls's (1971) contractarian theory of social justice to explore how judicial attitudes toward illiterates shifted as the society moved more and more to relations of formal obligation and contract. Stevens argued that the rights of illiterates suffer because their ability to exercise those rights is hampered by the rising value and authority of documents. For more on this matter, see Chapter 2.

Chapter 1. Literacy, Opportunity, and Economic Change

[1] In characterizing the economy this way, I recognize that many jobs do not require (and do not reward) advanced literacy skills of workers. However, I do want to emphasize that the prominence of symbol-wielding activity both in the private sector and the public sector that manages it affects all people in every place, whether they are directly engaged in these activities or not.

[2] For thoughts on formal knowledge as an economic resource, see Castells (1989), Drucker (1969), and Machlup (1980). Literacy researchers who have been paying attention to the impact of economic change on literacy include Gee, Hull, and Lankshear (1996); Gowen (1992); Hull (1997); Purcell-Gates (1995); Stuckey (1991); and Taylor (1996).

[3] Lockridge (1974) is an early and innovative study using signature rates to recover the rates and social impact of literacy in colonial New England. For one of many corrections and amplifications of Lockridge's study, see Perlmann and Shirley (1991).

[4] There is a vast literature on the history of mass literacy, especially its early growth. Graff's magisterial history (1986) is a good place to start. For treatments of the push and pull of literacy, see particularly Cressy (1980) and Vincent (1989), a provocative study that takes a critical look at the impact of literacy on working-class relations and the dynamics of upward mobility. I have been especially partial to studies of literacy that are grounded in material conditions and treat the literacy of ordinary people. See, for instance, Chartier (1987, 1989), Houston (1988), and Hurt (1972). Other good studies that focus on the ideological impact of literacy include, for instance, King (1994) and, for very early developments, Stock (1983). For relationship of literacy to recent American education, see Cremin (1988).

[5] For general treatments of the commercial and cultural stimulations of early printing, see Eisenstein (1979) and Davis's (1981) wonderful chapter, "Printing and the People," in Graff. For treatments of the American condition, Kaestle, Damon-Moore, Stedman, Tinsley, & Trollinger (1991), especially Chapters 2 and 5.

[6] In a study of popular literacy in Victorian England, Mitch (1992) showed that despite widespread literacy in the midnineteenth century, no more than 5% of the male work force and 3% of the female work force were in occupations that strictly required literacy (p. 14), although just over one half of male workers and two thirds of female workers were in occupations in which literacy was at least possibly an asset (p. 20). This study captured a period in which occupations were increasingly changing to make use of literacy. Drucker (1969, p. 284) also suggested that the lengthening of formal schooling in American in a sense forced the development of an information economy because educated people became unfit for anything but knowledge work.

[7] The best study of literacy and region that I know of is Gilmore (1989), a methodologically stunning treatment of literacy in the Connecticut River valley in the decades following the Revolutionary War. For other thoughtful methodological approaches, see Houston (1985). For comparative looks at literacy development in different economic settings, see Stephens (1987), and at vicissitudes of literacy in the face of political and social disorder, see Gallman (1988) and Gallegos (1991). For general historical treatments of schooling and region, see Kaestle (1983), especially Chapter 8.

[8] For sources of inequity by region and within regions in midtwentieth century, see Ginzberg and Bray's (1953) fascinating study of illiteracy and the military draft in World War II. Grubb (1987, 1990, 1992) has written a number of interesting articles treating literacy in terms of supply and demand and the cost to families of providing literacy for their children. For more on this issue, see Chapter 3.

[9] For a very interesting cost–benefit analysis of literacy acquisition as well as the development of family strategies for literacy and schooling, see Mitch (1992). Only one of the people that I interviewed reporting losing his literacy skills as a result of nonuse. The report was from a man who was born in rural Wisconsin in 1942 and graduated from high school in 1960. A heavy-equipment operator for his entire adult life, the man said, "I don't do enough writing. I got to the point where I'm a very slow writer and getting the words wrong because I don't do that much writing. I've found even some of the simplest words will trip me up. I'll write something down and go back and say, 'Boy, that's not spelled right. You should know that, but you don't.'"

[10] Perhaps the high drop-out rate in adult basic education classes could be explained by the deflation in the value of basic literacy, both as it spread to virtually all workers and as the advantages of advanced skills sharpened. The economic value of basic literacy (especially on top of the suppressed value of minimum wages) may not be worth the high investment of time and effort. On another front, many American workers are piling up obsolete knowledge and skills related to obsolete communication technologies and computer software.

[11] Although I use pseudonyms here, it is true that the farm journal that employed Martha Day and the gas station that employed Barbara Hunt both bore the same name. That small detail – which spoke so much about the economic changes that devastated family farming – inspired my decision to look more closely at the parallels and differences in the lives of these two women.

[12] Census of Agriculture (1991); also Saupe and Majchrowicz (1996, p. 96).

[13] In his history of rural America, Danbom (1995) wrote: "The first two decades of the 20th century represented a time of such rare prosperity for American farmers that the period is referred to as the golden age of agriculture. During this twenty-year period, gross farm income more than doubled and the value of the average farm more than tripled" (p. 161).

[14] For descriptions of the massive buildup of rural schools in the late nineteenth century as well as political and social organization of the schools, see Fuller's (1982) wonderfully readable history of the one-room school.

[15] Writing about the period between 1920 and 1930, Danbom (1995) observed: "Fewer farms and a declining labor demand on those that remained combined with the economic and social attractions of cities during the roaring twenties to increase the pace of rural-to-urban migration dramatically. The countryside suffered a net outmigration of 6.25 million people in the decade. Even though the rural birthrate exceeded the rural deathrate, there was still an absolute rural population decline of 1.2 million people between 1920 and 1930. Those most likely to leave were the young, whose family and property responsibility were usually minimal" (p. 196). In speaking of herself in this period, Martha Day remarked that she wanted to be a "Horatio Alger girl," referring to the author of popular turn-of-the-century rags-to-riches adventure novels.

[16] According to Evans and Salcedo (1974), this bonanza period for commercial farm publishing coincided with a rise in farm outputs and the appearance of a number of technological innovations. The 1950s saw a slackening in advertising revenue as the number of farmers declined and competition from mass-market magazines intensified (pp. 65*ff*).

[17] Interestingly, these strong teacher figures continue to appear well into the mid- and late twentieth century in the lives of many African Americans that I interviewed. Traditional forms of literacy sponsorship, including apprenticeship, held together for African Americans and grew most precious as they continued to be widely excluded from education and occupational opportunities connected to the new economy. For more on this phenomenon, see Chapter 4.

[18] See Walters (1996).

[19] Evans and Salcedo (1974, page 65).

[20] For more on the Country Life Movement as a social and educational policy, see Danbom (1995, pp. 167–175) and Tremmel (1995). Danbom traced the ambivalence of rural people to impositions of urban values on their education and consumer practices. He wrote: "The Country Life Movement was most significant for what its existence indicated about the evolving position of rural America in the nation. For most of the history of the country rural had been normal, and urban had been peculiar... Now farmers had become peculiar... Whatever its intentions and accomplishments, the Country Life Movement represented the diminished status and growing peripheralization of rural America" (p. 175).

[21] For an analysis of the impact of economic downturns on farm families, see Saupe (1989).

[22] Census of Agriculture, 1991, page 92.

[23] For more on this general transformation in work, see Nelson (1995), page 195.

[24] For a complete history of this organization through midcentury, see Brockhaus (1949).

[25] See Clark and Halloran (1993) for a provocative assessment of how oratorical culture was already being transformed by the end of the nineteenth century by values that stressed individual skill over collective voice. They suggest a direct line between this late oratorical culture and contemporary rhetorics of specialization and professionalization.

[26] In several parts of the interview, Barbara Hunt described her distaste for assigned writing, both in school and in catechism class. She was required to keep a journal during a class trip to Germany. "And I didn't really like that because the trip didn't turn out exactly what I wanted it to be," she explained. "So there were a few bad things in there and I don't want bad things in my diary so I didn't write everything down." On essay writing in catechism class: "You had to take the First Commandment and say what you believed about it. And I knew I was going to get in trouble if I wrote what I wanted to write. I can either tell the truth, the whole truth, or, I can just kind of, uh, I pretty much wrote what he [the priest] wanted to hear."

[27] In the same part of the interview, Hunt elaborated: "I hate when people don't make eye contact. I hate it when teachers are continuously at the blackboard or something and never look at you to see if you are learning."

[28] See Neth (1995) for descriptions of changes in social values that accompanied land transfer and mechanization in agricultural areas. She observed: "As farm families became more deeply enmeshed in the cash economy and as the nature of agricultural work changed, the rules of negotiation within families altered and the survival of the farm unit itself became more problematic. Women and children had to negotiate in a system that increasingly redefined the ways in which they could contribute to the farm economy and threatened the resources of the family and community base" (pp. 11–12).

[29] See Jackson (1975) for a pertinent discussion of the effects of literacy and print in objectifying social life.

[30] For some useful directions, see Giroux and McLaren (1989) and Shor (1980, 1982).

[31] Gee, Hull, and Lankshear (1996) explored how "fast capitalism," as they called it, forces new demands on thinking and language use in workplaces and in schools. They try to develop pedagogical approaches that can prepare students to function successfully – and more critically – under new economic structures. This book also exposes limitations and contradictions in workplaces and classrooms that can stymie the very critical and creative skills that the economy ostensibly demands and thereby underestimate the skills of workers and students.

Chapter 2. Literacy and Illiteracy in Documentary America

[1] See Stevens, especially Chapter 5. Later, he observed about the rule of contract: "When deliberate misinformation was not the issue, equal access to the informa-

tion contained in the contract was assumed. For the unlettered person not to avail himself of that knowledge was to be negligent... When the written word took on a life of its own, as often happened, the "worth" of liberty was considerably diminished for the unlettered person" (p. 207).

[2] Stevens saw growth in corporatism in the twentieth century as a period when contract law actually became less important than in former decades, when contracts were more typically between individuals. Regulation of contractual processes, including the development of standard contract language, became more accepted and upheld by the courts as a public interest issue (Stevens, 1988, pp. 185–186).

[3] In the Conclusion, I further explore implications of computer technology for issues of literacy, access, and justice.

[4] For more on how many low-income families navigate the complex accounting procedures on which their livelihood depends, see Taylor and Dorsey-Gaines (1988) and Cushman (1998).

[5] One of the most obvious cases of the creation of illiteracy for political ends involved the uses of literacy tests in the South to disenfranchise African American voters. Tests were used capriciously and inequitably to eliminate voters, a practice that continued in many places through 1965 (Stevens, 1988, pp. 79*ff*).

[6] For more on this point, see Heckscher (1988). He wrote about the rise of what he called "associational unionism" (p. 8), which depends "on influence more than on the power of confrontation" for effectiveness" especially by extending "employee rights by law rather than by collective bargaining. The last two decades [1970s and 1980s] have seen enormous activity in this area" (p. 9).

[7] For useful accounts of this period in union history, see Heckscher (1988) and Nelson (1988).

[8] Farr (1993) associated "essayist literacy" with written genres that are esteemed in the academy and noted for their explicitness, reliance on reasons and evidence, and impersonal voice.

[9] Kozol's observation in 1985 that the prison population represents the single highest concentration of adult illiterates was still holding true in the 1990s, with somewhere between 60% and 70% of prison inmates unable to read and write above a grade-school level. See Kozol, pages 13 through 14.

[10] For more observations about the survival system in African American cultural and economic life and its relationship to literacy learning, see Chapter 4.

[11] This legislation also initiated the first federal funding of adult basic education (see Stevens, 1988, p. 19).

[12] Like other "war on poverty" programs of the 1960s, Job Corps treated poor people as culturally deprived. In their brief history of the Job Corps, Levitan and Johnston (1975) listed three assumptions of the program:

First was ... that the success of disadvantaged individuals in the labor market could be measurably improved through basic education and skill training. Second was the hypothesis that much of the explanation for continuing poverty lay with the deprived, isolated, or debilitating environments from which most disadvantaged individuals came. Presumably, relocation away from these environmental obstacles could clear the way for educational, social, and employment gains. Finally, there was the belief that a significant number of individuals existed whose history of educational and employment failure could be reversed if they were given a carefully structured second chance when they were still in their teen years. (pp. 1–2).

[13] Levitan and Johnston (1975) report high drop-out rates among the youngest enrollees in the Job Corps program. In 1973, some years after Johnny Ames was enrolled, the average stay in the program for those under 18 years old was 5.3 months (p. 22).

[14] The first college programs for prisoners began in the 1950s, with big growth coming in the 1970s. According to Pollock (1997), 43 states have community college programs, 17 states offer four-year degree programs, and 6 states offer graduate programs. Education release was widespread in the 1970s but cut back in the 1980s (Pollock, 1997, 148*ff*). Interesting in terms of paralegal training was a 1987 federal appellate court ruling that required prisons to train inmates as paralegals if the prisons opted to forgo direct legal services to inmates. This same ruling also mandated free photocopying privileges and access to all library resources for all inmates (Pollock, p. 352).

[15] For professional discussions of counseling and rehabilitation in prison, see Whitely and Hosford (1979) and Scharf, Dindinger, and Vogel (1979); for illuminating historical perspectives, see Carney (1979). Whitely and Hosford (1979) observed that "it is the rare counselor involved in a correctional setting who does not find him/herself involved at some time in an altogether different (and possibly less valued) role: that of being a correctional or security officer" (p. 27). Together these articles relate the growing focus on communication skills as part of prison rehabilitation, the reliance on commercially packaged programs for self-help, and the demands for documentation of inmate progress as part of the parole process. For a useful overview of therapeutic writing generally, see Brand (1979).

[16] Pollock (1997) looked back: "The prisoner's rights movement swept into popular consciousness on the coattails of the broader reform of the civil rights movement. As public support for democratization of education, the workplace, and other institutions has receded, so too have the successes of litigation as a tool for reform of prison conditions" (p. 340). For more on the persisting influences of the civil rights movement on literacy learning among African Americans, see Chapter 4.

[17] See Coyle, 1987, page 17. Wisconsin prisons recognized inmates as citizen clients of libraries, independent of prison goals, as early as the 1920s when the State Library Commission adopted services to prisoner programs. They put small collections of books in libraries and made books and mail-order courses available from the state central library. The program was stopped in the 1930s for financial reasons (Coyle, 1987, p. 36).

[18] Mandatory education in American prisons dates back at least to the early 1800s, when Kentucky required prisoners to take four hours of literacy instruction on Sundays. Full-time teachers were assigned to New York prisons in 1847. Generally, prison education began in the form of religious instruction and evolved into rehabilitation. In this century, education became mandatory in some prison systems in the 1950s for inmates with less than a third-grade education (see Pollock, 1997, 141*ff*).

[19] Cornelius (1991) provided many descriptive accounts of settings for literacy learning among enslaved African Americans. Also see her earlier article, "'We Slipped and Learned to Read'" (1983).

[20] Johnny Ames showed me the list of titles that he read during his 16 years in prison. The topics ranged from religion, politics, sexuality, psychology, African American history, and sociology to Dale Carnegie–like self-help guides: more than 100 books in all.

[21] Dickey (1991) described the education and vocational program in a typical Wisconsin prison as consisting of math, social problems, business education, marketing, music, practical English, welding, auto mechanics, machine shop, printing, barbering, carpentry, steamfitting, cosmotology, food service, sewing, and clerical training.

[22] Johnny Ames felt that his understanding of racism learned in the blatant conditions of Jim Crow in the South served him well in a northern prison where, he said, the racism was more latent but no less virulent. He said he was able to negotiate the racist atmosphere better than some of his northern-born peers because he was able more often to know when to keep his mouth shut.

Chapter 3. Accumulating Literacy: How Four Generations of One American Family Learned to Write

[1] See Landes and Solomon (1992) for the dates on which each state passed compulsory schooling legislation.

[2] For a useful overview of the development of the graded school, see Vinovskis (1995), especially pages 112*ff.*

[3] For the role of reading in middle-class families, see, for instance, Heath (1983), Chapter 7, and Cochran-Smith (1984).

[4] In the nineteenth century, schooling levels among free white children generally rose with family prosperity, both because children's labor was less needed and because more money could be spent on schooling. For an economic analysis, see Horan and Hargis (1991) and Kaestle and Vinovskis (1978).

[5] See Danbom (1995), especially Chapter 8 for outmigrations from farm areas induced by World War I and other social factors. According to Cremin (1988, p. 230), high school enrollments increased tenfold between 1900 and 1940.

[6] Other members of Genna May's cohort recalled their European ethnic churches converting to English during the opening decades of the twentieth century. Henry

Schmidt (introduced in Chapter 2), born in 1908, began confirmation classes in German in his evangelical Lutheran church. Talking about that training, he said: "We didn't have Sunday school in those days. We had to go [to confirmation classes] every Saturday for two or three years, and then the last year, after public school was out, we had to go every day. That was in German when I first started. In our church, the minister preached in German and everything was German. But then they switched over when I was fourteen [1922] and I was confirmed in English anyway."

[7] For pertinent perspectives on European American Protestant women, literacy, and education, see Kerber (1976), Main (1991), and Riley (1969).

[8] Even as late as 1956, owners of the college were boasting that "we have no job placing students, particularly women," noting that there were six or seven jobs waiting for each female graduate. The number of office workers quadrupled between 1900 and 1940 (Beniger, 1986, p. 393). For useful contrasts in prospects between male nineteenth-century clerks and female twentieth-century secretaries, see Strom (1992).

[9] Of the men in this cohort who drove trucks and delivered milk, those who worked independently or for small businesses reported doing more recordkeeping than those who worked for larger, corporate condensaries. In the latter cases, office workers or foremen wrote out schedules and kept records of exchanges, as drivers at the most gathered signatures of receipt.

[10] Beniger (1986) suggested the information economy was an inevitable outgrowth of mass production, which separated producers from direct contact and communication with consumers. This split created a crisis of information and control that had to be restored through "control" technologies.

[11] The Palmer method of handwriting was developed by Austin Norman Palmer (1859–1927), a teacher at Cedar Rapids Business College. As a student of business, Palmer sought to develop a straightforward method of penmanship in contrast to curlicues and shaded calligraphy. The Palmer Method did not require students to form letters in precisely the same way but instead focused on muscular movement, posture, and paper position. By 1900, the Palmer Method was in general use in public schools. Palmer taught 50,000 teachers a year and ran summer institutes and correspondence schools. See Kernan (1984).

[12] Writing in 1933, Hettinger described how, in the early days of broadcasting, programs would "offer a small souvenir or useful gift to listeners who would write in to the sponsoring company or the station over which the program was broadcast" (p. 276). By 1932, nearly one third of companies on the air were giving something to listeners. After networks ended prohibitory regulations, commercial contests came into vogue in the early 1930s. Many of them invited writing in the form of endorsement letters, limericks, and word-building contests. Hettinger reports that contest magazines flourished briefly during this period (pp. 277–279).

[13] Other people born and raised in the 1930s and 1940s found the radio extremely important to their literacy learning, primarily because of the narratives and news shows. Burt Allan, a European American born in 1922 in rural Wisconsin, said he "used to wonder who wrote that nice stuff there that they put on." Christopher Farnspoole, also European American, born in 1933, said he always would "look for certain styles" in the many radio programs he heard, "especially the cynical ones that matched my own." Linda Spruce, a European American born in 1938 and raised in a series of foster homes, said, "I found creativity and creativity of thought on the radio." Darlene Smote, an African American woman born in 1942 in rural Mississippi, remembered listening to the radio show *The Romance of Helen Trent* with her aunt and being inspired to write her autobiography. "We used to listen to the stories and I would look at their point and think of mine. In between their words and mine, I would just write." Stanley James, an African American man born in 1920 in Kansas, reported that his family did not own a radio until 1935 but that his uncle used to bring over his crystal set, plug in his earpiece, and narrate baseball games being broadcast from Fenway Park. "He'd set right in the center of a circle and all of us would be around him and he would tell us what they were saying on the radio." Other people in this cohort reported no connection between radio and literacy learning, even though they listened regularly. Benjamin Lucas, a Jewish American born in 1936 and raised in New York City, said he regarded radio as a negative influence. "It was like TV today," he said.

[14] Susan Krauss, born in 1926 in Detroit, remembered listening to a program called *The Singing Lady*. "My mother would always put that on for us in the afternoon. It was a very charming woman who told stories for young children." Otherwise, Krauss associated the radio with her parents' love of music. "I recall we did our housecleaning every Saturday with the opera roaring around us. I learned a good deal about music from the radio," she said. "That was the only music, besides my piano, that I was in contact with."

[15] For corroboration of Sam May's account, see Thompson (1965).

[16] See Merritt Roe Smith's (1985) introduction to his edited collection, page 2.

[17] Four of the eight World War II veterans whom I interviewed said they did some sort of teaching while stationed in the armed services. One man taught agriculture and another helped to enroll soldiers in correspondence courses sponsored by the University of Maryland. Bill Short, a graduate of marine officer school, remembered censoring mail while stationed at Pearl Harbor. Soldiers in sensitive areas were not allowed to disclose their locations or to convey any other information of potential benefit to the enemy. Short recalled: "Somebody would try to use the name Pearl or something and I'd say, 'No. Forget it.' After the day was over, we had to read all this mail. The officers had to censor the mail. After you had a whole day in the field or something, then you'd come home and you'd get a stack of letters to censor. It wasn't any fun."

[18] Two immensely informative historical studies of the dissemination of writing-based information are Brown (1989) and Fuller (1972).

[19] For useful contemporary treatments of literacy and region, see Donehower (1997) and Purcell-Gates (1995).

[20] Although there was a public library in the village where Sam May attended high school, as a commuter he said he "didn't have any chance to go into their community library." He continued: "I never heard of anybody in our family ever going to a library for anything. But they collected their own books that they needed, bought them or borrowed them. A lot of book borrowing went on. Books had to be gathered up by the families. That's the story of rural America."

[21] Members of Genna May's cohort typically regarded their parents as competent, shrewd, intelligent, articulate, literate people who merely missed opportunities for schooling that later generations, including their own, would enjoy. Sidney Vopat (introduced in Chapter 2) regarded his father as a skillful salesman, even though he could not write. Martha Day (introduced in Chapter 1), born in 1903 in northern Indiana, said of her mother, who had left school in the seventh grade: "Oh, she was smart. She had educated herself in so many ways." Hope Moore, who was born in 1909 and attended secretarial college, was the daughter of grade school–educated parents. She discussed what she called the "literate" quality of her mother's personal letters: "It's not polished English, but it's good English. We all learned to speak correctly because our parents spoke correctly. They were good communicators. They used common sense. They had something that they passed on to me. The more schooling I had, the more I could do with it." Hedy Lucas, born in 1907, lived in a matriarchal household with her mother and aunt, both unschooled Jewish refugees from Poland. She recalled how her aunt would listen to her school essays before she turned them in to her teacher: "My aunt didn't read and write, either, but she used to have such beautiful thoughts. She would tell you what to write. She didn't know how to spell, but she would tell you how to write. And she would tell you if it was good. I used to finish it and read it for her, and if she said it was good, it was perfect. My mother and my aunt were smarter than I think a lot of people are with all the education."

The tendency to distinguish between being literate and being educated fell off among European Americans in subsequent cohorts but continued to be salient for African Americans well into the century as they continued to struggle for access to equal education. See Chapter 4.

[22] For a useful history of the development of children's literature during the twentieth century, see Viguers (1969). Viguers said paperback book fairs had begun in public schools by 1967. For an illuminating treatment of the selling of children's books, see the introduction in Jones (1987).

[23] See Allan Luke's (1988) perspicacious treatment of Dick and Jane.

[24] Yet even within military experience at midcentury, legible handwriting could bring rewards. Several of the World War II and Korean War veterans I talked with

said they stayed out of the line of fire by being assigned to desk jobs on the strength of their penmanship.

[25] For more on this era and its context, see Thornton (1996), Chapter 5.

[26] Distributive Education Clubs of America (DECA), or Delta Epsilon Chi, had its growth in the mid-1930s as federal funds became available for distributive education in high schools. The national organization was begun in 1947, through the sponsorship of the American Vocational Association. Sears Roebuck financed the first newsletter in 1948. In this era, DECA was sponsoring competitions in, among other things, table displays, merchandise manuals, and public speaking but soon after shifted its emphasis from retailing and distribution to marketing, management, and entrepreneurship. By 1969, DECA had a chapter in every state and a national advisory board was in place. By the 1970s, corporate sponsorship for DECA was growing rapidly as greater articulation was sought between the commercial education curriculum in school and the competitive structures of DECA. See Berns (1996); McClaure, Chrisman, and Mock (1985); and Paris (1985).

[27] Or else student organizations associated with recessive economies disappear completely. For instance, there was no Future Farmers of American Club in Jack May's high school.

[28] According to its Web site, the Future Problem Solving Program (FPSP) began in 1973 by Dr. E. Paul Torrance, considered the father of modern creativity, who developed FPS as a curriculum project for a talented-and-gifted program in Georgia. Interscholastic competition began in the 1974–1975 school year. The aim is to develop creative and critical thinking skills, communication skills, cooperation and teamwork, and research skills. It teaches a six-step problem-solving process. A Wisconsin chapter of FPSP began in the same year Michael May was born – 1981. (http://www.fpsp.org)

[29] Both of Michael May's parents changed jobs shortly after the interviews took place. In the late 1990s, Michael's mother was working for a newspaper and his father was apprenticing in elevator repair. Jack May sometimes was seeking out his father's help in reading diagrams associated with his training.

[30] Just as radio was an influence on literacy learning for members of Sam May's cohort, television inspired writing and literacy learning for members of Jack May's and Michael May's peers. Emilio Rodriguez, a Mexican-American born in 1959 in a Texas border town, said he developed his political and social consciousness by watching westerns. "I knew the destruction of the Indians was wrong," he said; "I just didn't understand why at the time." He also said he used to try to solve problems posed by television shows, "like how to get Gilligan off that island," he said. A white working-class woman born in 1968 said she used what she knew of television mysteries to write mystery stories in school, and a white middle-class woman born in 1969 said she got ideas for fictional stories by watching TV. An Iranian American boy born in 1978 used visual memory from television to think of settings and characters for his fiction writing. "I think about someone I saw on a show and use their characteristics and the way they act," he said. Bonnie Dickson,

a white, working-class woman born in 1974, wrote a letter to a local TV news program in protest of its negative treatment of raves. "I was helping them out with my opinion," she said. Several members of the youngest cohort reported influence of *Sesame Street* and other educational programs on their earliest reading and letter formation. Others in these cohorts reported no or negative influence on their literacy learning by watching television.

[31] For more on the origins and meanings of these developments, see Gee, Hull, and Lankshear (1996).

[32] I return to this issue in the book's Conclusion.

Chapter 4. "The Power of It": Sponsors of Literacy in African American Lives

[1] Similar analyses would pertain to the experiences of other groups in America, including Native Americans and Latinos, who have had to deal with systematic discrimination in employment and education throughout the history of the United States and whose literacy has lower status and market value in white-controlled arenas (see Chapter 6). White women also are an anomalous case, as their literate skills and education credentials were until quite recently passed up by economic sponsors and continue to be compensated less in relationship to white men.

[2] For the fascinating history of literacy and military buildup in World War II – and for evidence of what can happen when adult basic education efforts get serious – see Ginzberg and Bray (1953) and Goldberg (1951). For a treatment of the growing pressure of military technology on education skills of recruits, see Clark and Sloan (1964).

[3] See Stevens (1988, pp. 79–83) for an account of the uses of literacy tests in the South to disenfranchise African American voters. For treatment of the contemporary effects of standardized literacy tests, including racial discrimination, see Hill and Larsen (2000) and Sternglass (1997).

[4] See Cornelius (1991) for a full account of antebellum restrictions on the literacy of enslaved African Americans as well as the methods used by blacks and whites to circumvent these laws.

[5] See Washington (1912) and Smythe (1976, pp. 422–423) for African American literacy rates. Part of this spike was obviously due to the dying off of older African Americans who had not had access to schooling. But also see several chapters pertaining to this time period in Franklin and Anderson (1978) and Neufeldt and McGee (1990).

[6] According to Davis and Donaldson (1975, p. 163), in the 1930s nearly half of the states either required segregation or permitted it in the schools. During this period, expenditures for the education of black children were only half those for the education of white children. Schools for African Americans were separate, in poorer physical shape, and, in some cases, not even provided. Akenson and Neufeldt (1990, p. 180) reported that in some Southern school districts during

this period, spending for white students surpassed spending for black students by as much as 12 times. For other comparative statistics, see Ginzberg and Bray (1953). Regarding the lack of high schools, Anderson (1988, p. 186) wrote that "blacks in the rural South were excluded from the revolution in public secondary education that characterized the nation and the region during the period 1880 to 1935." For the shameful continuation of racial disparity in educational spending today, see Kozol (1991).

[7] For an excellent comprehensive history of the foundations of African American education, see Anderson (1988), Fraser (1999), and Vaughn (1974). See also titles that appear above in note 6. For more on the Freedom Schools, see especially Oldendorf in Neufeldt and McGee (1990).

[8] Royster (2000) suggested that the core cultural values of the African American survival system can be traced back to traditional African social and cultural practices (see her Chapter 3, especially pp. 82–87). Franklin (1984) treated some of these same values as they functioned as a critical response to the regime of slavery in America.

[9] For descriptions of how Protestant denominations competed for loyal believers, including African Americans, see Cornelius (1991). For a useful history of the tensions that led African Americans to leave white-controlled Protestant denominations, see Dvorak (1991). And see Morris (1984) for a useful treatment of cooperation and competition among civil rights groups.

[10] Fraser (1999) observed the distinctive meaning that church-sponsored education has had across time for African Americans, especially during the transformation of the school into a more thoroughly secular institution. He wrote: "In the early years of the nineteenth century, [African American churches] were not acting particularly differently from others for whom the distinction between religious and secular, public and private instruction was a vague and changing one. However, while many of the church-based schools of the early decades of the nineteenth century were missionary schools for 'other people's children,' in the African American community far more of the church-based schools were run by and for the community" (p. 68). For contemporary views, see Johnson (1999).

[11] See Lincoln and Mamiya (1990), Chapter 1.

[12] Morris (1984) observed: "The black church functioned as the institutional center of the modern civil rights movement. Churches provided the movement with an organized mass base; a leadership of clergymen largely economically independent of the larger white society and skilled in the art of managing people and resources; an institutionalized financial base through which protest was financed; and meeting places where the masses planned tactics and strategies and collectively committed themselves to the struggle" (p. 4). But the movement also at times pushed and pressured reluctant black churches and ministers to get involved (see Nelsen and Nelsen, 1975).

[13] For other testimonials from this period, see Litwack (1998).

[14] Bertha Nixon recalled returning from one of her absences from school and being put at the foot of the class. When it came time for spelling lessons, "It didn't matter how many in the fourth class or the fifth class, everybody is lined up in that class at that time. And, I say, if you are out of school, if you're at the head of the class today and if you are out tomorrow, when you come back, you go to the foot of the class. And, I say, I'll never forget the reason I know that I could have been a good scholar; I say, I was out and went to the foot of my class and in spelling class, *Pennsylvania* came all down that line and when it got to me, I spelled it. And I say right today I can spell *Pennsylvania*." Bertha Nixon said that she told this story to her grandson and then she spelled *Pennsylvania* for him, "and he said, 'Whew, Grandma!'"

[15] For excellent historical accounts of the complex situation of African American teachers during the first half of the twentieth century, see Fultz (1995a, 1995b).

[16] Although Bertha Nixon read religious materials and newspapers, she did not write much. "I can talk, talk, talk when I'm with somebody, but writing a letter? I don't know what to say." She also recounted how, when a daughter brought home a typewriter in connection with commercial education, she and other family members wasted a lot of time playing around with the typewriter. On the other hand, she was appreciative of her children's various interests in reading and writing and always supported her children in their learning, including staying awake until one of her sons got home from a job, after midnight, to sit beside him while he did his homework. "What he was doing, I knew I couldn't do it. But I got up and sat with him. He was studying banking or something and I'd get up and sit with him. It's not the help that the parents can give them. It's being with them."

[17] See Moss (1994) for a contemporary ethnography of literacy practices in three Chicago-area African American churches. Moss traced the similarities and differences between the sermon styles of what she called "manuscript" and "nonmanuscript" ministers.

[18] Kyle Barnes did not attribute these writing practices to church influences. He felt that they were an expression and production of his individual nature and were not modeled on religious texts.

[19] For a regional profile pertinent to the life of Frances Hawkins, see Crawford (1996), a book that chronicles, among other things, white resistance to the desegregation of schools in one rural Mississippi county in the late 1960s and early 1970s.

[20] For corroboration, see Gadsden (1993).

[21] For an excellent case study of community-school relations of one twentieth-century school in the segregated South, one that draws on oral testimony, see Walker's (1996) award-winning history.

[22] In the life-history accounts I collected, it was female teacher-relatives who did most of the informal teaching. Schwager (1987) reported that two thirds of the African American teachers by the turn of the twentieth century were women (p. 355). Also see Collier-Thomas (1982).

[23] *Wee Wisdom* is a nondenominational Christian magazine for children between ages 5 and 12. Sponsored by the Unity School of Christianity, it has been published since 1893 (Katz & Katz, 1992).

[24] See Fultz (1995a). For an account of the massive firings of African American teachers in the wake of the desegregation of public schools and subsequent decline in their ranks, see Hudson (1994) and Hooker (1970).

[25] For more on the history of apprenticeship and its relationship to knowledge, see Machlup (1980); and for a historical overview, Rorabaugh (1986).

[26] See Lincoln and Mamiya, 1990, page 180. The authors actually regarded this practice in a negative light for contributing to parochialism and interfering with the flow of new theological views, particularly black liberation theology, into mainstream black congregations.

[27] For a useful historical context, see Foner (1974), especially Chapter 7, and Lee (1963).

[28] I noticed this same tendency among other World War II veterans whom I interviewed. Several of them displayed maps, books, or news clippings as they recounted their military experiences to me.

[29] Franklin (1984) wrote: "While the black church and the black press should be considered central cultural institutions for Afro-Americans, the 'act of migration' (like 'the condition of enslavement') should be considered a central event in the interpretation of Afro-American cultural history. The movement of tens of thousands of rural farm people to urban areas in the South and North was a 'mass phenomenon' that was greatly influenced by economic conditions, but it was also driven by the individual and collective goals of the Afro-American population" (p. 194). For an engrossing history of this mass migration, see Lehmann (1991).

[30] See Donaldson (1991) and Reed (1991).

[31] Branch's biography-in-progress of Martin Luther King Jr. (1988, 1998) is especially good at capturing the decentralized efforts by scores of local citizens who made up the civil rights movement.

[32] See Nelson (1999) and Wolseley (1990).

[33] See Weems (1998) for more on African American magazine readership and its role in commercial advertising.

[34] For an excellent overview of the development of African American children's literature, see Harris (1990).

[35] For a description of seminary curriculums in the early part of the twentieth century, see Daniels (1925). For contemporary treatments of the composition of sermons by African American ministers, see Mitchell (1970) and Moss (1989).

[36] For a fascinating history of the fluctuating interest that corporate America has had in the educational and consumer development of African Americans, see Weems (1998).

[37] By 1950, 5% of black men and 4% of black women between the ages of 18 and 24 were enrolled in college. By 1975, those statistics had risen to 20% for men and 21% for women. (Smythe, 1976).

[38] See Cook-Gumperz (1986) for a historical treatment of the view of literacy as a decontextualized skill; see Street (1984), especially Chapter 1, for a critique of the hidden context of this form of literacy.

[39] Antonia Lawrence was encouraged to enroll in the medical technology program of a local community college by a pediatrician for whom she worked, a physician who also was providing medical care at the time for her young children.

[40] Very important work on what Ladson-Billings called "culturally relevant teaching" is now available and in critical need of wider enactment in America's schools. See Delpit (1995), Foster (1993), Gonzalez and Moll (1995), Ladson-Billings (1994, 1995), Lee (1993), Valdes (1996). For insightful ethnographic portraits of young children engaged in culturally relevant literacy, see Dyson (1993, 1997).

Chapter 5. The Sacred and the Profane: Reading versus Writing in Popular Memory

[1] For an account of the Bolton demonstration, see Laqueur, 1976, pages 124–125. For Laqueur's assessment of the role of writing in the politics of literacy in nineteenth-century Sunday schools, see especially pages 142*ff.*

[2] Furet and Ozouf, 1982, page 76. They observed: "Reading's original necessity – the ability to read the word of God – meant that it kept its claim to universality. It was an instrument of salvation, whereas writing ceased to be an art, to become a convenience... Let the poor, in fortune or in spirit, at least leave school able to read, and the good Lord will take care of the rest. Writing, on the hand, belonged to the 'civil' domain as people then called it, that is to the 'civilization' of men, as people were to say in the 18th century."

[3] See Furet and Ozouf, 1982, pages 166–191.

[4] It is interesting to note, however, that many reading assessments, including the National Assessment of Educational Progress (NAEP) in reading, depend on writing. In the NAEP exam, for instance, reading proficiency is gauged by short paragraphs that students must write in response to comprehension questions. The more organized and detailed the answers, the higher the students score. Writing is treated as if it were a transparent window into reading ability, even though the two are actually separate processes.

[5] For an interesting history of the origins of composition instruction in American public schools, see Schultz (1999), and for writing instruction in higher education, Berlin (1987).

[6] For various articulations of this new kind of literacy, see Langer (1999), Myers (1996), and Willinsky (1990).

[7] Bolter (1991) has suggested that interactive capacities of computers are breaking down traditional roles of readers and writers. Web-based texts are in a constant

state of potential revision; readers can change texts with which they interact; authorship in these conditions becomes more difficult to track and define.

[8] Whether computers are by design a decentralizing and therefore a democratizing technology or not has been variously debated. For a thoughtful treatment of these issues, see Selfe (1999).

[9] Among the people I interviewed, school libraries appeared to be used more heavily than public libraries, perhaps because visits to those libraries were required as part of school assignments. However, for many rural residents across the twentieth century, school libraries were more convenient and often existed in areas where there was no public library – although the provisions were sometimes minimal. A few of the older informants described school libraries as a "windowsill filled with books" or "a locked case with books in them." In 1956, the Library Services Act provided up to $7.5 million per year to provide library service to rural areas. More federal funding of school libraries followed in 1958 and 1965. Two of the people I interviewed worked in their school libraries, both as student volunteers.

[10] Computers as gifts were reported in the accounts of just a couple of the people I interviewed. Like typewriters, their purchase could be associated with going away to college. In two other cases, the gifts were mainly for entertainment. However, in other homes, computers were being bought for the same reasons that encyclopedias used to be bought – to enhance children's performance in school. In a follow-up interview in 1999, for instance, Jack May mentioned that he and his wife had just purchased a computer so that their children could type reports for school. "The teachers say that it doesn't matter if their papers aren't word-processed," he said, "but I think it really does." And in yet other homes, computers were bought in conjunction with parental work. For more on computers and their cultural and economic meanings, see Chapter 6.

[11] For discussions of the significance of the subordination of writing to reading in school, see Berlin (1990), Elbow (1993), Miller (1991), and Slevin (1986).

[12] See Heath (1981) for more on this point.

[13] But for a refreshing and inspirational account of state support of writing, see Talarico (1995).

Chapter 6. The Means of Production: Literacy and Stratification at the Twenty-First Century

[1] The National Assessment of Educational Progress Reading and Writing Report Cards illustrate the association of literacy achievement with race, region, family income, and parental education. As a group, students who reported higher levels of parental education, lived in the northeast and central regions of the country, attended suburban schools, and were not enrolled in the federal Free/Reduced-Price School Lunch Program outperformed other groups on proficiency tests in reading and writing. For more on the results, including improvements by racial minorities, see Donahue, Voelki, Campbell, and Mazzeo (1999) and Greenwald, Persky, Campbell, and Mazzeo (1999).

[2] Graff (1979) authoritatively established how literacy is deeply associated with other social ascriptions of gender, race, and class. That is, literacy is more regularly an outcome of social advantage than a cause of it. My argument is not meant to take issue with this basic dynamic, which, from all apparent social data, remains in place. However, it is important to consider now the changing status of literacy in production as a way to understand potentially new conditions in which social reproduction may be taking place. I argue here that literacy is now, more than ever before, a productive force that comes to be treated more than ever before as a site of investment and exploitation and that this process has direct ramifications for literacy learning. This process is enabled by the economic restructuring toward information processing, an economy that runs on what Bell (1973) has called "new intellectual technology" (p. 14) or what Smith and Parr (1989) called "brain intensive activity" (p. 42). Theoretical knowledge becomes what Bell called the "strategic resource" or "axial principle" of economic production (p. 26). Literacy – the ability to traffic in verbal and other symbolic forms – provides both access to and means of representing this knowledge. This is not to say that literacy is required or developed or rewarded at all levels of economic activity in the society, but it is to say that it has intensified status in production – more than when the economy was based principally in agriculture or manufacturing – and that the middle class, more than the working class, has a more advantageous location within this structure for access and reward in literacy. Also see Wright (1997), who confirmed "the increasing centrality of knowledge and information within the production processes of post-industrial society even within the manufacturing sectors of the economy" (p. 108). For implications of a growing income split between "symbolic analysts" and traditional production workers, see Reich (1992).

[3] Bourdieu and Passeron (1977) have provided foundations for understanding how schools reproduce political and economic inequity in societies in which ownership of symbolic power (including skills, expertise, and language styles) replaces ownership over the means of production as a source of individual and class dominance. Also see Bourdieu, 1991. Bernstein (1977) explored how schools rely on and reward experience with "elaborated" linguistic codes, a language style that he associated with middle-class social life, and reject or punish "restricted" linguistic codes that he associated with working-class social life. (But for explorations into the restricted quality of school discourse, see Wells, 1986). Astute and vociferous critics of social reproduction forces in American schools include Apple (1993, 1995, 1999), Apple and Weiss (1983), Giroux (1981), Giroux and Aronowitz (1985), and Shor (1980, 1982). Reports by schools on academic achievement, test results, and college continuance routinely sort out students by race, parental education, and family income as a kind of prima facie explanation of differential academic outcomes. In my experience, this accounting practice helps to rationalize and normalize inequalities by making them seem to be permanent features of the social structure rather than ongoing accomplishments of education practice.

[4] For a useful critique of this tendency, see Auerbach (1995).

[5] See Lareau (1989) for investigations into how cultural capital is cashed in or not during teacher–parent interactions in schools.

[6] The best two books I have encountered for explaining these transformations in material and historical terms are Beniger (1986) and Castells (1989).

[7] For fascinating facts about investment in computer technology, especially as it affects literacy education, see Selfe (1999).

[8] For a very useful treatment of Karl Marx's categories of basic productive forces, see Cohen (1978).

[9] Dora Lopez spent most of her grade-school years at a private Catholic elementary school, where her parents placed her after the public school to which she was assigned posted the lowest reading achievement test scores in the school district, blamed at the time on an experimental reading program in use at the school. She transferred back into the public system after eighth grade.

[10] Of course, native monolingual speakers of English take 12 years of instruction in the language and literature of English without having to justify it.

[11] In the county where Dora Lopez lived, per capita income, as reported by the 1990 U.S. census, was $15,542 overall, whereas Hispanic per capita income was $8,552.

[12] For more on the so-called digital divide, see *Condition of Education* (1997).

[13] Cohen (1978) observed: "Classes are permanently poised against one another, and that class tends to prevail whose rule would best meet the demands of production... There is a general stake in stable and thriving production, so that the class best placed to deliver it attracts allies from other strata in society" (p. 292).

[14] When asked, "Do you remember your parents reading to you at all?" Dora Lopez responded, "No." To the follow-up question, "Were there books in your house?" she answered, "Yes. All kinds of books. My mom used to work at the Bookstore when I was little, so we did have an extensive amount of books that she bought. And magazines. I had books in English and in Spanish." Raymond Branch said of himself: "I've never been a reader." Asked, "Do you remember your parents reading to you at all?" Branch replied, "Nope. Except for one homework exercise, which was to read with your parents. So I went home and read some *Wizard of Oz* with them for an hour, and that's about the only time I've ever read with them." Asked as a follow-up, "Were there children's books in your home?" Branch replied: "There were nursery school–level books – Richard Scarry and so forth – and my sister had a fairly large collection of those mystery books – Hardy Boys, Nancy Drew, and *Wizard of Oz* books and so forth."

[15] Just by way of crude comparison, the university that figures in these case studies is investing approximately $34 million a year on computer science plus information technology, a little over $4 million on its school of social work, and $1.5 million on the foreign-language department of which Spanish is a part.

[16] See, Heath (1983), Lareau (1989), and Snow (1991).

[17] Also see Lewis (1997) on the dangers of associating literacy merely with economic productivity.

[18] See Hawkins and Paris (1997) for how collegiate experience, for example, can exacerbate the digital divide among students.

Conclusion: Literacy in American Lives

[1] Sanderson (1991) wrote of England: "Levels of human capital in the 1850s curiously related more closely to GNP [Gross National Product] rankings of the 1970s rather than to those of Victorian times" (p. 27). Mitch (1992) provided a fascinating exploration of the spread of mass literacy and its effects on the value and use of individual literacy skills. Focusing on late nineteenth-century England, he investigates why it was that people were investing in the acquisition of literacy even when the economy in which they participated still required relatively little use of reading or writing. Also see Vincent (1989) on the processes of schooling in eighteenth- and nineteenth-century England. He wrote: "With few exceptions, occupational training remained embedded in productivity activity... Alone of the tools a child would need, reading and writing were to be gained away from the company of adults and apart from every other process of daily life" (p. 15). These conditions were changing dramatically by the end of the nineteenth century. See Mitch (1992), Chapter 2, for an interesting analysis of literacy requirements listed in job advertisements in various decades.

[2] What Castells (1998) observed about what he called "the network society" pertains to the current market economy generally: "The process of social exclusion in the network society concerns both people and territories. So that, under certain conditions, entire countries, regions, cities, and neighborhoods become excluded, embracing in this exclusion most, or all, of their populations... Under the new, dominant logic of the space of flows ... areas that are non-valuable from the perspective of informational capitalism, and that do not have significant political interests for the powers that be, are bypassed by flows of wealth and information, and ultimately deprived of the basic technological infrastructure that allows us to communicate, innovate, produce, consume, and even live, in today's world" (p. 74).

[3] See Graff (1979) and Soltow and Stevens (1981).

[4] Gilmore (1989) has provided a rich and fascinating account of the relationship between reading and commercialism in early America; however, the study also shows how access to literacy was affected by physical barriers, like muddy roads, that could slow the arrival of reading material to eighteenth-century communities in the upper Connecticut River valley.

[5] This ironic reassessment of the newspaper refers to readability formulas that emerged as part of school testing in the 1930s and 1940s, especially with the research of Rudolph Flesch. For a treatment of Flesch's Reading Ease Formula developed in 1948, see Kaestle, Damon-Moore, Stedman, Tinsley, and Trollinger (1991), pages 207–210.

[6] For an interesting account of writing assignments in nineteenth-century schools and their links to local experience, see Schultz (1999). The pedagogies Schultz described were still in use in rural Wisconsin schools through the first

three decades of the twentieth century, at least according to the memories of the people I interviewed.

[7] For the implications of these developments, see Castells (1998), and for an important account of literacy and recent immigration in Wisconsin, see Duffy (2000).

[8] See Mace (1998) for a study of literacy among mothers that is not focused on their maternal roles.

[9] Soltow and Stevens, 1981, page 193.

[10] See Kaestle et al. (1991), Part 3, for effects of mass-market print sales on the formation of consumer-based reading publics.

[11] Cremin (1990) took up this issue in "The Cacophony of Teaching," in which he suggested that complex economic and social changes since World War II, including the popularization of schooling and the penetration of mass media, have created "a far greater range and diversity of languages, competencies, values, personalities, and approaches to the world and to educational opportunities" than at one time existed. The diversity most of interest to him (and me) resides not so much in the range of different ethnic groups that are in society but in the different cultural formulas by which people assemble their education – or, I would say, literacy – experience.

[12] See Wilson (1997).

[13] For a rousing critique of political mean-spiritedness and historical amnesia in the literacy standards movement, see Fox (1999).

BIBLIOGRAPHY

Akenson, J. E., & Neufeldt, H. G. (1990). The Southern literacy campaign for black adults in the early twentieth century. In H. G. Neufeldt & L. McGee (Eds.), *Education of the African American adult* (pp.). New York: Greenwood Press.

Anderson, J. D. (1988). *The education of blacks in the South, 1860–1935*. Chapel Hill, NC: University of North Carolina Press.

Apple, M. W. (1993). *Official knowledge: Democratic education in a conservative age.* New York: Routledge.

Apple, M. W. (1995). *Education and power.* New York: Routledge.

Apple, M. (1999). *Power, meaning, and identity: Essays in critical educational and studies.* New York: P. Lang.

Apple, M. W. & Weis, L. (1983). *Ideology and practice in schooling.* Philadelphia: Temple University Press.

Auerbach, E. (1995). Deconstructing the discourse of strengths in family literacy. *Journal of Reading Behavior, 27,* 643–661.

Barton, D. (1994). *Literacy: An introduction to the ecology of written language.* Cambridge, MA: Blackwell.

Barton, D. & Hamilton, M. (1998). *Local literacies: Reading and writing in one community.* London: Routledge.

Becker, G. S. (1964). *Human capital: A theoretical and empirical analysis.* New York: Columbia University Press.

Becker, G. S. (1976). *The economic approach to human behavior.* Chicago: University of Chicago Press.

Becker, G. S. (1986). *An economic analysis of the family.* Dublin: Economic and Social Research Institute.

Bell, D. (1973). *The coming of post-industrial society.* New York: Basic Books.

Beniger, J. F. (1986). *The control revolution: Technological and economic origins of the information society.* Cambridge, MA: Harvard University Press.

Berger, P. L., Berger, B., & Kellner, H. (1974). *The homeless mind: Modernization and consciousness.* New York: Vintage Books.

Berlin, J. A. (1987). *Rhetoric and reality: Writing instruction in American colleges, 1900–1985.* Carbondale, IL: Southern Illinois University Press.

Berlin, J. A. (1990). Writing instruction in school and college English, 1890–1985. In J. J. Murphy (Ed.), *A short history of writing instruction from ancient Greece to twentieth-century America* (pp. 183–222). Davis, CA: Hermagoras Press.

Berns, R. G. (1996). *DECA: A continuing tradition of excellence.* Reston, VA: Distributive Education Clubs of America.

Bernstein, B. (1977). *Class, codes, and control. vol. 3: Towards a theory of educational transmission.* London: Routledge and Kegan Paul.

Bertaux, D. (Ed.) (1981). *Biography and society: The life history approach.* Beverly Hills: Sage.

Bertaux, D. (1984). The life story approach: A continental view. *Annual Review of Sociology, 10,* 215–237.

Bertaux, D., & Thompson, P. (1997). *Pathways to social class: A qualitative approach to social mobility.* Oxford: Clarendon Press.

Besnier, N. (1995). *Literacy, emotion, and authority.* New York: Cambridge University Press.

Bolter, J. D. (1991). *Writing space: The computer, hypertext, and the history of writing.* Hillsdale, NJ: Erlbaum.

Bourdieu, P. (1980). *The logic of practice* R. Nice, (Trans). Stanford, CT: Stanford University Press.

Bourdieu, P. (1991). *Language and symbolic power.* (G. Raymond & M. Adamson, Trans.). Cambridge, MA: Harvard University Press.

Bourdieu, P. (1998). *Practical reason.* Stanford, CA: Stanford University Press.

Bourdieu, P., & Passeron, J.-C. (1977). *Reproduction in education, society, and culture* (R. Nice, Trans.). Beverly Hills: Sage.

Bourdieu, P., & Wacquant, L. J. D. (1992). *An invitation to reflexive sociology.* Chicago: University of Chicago Press.

Bourne, J. M. (1986). *Patronage and society in nineteenth-century England.* London: Edward Arnold.

Branch, T. (1988). *Parting the Waters: America in the King Years, 1954–1963.* New York: Simon & Schuster.

Branch, T. (1998). *Pillar of fire: America in the King years, 1963–65.* New York: Simon & Schuster.

Brand, A. G. (1979). The uses of writing in psychotherapy. *Journal of Humanistic Psychology, 19,* 53–72.

Briggs, C. C. (1986). *Learning how to ask: A sociolinguistic appraisal of the role of the interview in social science research.* New York: Cambridge University Press.

Brockhous, H. H. (1949). *The history of the Wisconsin High School Forensic Association*. Unpublished dissertation, University of Wisconsin–Madison.

Brown, R. D. (1989). *Knowledge is power: The diffusion of information in early America, 1700–1865*. New York: Oxford University Press.

Carney, L. P. (1979). The counseling perspective in parole. *Counseling Psychologist, 11*, 41–47.

Castells, M. (1989). *The informational city: Information technology, economic restructuring, and the urban-regional process*. Cambridge, MA: Blackwell.

Castells, M. (1998). *End of millennium*. Volume 3: *The information age: economy, society, and culture*. Malden, MA: Blackwell.

Census of Agriculture (1991). Washington, D.C.: Bureau of the Census.

Chartier, R. (1987). Urban reading practices, 1660–1780. In L. G. Cochrane (Trans.), *The Cultural Uses of Print in Early Modern France*. Princeton, NJ: Princeton University Press.

Chartier, R. (1989). The practical impact of writing. In *Passions of the Renaissance. Vol. 3: A history of private life*. Cambridge, MA: Harvard University Press.

Clark, G., & Halloran, S. M. (1993). *Oratorical culture in nineteenth-century America*. Carbondale, IL: Southern Illinois University Press.

Clark, H. F., & Sloan, H. S. (1964). *Classrooms in the military: An account of education in the armed forces of the United States*. New York: Teachers College Press.

Cochran-Smith, M. (1984). *The making of a reader*. Norwood, NJ: Ablex.

Cohen, G. A. (1978). *Karl Marx's theory of history: A defense*. Princeton, NJ: Princeton University Press.

Collier-Thomas, B. (1982). The impact of black women in education: An historical overview. *Journal of Negro Education, 51*, 173–180.

Collins, J. (1995). Literacy and literacies. *Annual Review of Anthropology, 24*, 75–93.

Condition of education. (1997). Washington, D.C.: U.S. Department of Education National Center for Educational Statistics.

Cook-Gumperz, J. (1986). Literacy and schooling: An unchanging equation? In J. Cook-Gumperz (Ed.), *The social construction of literacy* (pp. 16–44). Cambridge, UK: Cambridge University Press.

Cornelius, J. (1983). "We slipped and learned to read": Slave accounts of the literacy process, 1830–1865. *Phylon: A Review of Race and Culture, 44*, 171–186.

Cornelius, J. (1991). *"When I can read my title clear": Literacy, slavery, and religion in the antebellum South*. Columbia, SC: University of South Carolina Press.

Coyle, W. J. (1987). *Libraries in prison: A blending of institutions*. New York: Greenwood Press.

Crawford, C. (1996). *Uproar at Dancing Rabbit Creek*. Reading, MA: Addison-Wesley.

Cremin, L. A. (1988). *American education: The metropolitan experience, 1876–1980*. New York: Harper & Row.

Cremin, L. A. (1990). The cacophony of teaching. In *Popular education and its discontents*. New York: Harper & Row.

Cressy, D. (1980). *Literacy and the social order: Reading and writing in Tudor and Stuart England*. Cambridge UK: Cambridge University Press.

Cushman, E. (1998). *The struggle and the tools: Oral and literate strategies in an inner city community*. Albany, NY: State University of New York Press.

Danbom, D. B. (1995). *Born in the country: A history of rural America*. Baltimore: Johns Hopkins University Press.

Daniels, W. A. (1925). *The education of Negro ministers*. New York: George H. Doran.

Davis, G., & Donaldson, O. F. (1975). *Blacks in the United States: A geographic perspective*. Boston: Houghton Mifflin.

Davis, N. Z. (1981). Printing and the people. In H. J. Graff (Ed.), *Literacy and social development in the West: A reader* (pp. 69–95). New York: Cambridge University Press.

Delpit, L. (1995). *Other people's children: Cultural conflict in the classroom*. New York: New Press.

Dickey, W. J. (1991). *From the bottom up: The Fox Lake Prison*. Madison, WI: University of Wisconsin Law School.

Donahue, P. L., Voelki, K. E., Campbell, J. R., & Mazzeo, J. (1999). NAEP 1998 Reading Report Card for the Nation and the States. Available at http://nces.ed.gov/nationsreportcard/

Donaldson, G. (1991). *The history of African Americans in the military: Double V.* Malabar, FlA: Krieger.

Donehower, K. (1997). *Beliefs about literacy in a southern Appalachian community*. Unpublished dissertation, University of Minnesota Department of English.

Drucker, P. (1969). *The age of discontinuity: Guidelines to our changing society*. New York: Harper & Row.

Du Bois, W. E. B. (Ed.) (1903). *The Negro church*. Atlanta: Atlanta University Press.

Duffy, J. (2000). *Writing from these roots: Literacy, rhetoric, and history in a Hmong–American community*. Unpublished doctoral dissertation, University of Wisconsin–Madison Department of English.

Dvorak, K. L. (1991). *An African-American exodus: The segregation of the Southern churches*. Brooklyn, NY: Carlson.

Dyson, A. H. (1993). *Social worlds of children learning to write in an urban primary school*. New York: Teachers College Press.

Dyson, A. H. (1997). *Writing superheroes: Contemporary childhood, popular culture, and classroom literacy*. New York: Teacher College Press.

Eisenstein, E. (1979). *The printing press as an agent of change: Communications and cultural transformations in early modern europe*. New York: Cambridge University Press.

Elbow, P. (1993). The war between reading and writing and how to end it. *Rhetoric Review, 12,* 5–24.

Evans, J. F., & Salcedo, R. N. (1974). *Communications in agriculture: The American farm press.* Ames: Iowa State University Press.

Faigley, L. (1999). Veterans' stories on the porch. In B. Boehm, D. Journet, & M. Rosner (Eds.), *History, reflection, and narrative: The professionalization of composition, 1963–1983.* Norwood: Ablex.

Farr, M. (1993). Essayist literacy and other verbal performances. *Written Communication, 8,* 4–38.

Foner, J. (1974). *Blacks and the military in American history: A new perspective.* New York: Praeger.

Foster, M. (1993). Educating for competence in community and culture: Exploring views of exemplary African-American teachers. *Urban Education, 27,* 370–394.

Fox, T. (1999). *Defending access: A critique of standards in higher education.* Portsmouth, NH: Heinemann.

Franklin, V. P. (1984). *Black self-determination: A cultural history of the faith of the fathers.* Westport, CT: Lawrence Hill.

Franklin, V. P. (1990). "They rose and fell together": African American educators and community leadership, 1795–1954. *Journal of Education 172,* 39–64.

Franklin, V. P., & Anderson, J. (1978). *New perspectives on black educational history.* Boston: G. K. Hall.

Fraser, J. W. (1999). Literacy in the African American community: Church and school in slave and free communities, 1802–1902. In *Between church and state: Religion and public education in multicultural America* (pp. 67–82). New York: St. Martin's Press.

Fuller, W. E. (1972). *The American mail: Enlarger of the common life.* Chicago: University of Chicago Press.

Fuller, W. E. (1982). *The old country school.* Chicago: University of Chicago Press.

Fultz, M. (1995a). African American teachers in the South, 1890–1940: Powerlessness and the ironies of expectations and protest. *History of Education Quarterly, 35,* 401–422.

Fultz, M. (1995b). Teacher training and African American education in the South, 1900–1940. *Journal of Negro Education, 64,* 196–210.

Furet, F., & Ozouf, J. (1982). *Reading and writing: Literacy in France from Calvin to Jules Ferry.* Cambridge, UK: Cambridge University Press.

Gadsden, V. (1992). Giving meaning to literacy: Intergenerational beliefs about access. *Theory Into Practice, 31,* 328–336.

Gadsden, V. (1993). Literacy, education, and identity among African Americans: The communal nature of learning. *Urban Education, 27,* 352–369.

Gadsden, V. (1997). Schooling, persistence, and family cultures: Intergenerational discourses within four generations. Lecture. University of Wisconsin School of Education, February 27.

Gallegos, B. P. (1991). *Literacy, education, and society in New Mexico 1693–1821.* Albuquerque: University of New Mexico Press.

Gallman, R. E. (1988). "Changes in the Level of Literacy in a New Community of Early America." *Journal of Economic History, 48,* 567–582.

Gee, J. P., Hull, G., & Lankshear, C. (1996). *The new work order: Behind the language of the new capitalism.* Boulder, CO: Westview Press.

Gere, A. R. (1997). *Intimate practices: Literacy and cultural work in US women's clubs 1880–1920.* Urbana, IL: University of Illinois Press.

Gilmore, W. J. (1989). *Reading becomes a necessity of life: Material and cultural life in rural New England, 1780–1835.* Knoxville: University of Tennessee.

Ginzberg, E., & Bray, D. W. (1953). *The uneducated.* New York: Columbia University Press.

Giroux, H., & Aronowitz, S. (1985). *Education under siege: The conservative, liberal, and radical debate over schooling.* South Hadley, Mass: Begin & Garvey.

Giroux, H., & McLaren, P. (Eds.) (1989). *Critical pedagogy, the state, and cultural struggle.* Albany, NY: State University of New York Press.

Goldberg, S. (1951). *Army training of illiterates in World War II.* New York: Teachers College Press.

Goldblatt, E. (1994). *'Round my way: Authority and double consciousness in three urban high-school writers.* Pittsburgh: University of Pittsburgh Press.

Gonzalez, N., & Moll, L. (1995). Funds of knowledge for teaching Latino households. *Urban Education, 29,* 443–470.

Gowen, S. G. (1992). *The politics of workplace literacy: A case study.* New York: Teachers College Press.

Graff, H. J. (1979). *The literacy myth: Literacy and social structure in the nineteenth-century city.* New York: Academic Press.

Graff, H. J. (1986). *The legacies of literacy: Continuities and contradictions in western culture and society.* Bloomington, IN: Indiana University Press.

Greenwald, E. A., Persky, H. R., Campbell, J. R., & Mazzeo, J. (1999). NAEP 1998 Writing Report Card for the Nation and the States. Available at http://nces.ed.gov/nationsreportcard/

Grubb, F. W. (1987). Colonial immigrant literacy: An economic analysis of Pennsylvania–German evidence, 1727–1775. *Explorations in Economic History, 24,* 63–76.

Grubb, F. W. (1990). Growth of literacy in colonial America: Longitudinal patterns, economic models, and the direction of future research. *Social Science History, 14,* 451–482.

Grubb, F. W. (1992). Educational choice in the era before free public schooling: Evidence from German immigrant children in Pennsylvania, 1771–1817. *Journal of Economic History 52,* 363–375.

Halloran, M. (1990). From rhetoric to composition: The teaching of writing in America to 1900. In J. J. Murphy (Ed.), *A short history of writing instruction from ancient Greece to twentieth-century America* (pp. 121–150). Davis, CA: Hermagoras Press.

Harris, V. J. (1990). African American children's literature: The first 100 years. *Journal of Negro Education, 59,* 540–555.

Harris, V. J. (1992). African American conceptions of literacy: A historical perspective. *Theory Into Practice, 31*, 278–286.

Hawkins, R., & Paris, A. E. (1997). Computer literacy and computer use among college students: Differences in black and white. *Journal of Negro Education, 66*, 147–158.

Heath, S. B. (1981). Toward an ethnohistory of writing in American education. In M. F. Whiteman (Ed.), *The nature, development, and teaching of written communication, Vol. 1*. Hillsdale, NJ: Erlbaum.

Heath, S. Brice. (1983). *Ways with words: Language, life, and work in communities and classrooms*. New York: Cambridge University Press.

Heckscher, C. C. (1988). *The new unionism: Employee involvement in the changing corporation*. New York: Basic Books.

Hettinger, H. S. (1933). *A decade of radio advertising*. Chicago: University of Chicago Press.

Hill, C., & Larsen, E. (2000). *Children and reading tests*. Stamford, CT: Ablex.

Hooker, R. W. (1970). *Displacement of black teachers in eleven Southern states*. Nashville: Race Relations Information Center.

Horan, P. M., & Hargis, P. G. (1991). Children's work and schooling in the late nineteenth-century family economy. *American Sociological Review, 56*, 583–596.

Hortsman, C., & Kurtz, D. V. (1978). *Compadrazgo in post-conquest middle America*. Milwaukee: Milwaukee-UW Center for Latin America.

Houston, R. A. (1985). *Literacy and the Scottish identity: Illiteracy and society in Scotland and Northern England 1600–1800*. New York: Cambridge University Press.

Houston, R. A. (1988). *Literacy in early modern Europe: Culture and education, 1500–1800*. New York: Harper & Row.

Hudson, M. J. (1994). Missing teachers, impaired communities: The unanticipated consequences of *Brown v. Board of Education* on the African American teaching force at the precollegiate level. *Journal of Negro Education, 63*, 388–393.

Hull, G. (Ed.) (1997). *Changing work, changing workers. Critical perspectives on language, literacy, and skills*. Albany: State University of New York Press.

Hurt, J. S. (1972). *Bringing literacy to rural England: The Hertfordshire example*. London: Phillimore.

Jackson, M. D. (1975). Literacy, communication, and social change. In I. H. Kawharu (Ed.), *Conflict and compromise: Essays on the Maori since colonialisation* (pp. 27–54). Wellington: A. H. & A. W. Reed.

Jacobs, J. B. (1977). *Stateville: The penitentiary in mass society*. Chicago: University of Chicago Press.

Johnson, J. H. (1989). With Bennett, L. Jr. *Succeeding against the odds*. New York: Warner Books.

Johnson, S. C. (1999). *The role of the black church in family literacy*. New York: Peter Lang.

Johnston, W. B., & Packer, A. E. (1987). *Workforce 2000: Work and workers for the twenty-first century.* Washington, D.C.: U.S. Department of Labor.

Jones, D. B. (1987). *Bibliography of the Little Golden Books.* New York: Greenwood Press.

Joyce, William L., David D. Hall, Richard D. Brown and John B. Hench, Eds. 1983. *Printing and Society in Early America.* Worcester: American Antiquarian Society.

Kaestle, C. F. (1983). *Pillars of the republic: Common schools and American society, 1780–1860.* New York: Hill and Wang.

Kaestle, C. F., & Vinovskis, M. A. (1978). From fireside to factory: School entry and school leaving in nineteenth-century Massachusetts. In T. K. Hareven (Ed.), *Transitions: The family and the life course in historical perspective* (pp. 135–185). New York: Academic Press.

Kaestle, C. F., Damon-Moore, H., Stedman, L. C., Tinsley, K., & Trollinger, W. V. Jr. (1991). *Literacy in the United States: Readers and reading since 1880.* New Haven, CT: Yale University Press.

Kerber, L. (1976). The Republican mother. *American Quarterly, 28,* 187–205.

Kernan, M. (1984). Write angles. *Washington Post,* 17 April, D1.

Kett, J. F. (1994). *The pursuit of knowledge under difficulties: From self-improvement to adult education in America, 1750–1990.* Stanford, CA: Stanford University Press.

King, L. (1994). *Roots of identity: Language and literacy in Mexico.* Stanford, CA: Stanford University Press.

Kozol, J. (1985). *Illiterate America.* New York: New American Library.

Kozol, J. (1991). *Savage inequalities: Children in America's schools.* New York: Crown.

Ladson-Billings, G. (1994). *The dreamkeepers: Successful teachers of African-American children.* San Francisco: Jossey Bass.

Ladson-Billings, G. (1995). Toward a theory of culturally relevant pedagogy. *American Educational Research Journal, 32,* 465–491.

Landes, W., & Solomon, L. (1992). Compulsory schooling legislation. *Journal of Economic History, 32,* 54–91.

Langer, J. (1999). Excellence in English in middle and high school. Albany, NY: National Research Center on English Learning and Achievement. Report No. 12002.

Laqueur, T. (1976). *Religion and respectability: Sunday schools and working class Culture, 1780–1850.* New Haven, CT: Yale University Press.

Lareau, A. (1989). *Home advantage: Social class and parental intervention in elementary education.* New York: Falmer Press.

Lee, C. D. (1993). *Signifying as a scaffold for literary interpretation: The pedagogical implications of an African American discourse genre.* Urbana, IL: National Council of Teachers of English.

Lee, U. (1963). *The employment of Negro troops.* Washington, D.C.: Center of Military History.

Lehmann, N. (1991). *The promised land: The great black migration and how it changed America.* New York: Vintage.

Levitan, S. A., & Johnston, B. H. (1975). *The Job Corps: A social experiment that works.* Baltimore: Johns Hopkins University Press.

Lewis, T. (1997). America's choice: Literacy or productivity? *Curriculum Inquiry, 27,* 391–421.

Lincoln, E., & Mamiya, L. H. (1990). *The black church in the African American experience.* Durham, NC: Duke University Press.

Litwack, L. F. (1998). *Trouble in mind: Black southerners in the age of Jim Crow.* New York: Knopf.

Lockridge, K. A. (1974). *Literacy in colonial New England: An enquiry into the social context of literacy in the early modern West.* New York: Norton.

Luke, A. (1988). *Literacy, textbooks, and ideology: Postwar literacy instruction and the mythology of Dick and Jane.* New York: Falmer Press.

Lummis, T. (1987). *Listening to history: The authenticity of oral evidence.* London: Hutchinson.

Lynch, J. H. (1986). *Godparents and kinship in early medieval Europe.* Princeton, NJ: Princeton University Press.

Mace, J. (1998). *Playing with time: Mothers and the meaning of literacy.* Philadelphia: UCL Press.

Machlup, F. (1980). *Knowledge: Its creation, distribution, and economic significance. Vol. 1: Knowledge and knowledge production.* Princeton, NJ: Princeton University Press.

Main, G. (1991). An inquiry into when and why women learned to write in colonial New England. *Journal of Social History, 24,* 579–589.

Martin, H. -J. (1994). *The history and power of writing.* (L. G. Cochrane, Trans.). Chicago: University of Chicago Press.

McClaure, A. F., Chrisman, J. R., & Mock, P. (1985). *Education for work: The historical evolution of vocational and distributive education in America.* Rutherford, NJ: Fairleigh Dickinson University Press.

Miller, S. (1991). *Textual carnivals: The politics of composition.* Carbondale, IL: Southern Illinois University Press.

Mitch, D. F. (1992). *The rise of popular literacy in Victorian England: The influence of private choice and public policy.* Philadelphia: University of Pennsylvania Press.

Mitchell, H. H. (1970). *Black preaching.* Philadelphia: J. B. Lippincott.

Monaghan, E. J. & Saul, E. W. (1987). The reader, the scribe, the thinker: A critical look at the history of American reading and writing instruction. In T. S. Popkewitz (Ed.), *The formation of school subjects.* New York: Falmer. 85–122.

Morris, A. D. (1984). *The origins of the civil rights movement: Communities organizing for change.* New York: The Free Press.

Moss, B. J. (1989). *The black sermon as a literacy event.* Unpublished doctoral dissertation. University of Illinois at Chicago.

Moss, B. J. (1994). Creating a community: Literacy events in African-American churches. In B. J. Moss (Ed.), *Literacy across communities* (pp. 147–178). Cresskill, NJ: Hampton Press.

Myers, M. (1996). *Changing our minds: Negotiating English and Literacy.* Urbana, IL: National Council of Teachers of English.

A nation at risk: The imperative for educational reform. 1983. Washington, D.C.: U.S. Department of Education.

Nelsen, H. M., & Nelsen, A. K. (1975). *The black church in the sixties.* Lexington, KY: University of Kentucky Press.

Nelson, D. (1988). *American rubber workers and organized labor, 1900–1941.* Princeton, NJ: Princeton University Press.

Nelson, D. (1995). *Farm and factory workers in the Midwest, 1880–1990.* Bloomington: Indiana University Press, 1995.

Nelson, S. (1999). *The black press: Soldiers without swords.* A film. Transcript available at http://www.pbs.org.

Neth, M. (1995). *Preserving the family farm: Women, community, and the foundations of agribusiness in the Midwest, 1900–1940.* Baltimore: Johns Hopkins University Press.

Neufeldt, H. G., & McGee, L. (Eds.). (1990). *Education of the African American adult.* New York: Greenwood Press.

Nicholas, S. J., & Nicholas, J. M. (1992). Male literacy, "deskilling," and the Industrial Revolution. *Journal of Interdisciplinary History, 23,* 1–18.

Paris, K. A. (1985). *A political history of vocational, technical, and adult education in Wisconsin.* Madison, WI: Wisconsin Board of Vocational, Technical and Adult Education.

Perlmann, J., & Shirley, D. (1991). When did New England women acquire literacy? *William and Mary Quarterly, 48,* 50–67.

Polanyi, K. (1944). *The great transformation: The political and economic origins of our time.* Boston: Beacon.

Pollock, J. M. (1997). *Prisons today and tomorrow.* Gaithersburg, MD: Aspen Publishers.

Popular Memory Group (1982). Popular memory: Theory, politics, method. In R. Johnson, G. McLennan, B. Schwarz, & D. Dutton (Eds.), *Making histories: Studies in history writing and politics.* London: Hutchinson.

Purcell-Gates, V. (1995). *Other people's words: The cycle of low literacy.* Cambridge, MA: Harvard University Press.

Rawls, J. (1971). *A theory of justice.* Cambridge, MA: Harvard University Press.

Reed, M. (1991). *Seedtime for the modern civil rights movement.* Baton Rouge, LA: Louisiana State University Press.

Reich, R. B. (1992). *The work of nations: Preparing ourselves for twenty-first century capitalism.* New York: Vintage.

Resnick, D. P., & Resnick, L. B. (1977). The nature of literacy: A historical exploration. *Harvard Educational Review, 47,* 370–385.

Riley, G. (1969). Origins of the argument for improved female education. *History of Education Quarterly, 9,* 455–470.

Rorabaugh, W. J. (1986). *The craft apprentice: From Franklin to the machine age in America.* New York: Oxford University Press.

Royster, J. J. (2000). *Traces of a stream: Literacy and social change among African American women.* Pittsburgh: University of Pittsburgh Press.

Ryder, N. B. (1965). The cohort as a concept in the study of social change. *American Sociological Review 30,* 843–861.

Sanderson, M. (1991). *Education, economic change, and society in England, 1780–1870.* London: Macmillan.

Saupe, W. F. (1989). *How family farms deal with unexpected financial stress.* University of Wisconsin-Madison: Comunities Economics Paper Series.

Saupe, W. F., & Majchrowicz, T. A. (1996). *Jobs in Wisconsin's farm and farm-related sectors.* Madison: University of Wisconsin Community Economics Series, No. 234.

Scharf, P., Dindinger, M., & Vogel, R. (1979). Keeping faith: Roles and problems of counselors in prison settings. *Counseling Psychologist, 11,* 35–40.

Schieffelin, B., & P. Gilmore (Eds.) (1984). *The acquisition of literacy: Ethnographic perspectives.* Norwood, NJ: Ablex.

Schultz, L. M. (1999). *The young composers: Composition's beginnings in nineteenth-century schools.* Carbondale, IL: Southern Illinois University Press.

Schwager, S. (1987). Educating women in America. *Signs, 12,* 333–372.

Scribner, S., & Cole, M. (1981). *The psychology of literacy.* Cambridge, MA: Harvard University Press.

Selfe, C. L. (1999). *Technology and literacy in the twenty-first century: The importance of paying attention.* Carbondale, IL: Southern Illinois University Press.

Shor, I. (1980). *Critical teaching and everyday life.* Boston: South End Press.

Shor, I. (1982). *Empowering education.* Chicago: University of Chicago Press.

Slevin, J. (1986). Connecting English studies. *College English, 48,* 543–550.

Smith, D. (1974). The social construction of documentary reality. *Social Inquiry, 44,* 313–37.

Smith, G. V., & Parr, R. L. (1989). *Valuation of intellectual property and intangible assets.* New York: J. Wiley.

Smith, M. R. (Ed.) (1985). *Military enterprise and technological change: Perspectives on the American experience.* Cambridge, MA: MIT Press.

Smythe, M. (Ed.). (1996). *The black American reference book.* Englewood Cliffs, N.J.: Prentice-Hall.

Snow, C. (1991). *Unfulfilled expectations: Home and school influences on literacy.* Cambridge, MA: Harvard University Press.

Soltow, L., & Stevens, E. (1981). *The rise of literacy and the common school in the United States: A socioeconomic analysis to 1870.* Chicago: University of Chicago Press.

Spellmeyer, K. (1996). After theory: From textuality to attunement with the world. *College English, 58,* 893–913.

Stephens, W. B. (1987). *Education, literacy, and society 1830–70: The geography of diversity in provincial England.* Manchester, UK: Manchester University Press.

Sternglass, M. S. (1997). *Time to know them: A longitudinal study of writing and learning at the college level.* Mahwah, NJ: Erlbaum.

Stevens, E. W. Jr. (1988). *Literacy, law, and social order.* DeKalb, IL: Northern Illinois University Press.

Stock, B. (1983). *The implications of literacy: Written language and models of interpretation in the eleventh and twelfth centuries.* Princeton, NJ: Princeton University Press.

Street, B. V. (1984). *Literacy in theory and practice.* Cambridge, UK: Cambridge University Press.

Street, B. V. (1993). *Cross-cultural approaches to literacy.* Cambridge, UK: Cambridge University Press.

Street, B. (1995). *Social literacies: Critical approaches to literacy development, ethnography and education.* New York: Addison-Wesley.

Street, B. V., & Besnier, N. (1994). Aspects of literacy. In T. Ingold (Ed.). *Companion encyclopedia of anthropology: humanity, culture, and social life* (pp. 527–561). London: Routledge.

Strom, S. H. (1992). *Beyond the typewriter: Gender, classs, and the origins of modern American office work, 1900–1930.* Urbana, IL: University of Illinois Press.

Stuckey, J. E. (1991). *The violence of literacy.* Portsmouth, N.H.: Boynton/Cook.

Talarico, R. (1995). *Spreading the word: Poetry and the survival of community in America.* Durham, NC: Duke University.

Taylor, D. (1985). *Family literacy.* London: Heinemann.

Taylor, D. (1996). *Toxic literacies: Exposing the injustice of bureaucratic texts.* Portsmouth, NH: Heinemann.

Taylor, D., & Dorsey-Gaines, C. (1988). *Growing up literate: Learning from inner-city families.* Portsmouth, NH: Heinemann.

Thompson, C. P., Skowronski, J. J., Larsen, S. F., & Betz, A. (1996). *Autobiographical memory: Remembering what and remembering when.* Mahwah, NJ: Erlbaum.

Thompson, G. R. (1965). The Signal Corps in World War II. In M. L. Marshall (Ed.), *The story of the U.S. Army Signal Corps* (pp. 174–182). New York: Watts.

Thompson, P. R. (1975). *The Edwardians: The remaking of British society.* Bloomington, IN: Indiana University Press.

Thompson, P. R. (1988). *The voice of the past: Oral history.* Oxford; NY: Oxford University Press.

Thompson, P. R. (1990). *I don't feel old: The experience of later life*. Oxford: Oxford University Press.

Thornton, T. (1996). *Handwriting in America: A cultural history*. New Haven, CT: Yale University Press.

Tremmel, R. (1995). Country life and the teaching of English. *Research in the Teaching of English, 29*, 5–36.

Valdes, G. (1996). *Con respeto: Bridging the distances between culturally diverse families and schools*. New York: Teachers College Press.

Vaughn, W. P. (1974). *Schools for all: The blacks and public education in the South, 1865–1877*. Lexington, KY: University of Kentucky Press.

Viguers, R. H. (1969). Golden years and time of tumult, 1920–1967. In C. Meigs, A. T. Eaton, E. Nesbitt, & R. H. Viguers (Eds.), *A critical history of children's literature: A survey of children's books in English*. New York: Macmillan.

Vincent, D. (1989). *Literacy and popular culture*. New York: Cambridge University Press.

Vinovskis, M. (1995). *Education, society, and economic opportunity: A historical perspective on persistent issues*. New Haven, CT: Yale University Press.

Walker, V. S. (1996). *The highest potential: An African American school community in the segregated South*. Chapel Hill, NC: University of North Carolina Press.

Walters, G. (1996). The ideology of success in major American farm magazines, 1934–1991. *Journalism and Mass Communication Quarterly, 73*, 594–608.

Washington, B. T. (1912). The Negro and illiteracy. *Independent, 73*, 766–768.

Weems, R. E. Jr. (1998). *Desegregating the dollar: African American consumerism in the twentieth century*. New York: New York University Press.

Wells, C. G. (1986). *The meaning makers: Children learning language and using language to learn*. Portsmouth, NH: Heinemann.

Whitely, S. M., & Hosford, R. E. (1979). Counseling in prison. *Counseling Psychologist, 11*, 27–34.

Williams, G. A. (1996). *The Christian Recorder: Newspaper of the African Methodist Episcopal church: History of a forum for ideas, 1854–1902*. Jefferson, NC: McFarland.

Willinsky, J. (1990). *The new literacy: Redefining reading and writing in the schools*. New York: Routledge.

Wilson, W. J. (1997). *When work disappears: The world of the new urban poor*. New York: Vintage.

Wolseley, R. E. (1990). *The black press, U.S.A.* (2nd ed). Ames, IA: Iowa State University Press.

Wright, E. O. (1997). *Class counts: Comparative studies in class analysis*. New York: Cambridge University Press.

INDEX

249